The Sacred Shift: Co-Creating Your Future in the New Renaissance

compiled by Hunt Henion

The Sacred Shift: Co-Creating Your Future in the New
Renaissance

Copyright © 2012 Hunt Henion

ISBN: 978-0-9822054-7-1

Edited by Rhonda Smith, PhD, DD

Printed in the United States of America
Shift Awareness Books
www.shiftawareness.com

TABLE OF CONTENTS

Authors

Adele Ryan McDowell
Adolphina Shephard
Alan Wilson
Alanna Hartzog
Anrita Melchizedek
Barbara Marx Hubbard
Bob Altzar Djurdjevic
Colin Whitby
Colleen Engel-Brown
Cynthia Sue Larson
Dale Ironson, PhD
Dave Stratman
Debra Hosseini
Diana Cooper
Edward Miller
E. Dee Conrad
Elizabeth J. Foley
Humanity's Team
Hunt Henion

John Spritzler
Judith Ray
Judith Stone
Linda Martella-Whitsett
Lou Bognon
Michelle Payton
Nina Meyerhof
Oren Cohen
Patricia Cota-Robles
Rabbi Michael Laitman
Rhonda Smith
Sharon K. Richards
Sophie Rose
Steve Bhaerman
Sylvia Klare
Uriel Light
Wayne Peterson
Wendell Fitzgerald

Revelations and Renaissance

If the Apocalypse comes, beep me.
Buffy the Vampire Slayer

It's the end of the world as we know it and I
feel fine.
REM

Preface

by Patricia Cota-Robles

We are in the midst of the greatest shift of consciousness Humanity has ever experienced. The anthology written by the eclectic group of authors in this amazing book clearly demonstrates that this shift of consciousness is occurring through people in all walks of life. When this Sacred Shift, which is often referred to as an Awakening, occurs within the heart and mind of an individual the person begins to "see with new eyes and hear with new ears." It seems as though his or her very first insight is the realization that all life is interconnected, interdependent, and interrelated. In other words, what affects one part of life affects all life. There is no separation. This means "We are One." We have all heard that statement but prior to the shift most people thought that was just a lofty platitude. Now we know that is not just a trite remark, it is a profound Truth. It means that literally there is no such thing as "us and them." Just for a moment contemplate what that means.

It means that every single thought, word, feeling, or action you express is affecting every person, place, condition, and thing on Earth. Depending on what your frame of mind and emotional state are at the time, with every breath you take you are either adding to the Light of the world or the shadows. That is quite a responsibility, isn't it? The intent of that knowledge is not to make you feel guilty or bad about yourself, it is to remind you of the fact that you are powerful beyond your knowing.

If every facet of life throughout the whole of creation is One with every other facet of life, that means that we are also One with our omniscient, omnipresent, omnipotent Father-Mother God, the Cosmic I AM, All That Is. We are truly Sons and Daughters of God and all that our Father-Mother God has is ours.

The Awakening taking place within the hearts and minds of people everywhere is proving that we are not the fragmented, fear-based aspect of our human ego that we had come to believe we are, nor are we just our physical body. The physical plane of Earth is not the only reality we abide in and our purpose and reason for being are not just to survive and gratify our physical senses; quite the contrary.

We are here to remember the Oneness of all life and to learn how to use our creative faculties of thought and feeling, and our gift of free will to co-create a new paradigm that will transcend the human miscreations of separation and duality we inadvertently created after our fall from Grace aeons ago. We are here to birth a New Earth. This will be accomplished by bringing into manifest form a New Planetary CAUSE of Divine Love. This in turn will birth a Renaissance of Love that will transform life on Earth, as we know it.

The time for us to accomplish this mighty feat is now! As the Hopi saying goes, "We are the ones we have been waiting for." All is in readiness, and through the unified efforts of Heaven and Earth our Victory is assured.

One of my favorite quotations from Buckminster Fuller states, "In order to create something new you do not try to change the existing model, you create a new model and make the old one obsolete." That is exactly what the Sacred Shift into Unity Consciousness is inspiring all of us to do.

Every single day there are billions of people on this planet who in one way or another turn their attention to a Higher Power and invoke the Light of God into their life. These heartfelt pleas are always heard and they are always answered. As a result, the Light of God is increasing on Earth and at long last Humanity is ascending out of our long exile in darkness. Now it is time for us to come together as the unified Family of Humanity we truly are to co-create a Renaissance of Love on Earth. That Love, which we all are, contains within its frequencies prosperity, abundance, peace, reverence for life, vibrant health, harmony, joy, and every other attribute of God. When we join together as one breath, one heartbeat, one voice, one energy, vibration, and consciousness of pure Divine Love with the intention of cocreating a Renaissance of Love, we will magnetize these patterns of perfection into our life experiences and birth a New Earth.

The veil is being lifted. The Awakening that is taking place is enabling Humanity to openly communicate with our God Selves and the Company of Heaven in ways that we have not experienced since prior to our fall from Grace. The information now pouring forth from the Realms of Illumined Truth is revealing that our New Renaissance of Love will involve many wondrous things including the Divine Alchemy of transfiguring our bodies and the body of Mother Earth from carbon-based planetary cells into the infinite perfection of 5th-Dimensional Crystalline-based Solar Light Cells. This process requires recalibrating our DNA into frequencies of Solar Light.

Scientists used to believe that our DNA was stationary and stagnant. We now know that our DNA is a shimmering, waveform configuration that is being modified by Light, solar radiation, magnetic fields, sonic impulses, thoughtforms, and emotions. When Humanity joins together to collectively imprint the genetic codes for our New Renaissance of Love onto the fluid field of unmanifest Divine Potential within our DNA, these patterns will ignite every cell in our bodies and lift us into alignment with our Solar Light Bodies of infinite perfection. This Solar perfection will then be secured in the nucleus of every atomic and subatomic particle and wave of life on Earth, transforming the body of Mother Earth into the patterns of perfection for the New Earth. Once this is accomplished, suddenly and miraculously nothing will be the same.

I am aware that for some those words may sound grandiose or too good to be true, but in reality they do not even begin to describe the transformation we will co-create on Earth through our Renaissance of Love. We have all been preparing for a very long time to accomplish this facet of Earth's unfolding Divine Plan. Know that you already have within you everything you need to accomplish this mission. You have all of the skill, talent, wisdom, strength, and courage you need to succeed. Now all you need is the willingness to take action and the tenacity to be the instrument of God you volunteered to be prior to this embodiment.

If there is any part of you that is resisting or doubting your part in co-creating a New Renaissance of Love on Planet Earth, just go within and listen to your heart; then you will know the Truth of which I speak.

Remember, "The Light of God is ALWAYS Victorious, and YOU are that Light."

Patricia Cota-Robles was a marriage and family counselor for 20 years, during which time she co-founded the non-profit educational organization "New Age Study of Humanity's Purpose." She now spends her time freely sharing the information that is being given to Humanity at this time by the Beings of Light in the Realms of Illumined Truth. Her website is **www.eraofpeace.org**.

The Book of Revelation

by Hunt Henion

Apocalypse, from the verb apokalypto, to reveal, is the name given to the last book in the Bible. It is also called the Book of Revelation. --From the Catholic Encyclopedia

Since the world hasn't come to an end yet, concerned people everywhere still talk about the Book of Revelation as if we're living in the days it describes. However, the classic understanding of that last book of the Bible, reprinted from the Catholic Encyclopedia (published in 1913) would indicate otherwise.

Excerpt from the Catholic Encyclopedia:

"It would be...wearisome and useless to enumerate even the more prominent applications made of the Apocalypse. Racial hatred and religious rancour have at all times found in its vision much suitable and gratifying matter. Such persons as Mohammed, the Pope, Napoleon, etc., have in turn been identified with the beast and the harlot. To the "reformers" particularly, the Apocalypse was an inexhaustible quarry where to dig for invectives that they might hurl then against the Roman hierarchy. The seven hills of Rome, the scarlet robes of the cardinals, and the unfortunate abuses of the papal court made the application easy and tempting. Owing to the patient and strenuous research of scholars, the interpretation of the Apocalypse has been transferred to a field free from the odium theologicum. But then the meaning of the Seer is determined by the rules of common exegesis. Apart from the resurrection, the millennium, and the plagues preceding the final consummation, they see in his (the author's) visions references to the leading events of his TIME." For the complete quotation from the Catholic Encyclopedia see: **http://exm.nr/wFPdy5**

Biblical scholars generally agree that the last book in the bible is a historical record. The only thing that history can't explain, as stated above, is the resurrection, the millennium, and the plagues preceding the final consummation.

1

The resurrection is the belief that "men will rise again with their own bodies from their graves. Right. That's going to happen.

The millenium is explained this way by the Catholic Encyclopedia: At the end of time Christ will return in all His splendour to gather together the just, to annihilate hostile powers, and to found a glorious kingdom on earth for the enjoyment of the highest spiritual and material blessings; He Himself will reign as its king, and all the just, including the saints recalled to life, will participate in it. At the close of this kingdom the saints will enter heaven with Christ, while the wicked, who have also been resuscitated, will be condemned to eternal damnation.

The dead who didn't follow the rules will be resuscitated, so they can burn in Hell forever? That makes me think the seer, who was banished to the island of Patmos, from where he wrote the book of Revelation, was the Stephen King of his age.

Even the Catholic "Church has wholly cast aside the doctrine of a millennium." It's a real eye opener to read the Catholic Encyclopedia describe his purpose for which "the seer" wrote the book, and where he got a lot of his material!

The bottom line is that the book of Revelation was written to influence Christians of that time, and the end of the world that it describes, according to the generally accepted "preterist" interpretation of the book, ended in 70 AD when Jerusalem fell. Look around. It's a different world today! No one goes to the book of Leviticus anymore to see who they can claim as slaves or who they are allowed to stone to death. So why do people look to the book Revelation for clues about the end of THIS world?

Don't let the cryptic language about horned beasts and seven seals spook you. It's all about an old apocalypse, which leaves Catholics and Jews and everyone else in the same boat -- with the same revelation: We need to look for clues to the future in our own lives and in the world around us today.

Sure, there will always be those who will interpret the ancient texts and tell you what to believe and what you should do about it. Still, it isn't truly a bonafide, relevant revelation unless it comes from within.

Hunt Henion has a Ph.D. in Religious Studies and has written books that can be found on his site: **www.shiftawareness.com**

Armageddon and Apocalypse both describe the end of an illusion.

Armageddon refers to the destruction that accompanies apocalyptic revelation. Yet, the destruction of your world is an illusion because your world is an illusion.

The apocalypse is lifting the veil of illusion, which can only be done once you realize your world is an illusion and you destroy this illusion.

See, you live in a dream, which looks more like a nightmare sometimes. You are just a projection of consciousness on this planet, what's behind the projector is your soul. Your soul is trying to direct the movie and watch it at the same time. It is hoping that you'll fulfill your role according to the script that was given to you before your incarnation. It waits patiently until you awake and realize that you are the dream and the dreamer, the creator of your world.

Once you awake to your Oneness with all that is, Apocalypse or Armageddon has taken place. Then your soul becomes the doer; by being in charge it co-creates Heaven on Earth.

Jeshua channeled by Sophie Rose, author of the channeled course *The Way of the Heart*, Teachings of Jeshua and Mary Magdalene, **www.thewayoftheheartcourse.com**

What is the Apocalypse Really?

by Rhonda Smith, D.D., Ph.D.

By definition an Apocalypse "is a disclosure of something hidden from the majority of mankind in an era dominated by falsehood and misconception, i.e., the veil to be lifted".

Well we certainly are in an era "dominated by falsehood and misconception". So we could say that the Apocalypse is in progress. Circumstances around the world are showing us what has been hidden, *i.e.*, the veil is being lifted.

One would think that is a good thing; however, a funny thing happened on the way to the forum; more falsehoods and misconceptions. Somehow Armageddon got mixed with Apocalypse. Maybe it's because they both start with the same first letter. Who knows?

Don't lose sight of the fact it is titled **The Book of REVELATION** not the book of destruction. Yes, revelations of what has been hidden can lead to various reactions such as violence. However, this is not "destined" to happen unless we choose it. Instead, these revelations can be used for us to choose a RESPONSE to them. That response can be an acceptance of the facts and moving forward to find a more positive way to direct those energies. That is where we are going, a new way to interact by glorifying the diversity and using those varied perspectives to move us forward rather than attempting to "kill" what's different.

So where did this book begin and why is it at the end of the *New Testament*? It is generally agreed that this book was written in 78 or 79 A.D. by a Jew named John on an island called Patmos to which he was exiled to by the Romans as a follower of Rabbi Joshua ben Joseph, *aka* Jesus, who taught "The Way" which was a branch of Judaism. The other thing to be aware of is the atmosphere and history of the time the book was written. So one would think it would be at the end of the Old Testament, not the New. This was written long before Christianity existed, nearly 225 years! The Christian Bible was not put together until around 300 A.D. at the Council of Nicea with the Romans leading the way.

So what made them put the *Book of Revelations*, the *Apocalypse*, almost like an appendix to the new testament? Well, there already was a tradition which had additional books other than the ones we usually think of as the *Old Testament*. Most of these books are still in the Roman Catholic Bible; however, they are not in the Protestant one. These books were called the *Apocrypha* and were part of the Greek translation (*Septuagint*) of the Jewish Bible and the Jewish traditions even though they were not accepted by the Protestants because they were not seen as part of the original Hebrew Scriptures. However, they were the books that John of Patmos knew and he understood that the Jews would understand the symbology he was using. That made the *Apocalypse* make sense.

Sometime in the 4th century, a Latin version (the language of the Romans) was created called the Vulgate which included the *Old Testament* as well as the *Septuagint* as well as a few other books and these additional books (*Septuagint* and the others) were called *Apocrypha* which was a term used to describe books that were "hidden away" because they were considered too esoteric or sacred for the common reader. By this time the *Apocrypha*, *Septuagint*, was an integral and important part of the Vulgate translation; however, there then was a German translation done by Martin Luther which collected the Apocrypha into an appendix. The Church of England borrowed this practice.

So we come to the *Book of Revelations* written after Christ's mission was finished and the Romans had spent years abusing the Jews. John knew about angels/demons etc from the Apocryphal books and knew the Jews would understand. He wrote a symbolic account of what was happening between the Jews and the Romans, much like the political commentaries of *Alice Through the Looking Glass* or *Gulliver's Travels*. It was meant to reveal to the world what was occurring and it was probably added at the end of the New Testament, even though it is totally different than the rest, simply because it didn't fit in the *Old Testament* because the *Apocrypha* had been left out.

Switching to Armageddon, it is only mentioned ONE place in the Bible, *Revelations 16:16* and it refers to a fortified Tell (small hill) outside Jerusalem which was built to protect the main highway which connected Ancient Egypt with Mesopotamia. There is nothing that speaks of a huge battle here. In this case, those of the doom and gloom brigade have definitely made a mountain out of a mole hill.

So we are already experiencing the Apocalypse, the revelation of what was hidden. So before you allow your emotions to panic, learn to question, seek the source and verify for yourself so that we all can move forward in truth.

Rev. Rhonda Smith has been teaching and practicing metaphysics for over 40 years. She also is the numerologist for the *Sedona Journal of Emergence*, a counselor, channel, Reiki Master Teacher, Chios Master Teacher and trained in other modalities. She can be contacted through **www.theawakeningcenter.com** or **www.theawakenet.org**.

Edgar Cayce's Interpretation on the Book of Revelation

by Hunt Henion

Edgar Cayce asked his guides about the true meaning of the Book of Revelation, and he got an amazing answer, which has relevance for all of us today. Unlike the universally scary symbolic interpretations of the book, this one is uplifting. According to Cayce's source, the book describes apocalyptic revelations about the fall of mankind and then the renewal of our Spirit and our ascension to our divine origins.

Personally, I can just see his guide taking Casey's question about the Book of Revelation and using it as an opportunity to squeeze in as many lessons as possible. (Guides do that sometimes, particularly with spiritual teachers.) From that point of view, the original intention behind the writing of the book is totally beside the many points. He simply takes the symbols included in the story of Revelation and extrapolates some very clever and practical interpretations.

Here's a quick summary:

John, the name given to the author of the Revelation, is sitting on the island of Patmos, where we're told he was "exiled", when the Spirit of Christ appears to him standing in the midst of seven candlesticks. The spirit of Jesus then tells John that the candlesticks represent seven churches and tells him to write down what he sees regarding them. John also sees God sitting on a throne with a book that has seven seals that no one can open except Christ.

Cayce's guide took this opportunity to discuss the seven churches and seven seals as the seven human chakras. If he had been talking to Cayce 50 years later, he would have undoubtedly worked in a discussion of the seven rays, which is a concept from the 6th Century, but wasn't popularized until Theosophy resurrected it in the late 19th century, and it didn't really become popular until fairly recently.

At any rate, our chakras are where the physical, mental and spiritual forces all come together, and according to Cayce, John is saying that anyone who can learn to balance these spiritual centers within their body can access the superconscious mind and thus rise above the need to reincarnate.

Below is a chart of which church and which seal is supposed to represent which gland :

CHURCH	GLAND	SEAL
Ephesus	Gonads	1
Smyrna	Ayden	2
Pergamos	Adrenals	3
Thyatira	Thymus	4
Sardis	Thyroid	5
Philadelphia	Pineal	6
Laodicea	Pituitary	7

Next, John sees four beasts and twenty-four elders around them. Also, Christ opens the seals, resulting in many Earth changes and releasing seven angels who sound seven trumpets, which are sounded one by one.

According to Cayce, Christ opening the seals is representative of John's mental and spiritual awakening within the throne of his own body. The four beasts are the four human lower animalistic desires, and the twenty-four elders are the twenty-four nerves leading from the brain to the five human senses.

So, the body is symbolized as a book that no one can open without activating the Christ consciousness within us.

Below are some more of Cayce's interpretations of symbols from the book of Revelation:

SYMBOL	MEANING
Paradise of God	The original consciousness of humanity before its fall into flesh
Tree of Life	The spiritual centers of the body, such as the heart and the pituitary, that can become perfectly synchronized
Angel of the Church	The intelligent force governing the spiritual centers or chakras within the body
Satan or The Beast	The force of self-centeredness, self-gratification, self-indulgence, self-righteousness, self-glorification, self-condemnation, ego, the "false god"
Book of Life	The collective unconscious record (memory) of all souls
Earth (and The book with 7 seals)	The physical body
Mountain of fire striking the Earth	The forces within the physical body, that are often at war with each other
New Jerusalem	The awakened superconscious mind
Nakedness	The exposure of faults
Seven lamps	The wisdom of the seven spiritual centers (Chakras) within the body

John then sees a very pregnant woman with twelve stars around her. Next to the woman is a dragon that is ready to devour the child once she gives birth. After the child is born, the child is taken to the throne of God. Then, a war in heaven occurs, and the devil and his angels are cast out of heaven to Earth. John also sees a beast rise out of the sea, and the world worships it.. John then sees a lamb on Earth, and angels proclaiming the fall of Babylon.

Cayce was told that the woman represents the development of humanity from the beginning. The twelve stars represent the twelve signs of the zodiac and the twelve corresponding patterns of human personality.

The child she bears is symbolic of the conscious mind. As the conscious mind is born, periods of rebellion occur as the soul matures. Divine intervention protects the conscious mind while the unconscious mind, from which it springs, retreats from our awareness to the unconscious level. This is, incidentally, the same meaning that Cayce attributes to the Adam and Eve story. Rebellion from the conscious mind causes conflict, which Soul simply rides out by remaining above it all, concealing a lot from the conscious mind in the subconscious.

The "beast rising out of the sea" is the human inclination to be ruled by selfish desires. These desires spring from the undisciplined intellect of humanity, which is worshiped in the material world. The human intellect that lacks a spiritual orientation separates us from the divine.

The lamb that John sees are the forces of the enlightened mind going into action. "Babylon" represents the human desire for earthly riches and success. That mindset is destroyed as humans become aware of consequences of separating themselves from the divine and from the lack us using their higher faculties.

SYMBOL	MEANING
Seven candlesticks, seven spirits	Perfection, symbolic of the 7 chakras and 7 rays
Six	Imperfection, the number for humanity
Mark of the beast	The unevolved selfish inclinations within humans
Mark of the lamb	The evolved divine force within humans
666	The unevolved animalistic force affecting our body, mind, and spirit

Chapter 15-18: Seven angels, seven vials of seven plagues, and a prostitute riding a seven-headed beast

Literal: John is shown seven angels each of whom holds a vial containing a plague which they pour upon the Earth one at a time. John then sees a woman sitting on a seven-headed beast with ten horns. The woman wears on her forehead the name Mystery, Babylon the Great, the Mother of Harlots and Abominations of the Earth. John is told the seven heads symbolize the seven mountains on which the woman sits and the ten horns symbolize ten kings. These make war against the lamb and the lamb conquers.

Interpretation

John is seeing within the soul of humanity, the collective unconscious, that the souls of individuals are purified and tested on seven levels of consciousness symbolized by the seven plagues being poured out by the seven angels. When all seven levels of consciousness have been purified, then and only then can a person control the physical, mental, and spiritual forces within his body.

Physical diseases arise from the misuse of the forces and self-gratification of the flesh, wars against universal truth. This brings about conflict in the world against groups and governments. The end of the seven ordeals comes when humanity's social institutions and concepts collapse, leaving universal truth to be realized.

The Prostitute of Babylon symbolizes humanity's desire and lust for riches and gratification of the flesh. The beast it rides on are man-made ideas stemming from self-gratification. It is explained to John that these forces have taken control of the seven spiritual centers of the human body, thereby becoming possessed and ruled. However, as the highest forces of evolving humanity overcome the forces of self, even the ten basic urges of the body, symbolized by the ten horns, will in time fulfill the divine pattern. As the divine nature in humanity becomes less realized, society is destroyed by its own hand through self-gratification.

SYMBOL	MEANING
Seven plagues	The purification and tribulation experienced by souls in order to overcome negative karma
Vials of God's wrath	Karma, eye for an eye, sowing and reaping, the consequences of our negative acts
Armageddon	The spiritual conflict within humans
False prophet	Self-delusion

In chapters 19-22, John sees rejoicing in heaven and the appearance of Jesus Christ. An angel casts the devil into a bottomless pit for one thousand years, and then John sees a new heaven and a new Earth suddenly appear.

According to Cayce, this means that when a critical mass of humanity finally recognizes the divinity within, we all will turn away from our short-sighted, selfish ways. Separation will disappear, and the enlightened, or "Christ", pattern emerges.

John comes to believe (as referenced in Rev 19:7) that the merging of his evolved self with his divine, superconscious self, must also take place in all humanity. This fulfilled evolution of mankind, the recognition of our divine self, IS the "second coming of Christ".

For a period of one thousand years, only those evolved souls who are in harmony with their divine self and all of humanity will be permitted to incarnate on the Earth (Rev. 20:4). At the end of this period, the others of a lower vibration begin to incarnate, ringing with them another round of wars and plagues from the pursuit of their selfish desires.

This is the final chance for all to expiate this karma. After one last self-indulgent fling, all that is not divine will be purged. (Rev. 20:14).

The new heaven John sees in the new, enlightened state of human consciousness, and the new earth he sees is our body brought into harmony through the balancing of our seven spiritual centers or chakras. The human mind at this point is now evidently ascended, because it's one with the divine AND is totally free from outside limitations.

John states that if anyone adds or takes away from this book, that person will experience the plagues in this book. Scary stuff until you realize that he's just making the point that since The book is the human body (through which we learn our soul lessons), there can be no shortcuts without causing consequences to the body

Hunt Henion reviews inspirational books and is the originator of the Don Q Point of View Seal of Approval. His own books are described at **www.shiftawareness.com**

There is no doubt in my mind that Barbara Marx Hubbard – who helped introduce the concept of futurism to society – is the best informed human now alive regarding futurism and the foresights it has produced.
Buckminster Fuller

The Universal Human

by Barbara Marx Hubbard

The universal human is a name for the next stage of human evolution. It may eventually become our name for the new species that is now emerging from within so many of us. We have arrived here passing through many other stages well recognized by scientists: *Homo habilis, Homo erectus, Homo neandertal, Homo sapiens, Homo sapiens sapiens.* There is no reason to suppose that evolution stopped when it achieved our big brain!

In fact, there is evidence that for the past few thousand years, there has been emerging out of *Homo sapiens sapiens*, a more universal human. This new type of human began to appear about 5000 years ago in Israel, India, Persia, Greece, China, the Middle East. We identify some of these humans as Isaiah, Buddha, Zoroaster, Socrates, Plato, Aristotle, Lao-tzu, Confucius, Jesus, Mohammed and others, advanced human beings who gave fuller expression to the Great Creating Process in themselves. In these people the Consciousness Force Itself broke through into human awareness. Indeed, these advanced beings founded the religions and the ethical systems of the world, calling all of us to evolve to a higher state.

But most of us could not experience what the evolved humans did. The teachings of the originators were codified and became dogma for those who could not experience the truth themselves. And often this dogma fostered obedience to outside authorities, rather than inspiring people to recognize the great Source within.

Now, during our current planetary crises, these old codified systems are breaking down and changing. Many people are leaving organized religion behind and experiencing the awakening of Spirit within themselves. They are listening to the voice of their Higher Self, the One Voice calling us all to grow in consciousness and to recreate our world. The Era of the Holy Spirit incarnating has begun.

In this awakening it has become clear to many that it is self-conscious humans feeling separate from each other and from nature, who are threatening our world. At the same time, if we look closely, there is also arising, for the first time, a more universal humanity.

Our crisis is inducing the birth of a more universal human. We are the crossover generation moving from one phase of evolution to the next! Although barely perceptible, as were the earliest humans in the pre-human world, a young Homo universalis is emerging everywhere, in every culture, faith, and background. The signs of our emergence as universal humans include an unconditional love for the whole of life; a powerful, irresistible passion to unite with Spirit within; and a deep heart-felt impulse to connect with others and co-create a world equal to our love and our capacities.

As we pass through our crises, as we successfully birth ourselves into a more universal humanity, we will emerge capable of co-evolving with nature and co-creating with Spirit. We will be able to solve our problems. We will be able to co-create a new world.

During these transition times it is important to stabilize our consciousness as universal humans. We can do this by practicing authentic relationship with others of similar intent and reminding one another of who we are. When we intend together, we build a collective field of resonance that can support our conscious evolution. Our job is far easier when we offer each other the support of staying awake together.

For more on the universal human, see Barbara's books: *Emergence: the Shift from Ego to Essence* and her soon-to-be-published *The Secret Journal: How to Birth the Universal Human in Yourself.*

Barbara Marx Hubbard has been called "the voice for conscious evolution of our time" by Deepak Chopra and is the subject of Neale Donald Walsch's new book "The Mother of Invention." A prolific author, visionary, social innovator, evolutionary thinker and educator, she is co-founder and chairperson of the Foundation for Conscious Evolution. She is also the producer and narrator of the award-winning documentary series entitled Humanity Ascending: A New Way through Together.

For more information about Barbara Marx Hubbard please visit: **www.evolve.org**

Show and Share Your Light

by Adele Ryan McDowell, Ph.D.

This is the moment. There are no more warm-ups: practice is over. It is time to suit up and get in the game. Our souls have been preparing for this moment for lifetimes. We have arrived at the tipping point of our evolutionary consciousness and have chosen this moment in time. We raised our soul hands to be here now, to tip the balance in favor of an evolved and expanded humanity. Our mission is to add our personal light, like a pearl on a string, to the web of energy surrounding the planet.

But holding and maintaining – and sometimes even finding -- our light can be tricky and tenuous as we ride the chaotic waves of change. The personality part of us, the little self, wants life to return to "normal" --whatever normal used to be. The soul part of us is straining at the bit; eager to be of service and lead from the heart. Our soul understands completely that each and every one of us is connected. We are all one, and we are here to help each other learn the lessons of compassion, acceptance, forgiveness, peace, oneness, and, ultimately, unconditional love for all.

Many of us sojourners on the path have been working hard to discern our deeper selves and unfold in expanded consciousness. We have steeped ourselves in personal growth studies; we have read mountains of books, listened to countless tapes and CD's, attended workshops and lectures, and talked and talked -- and talked some more.

Now, we are called to step out of the boxes that hold us back and keep us in the shadows. Fear, unworthiness, and incompleteness no longer serve us -- or the planet. This is not the time for martyrs or shrinking violets. Nor do we need to step into one another's karma or participate in dramas. These are our moments to detach with love, trust our hearts, and listen to our inner knowing. We are standard-bearers for the shift in consciousness and move towards unity.

As healers, light workers, peacemakers, spiritual warriors, and bridge builders, we are called to claim the unique amalgams of our respective experiences and gifts. We are called to bring forth our most light-filled selves by way of our actions, choices, thinking, and intentions. Everything counts. In other words, every action we take, every thought we have, every choice we make, impacts the balance of light and dark on this planet. Our purpose is to illumine the darkness and increase the light. This is our moment to show our high-vibratory selves. This is our moment to shine.

And to aid and abet this unfolding process, here are four steps to up your energetics, increase your coherence, strengthen your connectivity, support your authenticity, and encourage your brilliance:

1. Practice mindful heart service

Every spiritual tradition speaks of the power of love and compassion. This is not a new concept. We all are familiar with this, but where we tend to fall short is that we forget the power that our individual hearts can generate.

When we practice mindful heart service, i.e., sending out intentions with loving detachment, blessings, beams of light, waves of gratitude and appreciation, and offerings of compassion, we shift the energies and enhance the light.

The power of the heart is our catalyst for change. When charted, our positive emotions create a resonance that looks like even, looping waves; whereas, negative emotions are reflected by spiky, uneven patterns. Our resonance and, equally, our non-resonance impact one another.

Heart service is practical, do-it-yourself transformation that serves us both personally and globally.

2. Aim for morphogenic resonance

What do I mean by these words? I am talking about pooling our collective energy fields and having us all swim in one, high vibratory pond.

Imagine that you turn on the lights in your darkened home on your darkened street. Imagine that the neighbor across the street does the same and, then, another neighbor, two streets over, turns on their house lights. And so it goes. The idea is that as you turn on your Light, you not only help others, you also lay down the tracks to create new energy grids and foundations for higher vibrations. More simply, light begets light and this means we all pulse and oscillate together at this higher frequency and share the same energetic wavelength.

Here are six ways to become more morphogenically resonant:

• Become responsible for yourself, your thoughts, and your actions. Do not give your precious power and energy to anyone.

• Override the energetic imprint of fear. Fear eats away at your energy and strength; it makes you a victim. You and you alone are responsible for the part your fear or lack of fear weighs in on mass consciousness. And fear is a learned trait that is based on the past. You can pull your fear out of its dark corner, bring it into the light of your consciousness, and accept the lesson it teaches. Reframe fear: consider that the personality part of you has simply forgotten what your soul already knows.

• Consistently choose light over dark. Every choice you make, counts. Act with integrity, and shepherd your light carefully. It makes a bigger difference than you realize.

• Move beyond duality. It is time to think "and and" as opposed to either/or. There is room at the table for everyone. Separateness is an illusion – and a very good one at that – but know that each and every one of us is a light-bearer. We all are card-carrying, battery-pack wearers of the Light.

• Celebrate community. We humans are interdependent on one another. It is time to bring down our walls and work together for the planet, our children, and our future. This is the key to our regeneration.

• Connect with Source. What better way to enhance your light than to power up with our primary source. We all need to recharge our battery packs. Consistent connection and practice (with whatever face or name you call the Divine) helps to remind each of us that we are, indeed, fractals of the Divine. We are vibratory beings carrying light code matrices.

3. Don't push; allow

As hard as we have worked to make order and sense out of our lives, there comes a moment in our evolutionary development, when we are called to relinquish our tight grasp on the steering wheel of life. There is no more fighting, resisting, pushing, or pulling; there is simply the conscious and active choice of letting go and allowing ourselves to be present to what comes before us.

Now, we find ourselves in the flow. We have merged our individual light with the Light. We swim in the channels of high vibration and a unified heart.

And there are benefits: Life gets to be more fun, and less robotic. Creativity thrives. Intuition and telepathy are significantly enhanced. Synchronicities and mysteries happen frequently. We learn the lessons that only joy can teach, and the Light keeps getting brighter.

4. Sparkle

Light is an amazing phenomena. We know when it is missing. Light can shift and change in its intensity, spectrum, and bandwidth. Light is an energy that has the power to heal and the power to destroy.

When you raised your soul hand to be here, you said, "Yes!" to awakening and enlightenment. The next step on that ladder is self-remembering. It is time to remember the depth and breadth of your soul, the power of your heart, and the Light that you are. Given the state of the world, it may sound heretical, but the more joy, zip, and sparkle you have in your life, the better it is for you, your family, and the planet.

It is time to walk into your magnificence. Show your beauty and allow your authentic self to be seen. Be outrageous. Be creative. Be passionate. Be alive, and take your soul out for a spin. Shine your light and sparkle, sparkle, sparkle. You will make all the difference in the world.

Adele Ryan McDowell, Ph.D., is the author of the Amazon best-selling Balancing Act: Reflections, Meditations, and Coping Strategies for Today's Fast-Paced Whirl and a contributing author to the best-selling anthology, 2012: Creating Your Own Shift. Her next book, Help, It's Dark in Here, will be released in 2012. You can learn more about Adele and her thinking at **http://theheraldedpenguin.com**

Who Hit the Fast Forward Button?

by Adele Ryan McDowell, Ph.D.

Who hit the fast forward button? Doesn't it feel like time is whizzing by? Do you remember last week? Doesn't it feel like last week was a month ago?

Science-types tell us the world has, indeed, accelerated. I have heard it said that our 24-hour days are really more like 16 hours. So, good, we're not crazy, lazy or inefficient. The universal ticker has just picked up its pace. That said, I'm getting dizzy with the whirl and spin of it all.

Here's an interesting anecdotal fact: the amount of information made available every five minutes in today's world is the equivalent to the entire body of knowledge during the Renaissance. We live in the Information Age and we're bombarded non-stop with news, data, media events and the like. Simply trying to stay on top of the latest and greatest information can make us feel winded and breathless, as if we're madly dashing to an ever-changing and elusive finish line.

We have seasons, hours of light, and hours of darkness. Yet, time is more subjective than objective. In childhood, it seemed as if every week was a very long stretch of time. Christmas was very, very far away and birthdays couldn't come fast enough. In adulthood, time is like trying to catch a butterfly bare-handed. It slips through our fingers and flits away. It is ephemeral. Challenges, stressors and demands for our time increase daily, hourly. There is never enough time to get it all done. Some of us stay up way too late, and the morning folks are up at the crack of dawn. We all fall into bed exhausted with the perpetual push of attempting to get it all done. No matter how hard we work, we can't hold time.

Mindfulness experts tell us that if we s-l-o-w d-o-w-n and are in the moment, we will have a fuller, expanded experience of time. I do know this to be true. If I take a breath and am fully aware of what I'm doing, I have a more memorable experience; I have also increased the probability of remembering what I experienced.

For me, slowing down has been another of those good

ideas I'll get to when I catch up and get it all done. If I think about it, I realize I have been doing what I call fast-food time -- gobbling it all down without any real sense of nourishment or satisfaction, much less any solid memory of my experiences. So, ok, I'm aware and cognizant. I want to slow down, but here is the kicker. The world is going faster. Can you say vr-r-r-room? We live – and if you are a metaphysical type, you know we choose to live now – in this period of enormous transition. We are moving through a shift in the ages. December, 2012, via the Mayan calendar, is seen as a pivotal point in this cosmic shift of consciousness, where we recognize that we are all connected, energetically bound, and in this cosmic soup together. As with any shift, there is an attendant change in consciousness.

Remember, we are living in the Information Age; technology by itself has expanded our awareness. As an example, there is a pervasive desire to honor Mother Earth, to stand up against abuses and ensure that no child goes to bed hungry. We see our world erupting with change. People are reaching out to one another, working to make a difference and equalize the inequities.

As we know, everything is energy; thus, everything is vibration. We know our expanded collective consciousness raises the vibration. And.... drum roll, please ... the higher the vibration, the faster the time. Take that statement in; it confirms that we are chugging forward in vibration, consciousness, and time.

And that brings me to this provocative statement I recently read: Given the acceleration of time, 20 days now feels equivalent to one year of time. Think about that. Doesn't that statement ring true to you?

It rings true to me and I know time is whizzing by. I also know we can't control time. The more we try to control time, the more we feel hammered by the demands of time and energy.

My solution?

I no longer try to beat time into submission, forever bloodying and depleting myself in the process. I am going for the more difficult and counter-intuitive responses. I am taking a walk on the wild side and putting self care at the top of the list. I know ... who has time for that? I realize that everything may not get done, but, hey, if I am going to ride the waves of accelerated time and consciousness shifts, it only makes sense to honor the expression of consciousness I have chosen for this lifetime. Really, if not now, when?

Further, with a great leap of courage, I'm opting to use the gourmet variety of time – you know, the kind of time you savor, one bite at a time. This will be tricky as well; I have grown accustomed and habituated to the race and rush of life. That said, gourmet time offers an option of savory moments in lieu of being whirled senseless by a freight train of constant movement. I am putting down my universal remote control and simply, scarily, allowing things to unfold without my unnecessary prodding and pushing.

Today, I am going to float on the river of time and see where it takes me. Care to join me for a ride on the current?

Adele Ryan McDowell, Ph.D., is the author of the Amazon best-selling Balancing Act: Reflections, Meditations, and Coping Strategies for Today's Fast-Paced Whirl and a contributing author to the best-selling anthology, 2012: Creating Your Own Shift. Her next book, Help, It's Dark in Here, will be released in 2012. You can learn more about Adele and her thinking at **http://theheraldedpenguin.com**.

Revelations for the New Era

Channeled by Lou Bognon

The era before you is another golden age when your soul's longing will continue to get still deeper and deeper for a higher and higher connection to its Creator. You are now home bound, on your way to that most wondrous reunion, and you shall soon be welcomed into the heart of Light, from where you departed aeons ago.

Imagine a great upward spiral and know that from its end point, which is your own divine presence, you are now reaching half point through that spiral. By the year 2012 you will all have completed enough cycles on the same spiral to finally understand this image we are giving you of your current place in your own personal spiral of light and evolution.

By the end of 2012, much of humanity will understand and have integrated the inner knowledge that they are Love manifest, that all life forms are Love manifest, and this, Beloved, is another great revelation for your time!

The blessings of such a revelation will manifest and eventually translate into a quantum leap in the way you relate to each other and in your relationships to all of life's expressions. A lot of you already have this consciousness, but what will be most wonderful to watch is for this same consciousness to finally affect all and then become the new golden age standard for all of the Earth's humanity. This is nearer than you think, indeed.

The next few years are crucial to this evolutionary leap. ... you are indeed free to choose to do this leap in painful and chaotic ways, or to embrace the Love that you are, and make the leap within the divine law of Love.

In this, your mother planet will also follow your choices. How you will use your divine gift of free will, will to a great extent determine how she chooses to use hers as well. If you choose chaos, she will give you some of it, and lots of it too --should a little not be enough to wake you up to make your choices with Love.

Watch; as even as we speak, she is active in the same spots over and over again...expect her to become relentless in the places where her children neither listen, nor learn.

Now, understand Beloved that all laws are called laws because of their inherent qualities to be heeded and obeyed, or broken and ignored; and in this, the Divine Law of Love is no different, even though our loving Father-Mother-God also gives us the use of free will. You remain free to either obey this or any other law, thus learning in one single leap of faith or, through what are often very painful experiences, even entire lifetimes.

Such has been the path for most of you, lifetime after lifetime, for you were not taught any other way. Now you are being taught differently, now you are being reminded that you alone have the power of your choices.

How much easier it is Beloved, to just live the law, and thus think, move, speak and act within Love. This is in essence what, we, at the Council of Love and Wisdom, have come to *re-mind* you of at this most sacred time.

In closing, we would Love to give you a few final pointers to guide you closer to the divine law of Love:

You know **you are Love when you experience joy** at being alive and at doing all the things that bring true and lasting happiness to your heart and soul, and to those around you. For some of you, that may be contemplating the stars. For others, it may be reading; and yet for others, it may be gardening, painting dancing, singing, or the pursuit of any other creative endeavour.

Learn, once and for all, what it really means to be an eternal soul – eternal means forever and soul means spirit. So, forever your spirit lives. You have lived before and you will live forever. And it is not your human or scientific discoveries of a hypothetical elixir of eternal life that will grant you eternity. That is already your divine right -you are already eternal. All that changes are only in your outer form.

Now with that comes a truly awesome responsibility and hopefully this book will guide you further in that understanding. Just as you would create, say a lovely corner in your garden, filled with beautiful flowers and special plants and objects, a place you would want to go to, to enjoy the beauty and the energy that you would have created, the Creator creates you and all things in order to experience Himself-Herself in all of His-Her infinite magnificence

So, in a sense you could not only just imagine the Creator

anywhere and everywhere --that is why He is said to be Omnipresent and Omnipotent; but he could be said to be equally the garden and the gardener, the rose and its perfume, the rain and its drops, you, yourself, as a body and a soul, reading these words with all you are feeling and being this very instant.

He is inspiring this book and feeling what his creation feels through your own individual and collective feelings. He feels your joy as you integrate and discover these very words. That is what we mean about you being God's perfection manifest. He created you so that you could beam back to Him the very Light with which he has infused Life within your being.

Take a deep breath then.

Close your eyes and know that you are, this very instant, the lungs, the eyes, the heart and the body of Father-Mother-God Himself-Herself. If only you could remember to feel this way more often...

There was much Beloved, that was made complicated and mystified about the truth of God's Love for you. When we say that you need to unlearn many things you think you know about Love, we think specifically about those teachings that insist that you need to become worthy of God's Love.

Nobody becomes, you do not become, worthy of Father/ Mother God's Love because you already are Love. Always remember that our Father-Mother-God's Love is unconditional. Nothing you do, say or don't do or don't say will ever be able to change that.

Our Beloved Brother Jesus tried to teach you this during his earthly sojourn, and what He said was that you needed to learn to Love yourselves and each other as FatherMother-God Loves you. He explained that indeed all you needed was to learn to accept that Love. The part of you that is Divine-mind, understands this perfectly. The human-mind aspect does not – and there lies the problem with humanity in your dimension. It's the problem of duality. You see yourself as your body-mind, or as a body that possesses a soul. But what you really are is an eternal soul visiting a temporary abode, which is all your human body really is.

...It is time for humanity to fully come into this understanding by letting go of all negative, imperfect and fear-based teachings about God's creation, for God's creation can only be, and is only, Perfection. All the rest is and shall always remain human creation and human invention.

Let this myth go Beloved, for sin is a human invention. The very notion of sin needs to be unlearned, revised and called by its proper name: mistakes. You all make mistakes, errors of judgement and action, some far more serious than others, we have to concede, but that is how all souls learn. Look at what you call sins as opportunities to learn, as potential lessons you may have to redeem in this or in another lifetime, for you are all eternal.

If you were to treat yourselves and each other with Love and compassion, each time one of you would fall prey to temptation, or make some other sort of mistake, you would through your Love, remind each other that that is how you learn from and teach each other.

Knowing that you and God and every other of God's creations are inseparable, is Love.

Doing something that brings joy to another, is Love.

Love is treating others with kindness, fairness, honesty, compassion, helpfulness, caring. If Love can be said to have ingredients, then those are some of the ingredients of godly expression in action. (Taken from: www.mathewsbooks.com *)*

. ..The law of Love says that no soul walks alone along this treacherous path called

life on Earth.

The above is an excerpt from her book The Divine Laws by The Council of Love and Wisdom, channeled through Lou Bognon. Lou Bognon is a spiritual healer since childhood and author of five spiritual books based in South Africa. She is also a broadcaster within the African Continent inspiring millions of listeners in English and French.
website **www.loubognon.com**
email: lou@loubognon.com

The New Renaissance

by Hunt Henion

Renaissance means rebirth, and THE Renaissance, a period roughly from 1350 – 1600, is known for a tremendous rebirth of awareness and knowledge. Up until that point, The church had explained everything to the illiterate masses in simple terms of an unknowable God. During the Renaissance, attention began to shift to science, art, and to humanity.

In the big picture, I see the Renaissance 500 years ago as a renewal of the statement humankind made when we built that temple to ego 5000 years ago in ancient Babylon. However, it was a necessary statement. After the tower of Babylon was constructed, (as the story goes) the common language of love and mutual concern was lost as individual pursuits began to occupy an increasingly large place in the thoughts of the people. This path of individual accomplishment and self-discovery was magnified and multiplied during the Renaissance.

At that time, great strides were made in science, culture and socio-political notions, all based on the rediscovery and application of classical thought and texts. Today, we are once again examining the ancient wisdom in hopes of putting our world in perspective.

It's interesting that the original Renaissance started with the Black plague in Europe in 1347. The exclusive positions of power of the royalty and the Church were also beginning to be threatened. Today, the power structures of our economic and social systems are in a similar deconstruction period, and I can't help wonder what single event will come to be recognized as the catastrophe that launched us into our new Renaissance.

During the Renaissance, Pope Julius II (the reincarnation of whom is one of the authors of this anthology) commissioned Michelangelo to paint the Sistine Chapel, one of the most magnificent and ambitious creative pursuits in history – one reason it's represented on the cover of this book. Another reason has to do with the symbology of getting in touch with each other and with our source.

The invention of the printing press during the last Renaissance also was a monumental accomplishment. In fact, it was probably the most important contribution to humanity in over a thousand years! It made duplicating manuscripts and music practical.

The landmark Renaissance publication would have to be The Gutenberg Bible in 1454, which revolutionized European literacy. The innovation of printing has also revolutionized our personal connection to each other. However, while personal notes were carried by rider during the first Renaissance, now they're carried at the speed of light on the internet.

This new quantum leap to an entirely new level, or Renaissance, brought to us by the world wide web, now allows us to access the knowledge of others that would otherwise be unobtainable, even as it permeates our global mental grid.

Technology is uniting us, and the realization of this unity is the hallmark of our new Renaissance. We're discovering our interconnectedness and what we all have in common as the world seems to becoming smaller all the time. The birth of new systems and the collapse of the old is unsettling. Still, when dust settles, this new Renaissance will be understood as a paradigm shift that we made sacred by our cooperative co-creation of it.

Hunt Henion writes on Practical Spirituality for The Examiner and is the author of books that can be found at **www.shiftawareness.com.**

Transition through Apocalypse

by Diana Cooper

2012 marks the end of a 260,000 cosmic era which is the end of the experiment of Atlantis. This period included the 1,500 period of the Golden Age, which was the last time the light truly shone on Earth. Everyone had a golden aura as well as awesome gifts and an understanding of the power of deep relaxation. After that the frequency of the planet fell to the third dimension. Five of their twelve chakras were closed down so that only seven remained active and 44 codons of DNA were switched off, leaving only 20 enabled. 44 is the vibration of Golden Atlantis and those codons contained their special psychic and spiritual gifts of telepathy, telekinesis, powers of manifestation, clairvoyance, clairaudience, levitation, teleportation, self healing and many others.

The frequency of Earth is now rising again. Our planet moved into the fourth dimension in 2010 and will return fully to the fifth dimension by 2032, the start of the new Golden Age.

Babies are already being born with their 12 strands of DNA intact but the density of the planet is still so low that they cannot use this and may demonstrate such conditions as autism. However, more adults are opening their twelve chakras and starting to activate their gifts, allowing an atmosphere within which these psychic children can start to demonstrate their potential. It is estimated that in twenty years time 17% of the children will have their 12 strands of DNA switched on at birth. This number would be increased if more adults open their 12 chakras. Here are some of the things that will accelerate the rise in frequency.

Cosmic moments

11.11 is a number vibration which was set in the collective consciousness aeons ago. It activates the new at a higher frequency than the old. At 11.11a.m on 11.11.11 and 12.21.2012 (which adds up to 11) there are cosmic moments. These are instants of total silence in the universe, when the portals of heaven open and Source energy pours into the planet, triggering awesome possibilities. It will help to step individuals and the planet up into higher frequencies.

The opening of the fifth dimensional planetary chakras

On 21st December 2012 the twelve fifth dimensional chakras of our planet will open. As the Stellar Gateway in the Arctic awakens it will fully expand like a chalice to receive an inpouring of Source energy! The entire planet will be bathed in Source light.

Awakening of six cosmic pyramids

The opening of the twelve planetary chakras will trigger the awakening of six cosmic pyramids which were built by the High Priests and Priestesses of Atlantis after the fall. These are in Greece, Tibet, Mesopotamia, Machu Picchu, Egypt and the Mayan pyramid. Only the Egyptian and Mayan pyramids remain in physical form. The others have been destroyed but remain energetically active. They will reconnect to the wisdom of the stars and spread that round the planet.

Opening of the cosmic portals

33 cosmic portals containing the light of the twelve rays plus the silver ray and the Christ light will open in or around 2012. In my book 2012 and Beyond there are maps of the locations of the 12 planetary chakras and the 33 cosmic portals and information about them.

Activation of the crystal pyramids from the Dome

During the golden era of Atlantis the experiment was protected by a dome of crystal pyramids, set in a triangular formation. This was also a power generator and communications system. After the fall six of the crystal pyramids from the dome were placed over the six cosmic pyramids, one over Mount Shasta and one over Uluru in Australia, to keep the frequency high. The remainder were returned to the inner planes. In 1987, at the Harmonic Convergence, these were all strategically placed around the universe. They are connected to each other by pure love and are waiting to be switched on. As the spiritual heart chakra of the planet opens in Glastonbury in 2012 it will connect to the cosmic heart and this will ignite all the pyramids. Then the heart centres of all the planets, stars and galaxies in this universe will connect. When they are all linked, the pyramids will swivel and join their energy to that of the Great Crystal Pyramid in Hollow Earth, waking its wisdom. They will all merge their divine essence by 2032 and bring our universe fully into the fifth dimension.

The ascension of all the universes

There is a huge current of movement taking everyone and everything higher. 2012 marks the start of the ascension not just of this planet or this universe but of all the universes. The first dimensional universe will move into the second dimension, the twelfth will be
absorbed into the Godhead and a new first one will be created. We have a twenty year window of opportunity and change. The wise ones of old plus highly evolved souls are incarnating on Earth to help us.

Changes in Society

Economies

So what does this mean for our society? All businesses that are not in alignment with the new paradigm will collapse. This includes all the huge dinosaur companies who are only interested in profit. Big impersonal schools, hospitals, banks and political constructs must change or go. The higher selves of those who are not doing work that brings them joy and satisfaction are causing them to be made redundant or go out of business. Many are then going through an initiation to a higher spiritual level where they will automatically attract the perfect work for their soul. For many, this will be a very challenging process. Businesses working with integrity for the good of nature, animals, people and the planet will succeed.

The economic structure of this planet is rotten and this too will be swept away. The world economy must move at a faster frequency and will evolve until it operates with honour, openness, honesty, integrity and fairness. This, too, will dissolve as money ceases to have relevance after 2032. Then people will exchange goods locally within their fifth dimensional communities.

Oil and power

The oil that we are spiritually allowed to access will run out in 2012. There will be more oil available but humanity will create huge karma if we use it as it is for the protection of the tectonic plates. In any case all forms of transport will become increasingly expensive so that it will no longer be viable to fly goods across the world. Eating and producing locally will become the order of the day.

International peace

The boundaries will come down between countries as people start to honour each other's cultures, so that by 2032 there will be international peace. People will be welcome wherever they go. However, because of the destruction caused by the purification of the planet it will be less easy to travel. Bicycles and water transport will become popular again.

Planetary cleansing

All the dark places on the planet must be cleansed. This is already starting but will really take place between 2017 and 2022. In my book Transition to the New Golden Age in 2032 I forecast what is to happen throughout the world including each State of the US. However, even where there is negative stuff to be purified, incredible positive spiritual happenings and energies are to be released to assist the process. Yes, it will be challenging but the lessons will bring about humility, co-operation, friendship and an opening of hearts and minds.

Countries will help each other. Traditional enemies will become friends. Women will be empowered.

Religion into spirituality

It is time for human made constructs and dogma to be dissolved and by 2032 religions will become truly spiritual.

Spiritual technology

Children are already being born whose brains are configured to understand and work with new spiritual technology which is currently beyond our comprehension. At a time when people en masse are opening up psychically and spiritually, they will be inventing ecological forms of transport and power. Communication networks will be at a high frequency and most will be able to link telepathically. We will control the weather for the highest good of all and we will start to listen to the wisdom of beings from other planets. For the first time since Atlantis people will be happy and contented.

The next twenty years offers the greatest opportunity for spiritual growth that there has ever been on this planet. We are asked to watch our thoughts, connect with the angelic and elemental realms and do our part to help in this massive transition to the new Golden Age.

Diana Cooper is author of 24 spiritual books and Founder of the Diana Cooper School. **www.dianacooper.com**

You Are The World

The light of God surrounds me;

The love of God enfolds me;

The power of God protects me;

The presence of God watches over me.

Wherever I am, God is!

Unity affirmation by James Dillet Freeman

Revelation to Renaissance to the World Through You:
The Spiral of Evolution

by Rhonda Smith, D.D., Ph.D.

How does this all connect? The revelation of what has been hidden leads you to reevaluate what you thought was true. Finding that truth may lead to a new belief and perspective on the issue (renaissance) which tends to bring about a rebirth of understanding and a shift in your beliefs and perspectives which, in effect, shifts your energy. As we all know from the quantum physicists, everything is energy and all energy is connected and commended by your consciousness. So when you shift your energy, you effect the world through that connection.

This is the process we are all working to understand, accept and integrate. Many, if not most or all, in the group consciousness have been "programmed" to believe what they do, feel or think does not matter. However, it MATTERS A LOT. It matters because what you do, feel and think effects your energy field and, thereby, the world. Don't go into fear please. In spite of what you've been taught both directly and indirectly, you have complete command of you. To exercise that command means making all your choices CONSCIOUSLY. Making choices consciously means you are aware you are choosing and what you are choosing. Also, never lose sight of the fact that not making a choice is also a choice.

Given this underlying process of creation, what is the significance of this year? In addition to having experiences to assist us to accept and integrate this process, we are being asked to use that awareness to build our own personal foundation which is composed of our beliefs, perspectives and balancing of all our energies.

The corners of this foundation are the four basic vibrations within all of us. Getting them in balance is what puts you on a firm foundation for future growth and evolution. We have all had lives and had life experiences with one of these energies dominant in order to gain understanding of "how they work" in order to master them and use them for our own growth. Now it is time to bring them together for both yourself and the world.

So what are these 4 energies? Three of them have been obvious in our physicality, one is being assisted to manifest so we have our complete foundation, all four corners.

They are the solar male, lunar male, lunar female and solar female. We all have been hearing for several years that it's important to balance the generic male and female energies irrespective of what gender body we have chosen. Now we're on the home stretch and need to be conscious that, like everything else in the physical, there are two sides to the male/female coins. The Solar Male energies are energies of action (the warrior) while the Lunar Male energies are energies of reception (the priest/guru). The Lunar Female energies are energies of reception (the Oracle of Delphi). These three energies have been present in our experiences for a long time.

Since the females gave the males the opportunity to "run things", we had a lot of aggressive behavioral experiences. However, when the "boys" came up with the concept of chivalry, we did see some changes, another renaissance if you will. That was followed by the Renaissance where, at least in the art, the female form was glorified beginning with Titian. However, the solar female (active) energies were still suppressed. Personally, I believe it was because the males were subliminally afraid that they would "lose control", "lose power over".

The latest Renaissance, there have been many throughout history, is this period. It actually has been going on for some time. We have seen women business leaders coming forward in increasing numbers. It is this energy that is being activated to complete our foundation for the future.

We have been given clues to this for hundreds of years. The most noted artistic representation is the ceiling of the Cistine chapel. The picture of "God" reaching out his right hand (left brain/female) to Adam demonstrates that when humankind was created Adam in the male physical body was infused with female energies.

In addition, if you look at the whole picture on that ceiling, you see that the male "God" is holding the female "Goddess" extremely close with his left arm (right brain/male). So you have the male side and the female side united. I don't believe anyone would argue that the male "God" (Divine Mind) and the female "Goddess" (Divine Heart) are out of balance.

So what makes me say that there is a receptive and active male and female? Just look around. We have taken either a male of female body and, in my experience, both males and females can be quiet and receptive as well and verbal and active, or sometimes nonverbal and active. Both qualities exist in us all irrespective of the gender body we've chosen to manifest. So, as the physicists say, everything, including us, is energy vibrating at different frequencies. We, in this transition, are integrating all those energies into our physical body so we stand on a firm foundation to move forward in our evolution.

We are experiencing all of this now. We have revelations of what has been hidden, we are changing our perspective and rebirthing our Selves as a result and, because everything is energy, our progress effects everything else, the world.

One final comment, we have selected this time for this final balancing act because it coordinates with all the solar and lunar flares we are experiencing to bring in the complete love of all four of our basic aspects. So use the S.T.A.R. principle from the Golden Dolphins and Surrender, Trust, Allow and Receive willingly. We have Nina Brown, www.crystalsinger.com, to thank for the Golden Dolphin information.

Rev. Rhonda Smith is a minister, mentor, author and numerologist. You can find out more at **http://www.theawakeningcenter.com**.

The Golden Thread

by Hunt Henion

Everyone reaches for the divine in different ways. Still, the fact that we're all doing what we can to better know the essence of things, demonstrates the golden thread that runs through the hearts of people from every walk of life and from every faith. Below are some examples of the ways these hearts reach for the divine every day:

Did you know that the word *Islam* comes from an Arabic word meaning "peace" and "submission?" Islam teaches that one can only find peace in one's life by completely submitting to the divine Source (Allah). The universal Muslim greeting is "Salaam alaykum," which means "Peace be with you". It's important for a Muslim to pray five times each day in order to maintain that peace and their connection to The Almighty.

Jewish rituals and religious observances are also designed to constantly remind them of their connection to God. **Jewish law** (*halakhah*, lit. "the path one walks.") *Halakhah* governs not just religious life, but daily life: how to dress, what to eat, how to help the poor, etc. Observance of *halakhah* shows gratitude to God, and brings the sacred into everyday life.

The Hebrew word *mitzvot* means "commandments." Although the word is sometimes used more broadly to refer to rabbinic (Talmudic) law or general good deeds, it really refers to the divine commandments laid down in the Torah.

The Jewish philosopher Maimonides made a list of the 613 commandments he found in the Jewish Bible. In addition to the 613 *mitzvot*, Jewish law incorporates a large body of rabbinical rules and laws. These are considered just as binding as the *mitzvot*, and this is all designed to bring the divine into their lives in every possible way.

The Jews, Christians, and the Muslims see themselves as totally different communities, with totally different interests. However, Islam reveres Jesus Christ and His Mother, as well as John the Baptist. Also, all three cultures recognize Abraham as the "father of all believers." "*Al-Khader*" is the Islamic identification for St George, and there's a town near Bethlehem by that name, which demonstrates yet another connection between these two supposedly polar opposite religions.

The displaced Palestinians are also a blend of these cultures. Christians, Jews and Muslims all live in the Palestinian areas in relative harmony. There's religious tension, but they generally get along, recognizing a common language, a common faith in one God/Allah, and a common history and heritage. They unite in heart and mind at funerals and weddings, in churches and in mosques. And I have to wonder if these people had a secure place in the world, if they might help heal the rift between the oppositional forces of their neighboring Jewish and Muslim brothers.

The bottom line is that the secret to getting along as well as getting comfortable with our purpose in life is a matter of focusing on our unity with those around us:

"We attribute our question about the meaning of life directly to the lack of unity. The Light is manifested in unity... It turns out that **the meaning of life for us is to be connected with each other**." --From Rabbi Michael Laitman's Aug 1, 2011 blog titled *Unity Is A Jewelry Box With A Secret.*

"The big issue is whether there can even be a future without religious harmony,"

"To build religious harmony is to build a future for humanity. It's not going to be easy but I say let's do it. Bring it on." -- Rev. Paolo Dall'Oglio, an Italian Jesuit, who restored an ancient monastery in Syria and is currently fostering dialog between Christians and Muslims.

"Don't speak to me about your religion; first show it to me in how you treat other people. Don't tell me how much you love your God; show me in how much you love all God's children. Don't preach to me your passion for your faith; teach me through your compassion for your neighbors. In the end, I'm not as interested in what you have to tell or sell as I am in **how you choose to live and give**."--Newark mayor Cory Booker.

Living and giving is what it's all about! Throw in caring and sharing and suddenly you've discovered the golden thread that links all religions together.

Just look at all these ways to phrase the Golden Rule:

> **Christianity** ~All things whatsoever ye would that men should do to you, do ye so to them; for this is the law and the prophets. Matthew 7:1
>
> **Confucianism** ~ Do not do to others what you would not like yourself. Then there will be no resentment against you, either in the family or in the state. Analects 12:2
>
> **Buddhism** ~ Hurt not others in ways that you yourself would find hurtful. Udana-Varga 5,1
>
> **Hinduism** ~ This is the sum of duty; do naught onto others what you would not have them do unto you. Mahabharata 5,1517
>
> **Islam** ~ No one of you is a believer until he desires for his brother that which he desires for himself. Sunnah
>
> **Judaism** ~ What is hateful to you, do not do to your fellowman. This is the entire Law; all the rest is commentary. Talmud, Shabbat 3id
>
> **Taoism** ~ Regard your neighbor's gain as your gain, and your neighbor's loss as your own loss. Tai Shang Kan Yin P'ien
>
> **Zoroastrianism** ~*That nature alone is good which refrains from doing another whatsoever is not good for itself.* Dadisten-I-dinik, 94,5

Beliefs give each of these religions historical and cultural context. However, as you can see from the above, the real substance, or the spiritual path that each of these faiths follow, is remarkably similar.

Think substance! Think of what's beneath the beliefs. Let's focus on the golden thread that runs through all religions and give peace a chance.

...

Can you step back from your own mind and thus understand all things? --Lao Tzu

46

"If you've ever watched a flock of birds move in the sky in unison, or a school of fish turn and dart around as if they were one body, you've witnessed firsthand, the divine reality of the One Spirit and the ways of home we've all but forgotten. We had to set up limits separating ourselves from God in order to play our games and learn our lessons in the earthly world. Still, that was *then*, and this is *now*. And now, as I stand alone on the ground, watching the birds fly together, the longing to go home and fly in unison with kindred souls is often overwhelming." -from *Memories of Home*, in my book,

The BIG Fake-out, the Illusion of Limits

In the beginning...we were one. Then, some say we fell from grace. Others explain that taking that bite out of the fruit of the knowledge of good and evil was a good thing. However you see it, that era of individual interests ueber alles seems to be coming to an end. Thank God.

Our Western society is rooted in the Greek philosophy that conquered the community-oriented Persians and set up competing independent city states. Competition is another aspect of this individualistic mindset. We're raised to believe that competition is healthy, and we should strive to get ahead of everyone else. Yet this ethic has (according to a

A UN study resulted in a situation where two percent of the people own over 50% of the world's assets, and half of the world's adult population account for barely 1 percent of global wealth.

These are just statistics until you look into the faces of the 30,000 people who die each day because of poverty related issues. **http://everythreeseconds.net/**.

We'll get into economic solutions in the last section of the book. For now, it's just important to understand that as admirable as personal ambition is, taking the time to care about others is sort of a prerequisite to being a descent human. The answer to all of the world's problems is simply to shift away from competition and back toward caring, sharing and cooperation.

There are still many things to figure out, and this book takes a stab at the biggies. It also tries to focus on some simple truths that have gotten lost as our Individual paths have taken us far from our innate understanding of our unity with others. In Yogananda's classic, Autobiography of a Yogi, he says that "Love is simple, everything else is complex."

This complexity is a result of our run-away human egos, which divides us. Ego finds fault, and in thinking things through, believes it knows more and better with every new thought. Lines are drawn, good and bad are defined, and life becomes a battle instead of the harmonious creative adventure that it can be when we are willing to step outside of our personal position long enough to care and share with others.

Your ego can be your best friend if controlled, but otherwise acts like your big brother commanding your attention to ensure you come first. We certainly promote the idea of self-preservation, and self-love but not at the expense of other souls. In long gone times your ego ensured your survival, but that is no longer necessary as it is your Light that now protects you. The more you think and act in Love and Light the more you attract, and place yourself beyond the attention of the dark Ones. Perhaps you can see how your civilization divides itself into two factions, and you are in a time when they will draw further apart. Even your way of thinking becomes quite different when you allow the Light to take over. Suddenly you are One with all life... - From the July 20, 2011 channeling of SaLuSa

This section of the anthology will describe the various ways in which people are turning our historic individualistic orientation into community awareness and concern. It discusses our unity with all of the world in down-to-earth ways, and in some ways that will stretch your awareness. Realizing that we ARE one with all that we perceive around us is just one manifestation of our raising consciousness. Doing something about it is another manifestation—one that we will mainly get to in the last two sections of this book.

Hunt Henion holds a PhD in Religious Studies and compiled the predecessor to this book, the #1 Amazon Best Seller, 2012, Creating Your Own Shift. **www.shiftawareness.com**

Speaking Personally about My Religious Journey in Christ

by Judith Stone

"Christ be with me, Christ within me, Christ behind me, Christ before me, Christ beside me, Christ to win me, Christ to comfort and restore me, Christ beneath me, Christ above me, Christ in quiet, Christ in danger, Christ in hearts of all that love me, Christ in mouth of friend and stranger"

This prayer from the Breastplate of St. Patrick reminds me that, while I am not always awake to it, the Divine presence is all around me. The New Testament speaks of the "God in whom we live and move and have our being."(Acts 17:28)

"In beauty I walk
With beauty before me I walk
With beauty behind me I walk
With beauty above me I walk
With beauty around me I walk"

This portion of the Closing Prayer from the Navajo Way Blessing Ceremony, called "Walking in Beauty," reminds me of the Saint Patrick's prayer.

Both of these prayers are foundational to my understanding of religious life, and to my own Christian journey. I grew up in a Christian home and in the United Methodist Church. Then, after a twelve year long hiatus from the church, while studying art at the University of California in Berkeley, I unexpectedly found a doorway that led me back to Christ, and more astonishingly back into a Christian Church. That doorway was "paying attention." Paying attention beyond self.

John Downing, O.D., PhD, my eye doctor, says, "Attention is the outward expression of soul." The making of art is all about paying attention: to color and line, to form, texture and design, to the beauty of the human body and of creation, to the sensibilities and art work of others, and to one's own soul. As I was struggling to make a problematic composition start to "sing", one of my Art Teachers at Cal, Sidney Gordin, counseled, "Listen to the voice within."

Though I did not know it then, his words would take me back to God.

Deep attention to life can forge a connection to the eternal mystery: to the profound beauty, in which we walk, to the Christ around, above, within, before, and restoring and healing all creation. Christ in the mouth of Sidney Gordin my Jewish professor.

Central to Christianity is the reality of Incarnation. The word incarnation is derived from the same root word as "carne" and "carnal". It could literally be translated as "in the meat." Incarnation speaks of the mystery that God is present in the very flesh of everyday life, in the flesh of the world. John Keating puts it like this: In Jesus, "God has become one of us, breathing our air. . Through his humanity the whole material universe has become divine. . . By becoming a human being [God] is in the heart of all creation, in every part of it . . . By his breathing the atmosphere is sacred. By his eating, food is sacred. Now every sense experience conveys the mystery of Christ. He gives himself to us in everything that happens.

"The Word was made flesh"— made a part of creation, made matter—and dwells among us." (1)

Matter matters! The whole of material creation matters, the whole cosmos matters, because it is an expression of the Divine.

Now, long story short, I am a United Methodist pastor. Have been for 32 years. The founder of Methodism, John Wesley, said over and over again, "The world is my parish." That is like saying the world is my church, my cathedral, the realm of the sacred, or the world is my kin. It is also saying the world is "where it's at", what religion is all about. Because, in Wesley's understanding, the here and now matters to God, Wesley started the first free clinics in England, and wrote a herbal compendium for those without access to doctors, hospitals and health care. He started loan programs for the poor, visited those in prison, opposed slavery, and child labor. The tangible presence of God in creation affected how Wesley lived, and how he treated others.

Here's another Wesley quote, "as for matters of Doctrine, we (Methodists) think and let think, but if your heart is as my heart, give me your hand." Wesley focused on that which connects, rather than focusing on differences. He saw Christ in the mouth of friend and stranger.

I think it has something to do with Wesley that I do not think of religious life as distinct from ordinary activity in the world. It is not when we stop to pray, or something for special days and times, ceremonies! My sense is that religious feeling connects us more deeply to everyday activities, to creation and to others.

Nor do I think of religious practice as a form of achievement, leading to some kind of elevated status. I feel uncomfortable with the idea that religious practice makes us 'holier' or 'more Godly' than others. Nor do I feel that its main purpose is to make us "good" people." though it may impart ethical responsibility. Jesus said to his disciples "Good, good, why callest thou me good? There is none good but God alone." (Luke 18:19, Matthew10: 18, Mark 10:18) I am uncomfortable with the notion that religious life in any way separates people from each other. (For example, into good versus bad people, or into those deserving eternal reward or eternal punishment). When I took a confirmation class to a Buddhist Sitting Group, the priest Bruce Fortin, told us the Buddha would likely be uncomfortable if called a Buddhist, because that identity has the power to separate. The Buddha did not see himself as separate. I am with the Buddha on this. If following Christ, or companionship with Christ does not lead me to see the beauty in the Buddha, I do not wish to be a follower.

The word religious comes from the word "religio" which means to bind together. (2) The idea that one person is holier than another, or has achieved an elevated religious status, evaluates and divides rather than binds together. If the intent of religion is to bind together, then any religious practice that elevates one person above another, or separates one person from another seems at best an illusion or self-defeating.

Herman Waetjen, one of my New Testament Professors insisted that Jesus Christ practiced "radical horizontality." The letter to the Philippians (2:6) says "Jesus being in the very nature of God, did not count equality with God a thing to be grasped, but emptied himself." The message of Jesus is that God comes to be with us, not above us, to connect with us and to connect us to each other.

I love the word "religious" and prefer it to "spiritual" because it communicates this "meaning-sense" that, at its depth, religious life is all about "connective tissue." Here is how I would put it: because of God the whole cosmos is a matrix of connective tissue. I experience Christ as the connective tissue of God, linking God to the flesh of the world and linking us to creation and to each other in "radical horizontality".

This is the beauty in which we walk: the divine before us, the divine within us, the divine beneath us and above us, the divine comforting and restoring us, the divine in mouth of friend and stranger.

Religious life is, from my perspective, about the radiant, the luminous "everywhereness" and "ordinariness" of God, of the sacred. So then, in my understanding, religious practice is simply seeking to live within that framework, or understanding, or living toward that horizon: the interconnectedness of all life in God. It is seeking to make an inward experience, real in outward action.

Hard to do! So often I get disconnected and fragmented. In a world of broken connections and broken-souls, I get caught up in the illusory. I miss the deep connections. Practice, for me, is about reconnecting to life, to creation, to others, to my own soul, to God, to truth, to the mind of Christ. Practice is for the sake of my own soul. Prayer and silence, study, spiritual reading and conversation, all help me to reconnect. So does art, beauty, listening to music, being in nature, friendship, being aware that I am a part of the circle of life. Here are some other re-connecting practices: confession (entering the truth of my life, when it is not very pretty), practicing forgiveness and self-compassion, participating in community worship, practicing what Jews call "world repair" and Christians call social responsibility, entering the common reality of suffering. John Wesley said, "All

Holiness is social holiness." I think he was talking about the interconnectedness of all of life.

Then there is the experience of grace. The Transcendent connects to us, pays attention to us, comes close to us, touches us, and is with us. When I ponder this it is beyond wonderful! We can't make grace happen. But it does happen: the grace of the mystery, amazement at the privilege of being alive, beauty, the sense that, imperfect as we are, we belong here, that we have something to offer the cosmos, the sense that for all the brokenness around us and within us, that connective tissue is stronger than the forces of separation. Jesus at the cross makes a big statement with his life about that. In him the connective tissue of love is incomprehensibly stronger than all our capacity for disconnection (and the darkness and tragedy that are its outcomes). He reminds us that God is everywhere "in it all with us," as the connective tissue that weaves all of life together in profound care.

Rev. Judith Stone is the pastor of the United Methodist Church in Sebastopol, CA. She is a published poet, leads spiritual retreats, was the Denominational Environmental Justice Cocoordinator for her Region. She is currently on the Board of the Nomina Center for Spirituality and the Arts in Santa Rosa California. She has been a United Methodist pastor since 1979. United Methodists are a Christian Denomination known for their focus on both the inner life and outward action. Valuing reason, experience, tradition, and scripture, they take the Bible seriously, but not literally.

(1)Thomas Keating, "And The Word Was Made Flesh," Crossroads Publishing Company, New York, 1983 pg. 20

(2) Modern scholars such as Harpur and Joseph Campbell favor the derivation from ligare "bind, connect", probably from a prefixed re-ligare, i.e. re (again) + ligare or "to reconnect," which was made prominent by St. Augustine, following the interpretation of Lactantius. In The Power of Myth, with Bill Moyers, ed. Betty Sue Flowers, New York, Anchor Books, 1991. ISBN 0-385-41.

Being in the Church in a Time of Change

by Rev. Judith Ray

It's easy for me to criticize the Church. After all, I've been an insider my whole life, being a Christian in a variety of traditions. I was baptized as an infant in the United Methodist Church. Later, I was confirmed and received my first communion there, a very holy experience for me.

Though my parents were not especially involved, my grandmother was. I was known as Hazel's granddaughter and enjoyed a sense of belonging there, of being connected with that community. But the connection wasn't just within that small community of faith. It extended out into the world as we learned about what missionaries such as Albert Schweitzer were doing in distant parts of the world. Missionaries visited our church too, and told us of their experiences. It all nurtured a sense of being connected, at least in a small way, with something far beyond my personal experience.

Unlike most, if not all of my peers, I enjoyed going to Sunday School and also worshipping with the adults. The stories of Jesus fascinated me, especially the stories of Jesus healing blind people, no doubt because I was born with a myriad of eye problems and wanted healing for myself.

The possibility of such healing became real one Easter Sunday. I had learned that Jesus had been crucified and died, but that he had become alive again, resurrected, and was a living presence in our lives, now. The power of this transformation was dramatically brought home to me in worship that day. The whole congregation processed into the sanctuary, each of us carrying white calla lilies. At the front of the church was an ugly wooden cross wrapped in chicken wire. As we passed by the cross we placed our calla lilies into the holes of the chicken wire. When the last few lilies were put in place and we had taken our seats in the pews, everyone could see that the ugly wooden cross had been utterly transformed into a display of magnificent beauty. It is an image indelibly imprinted on my mind.

As a result, in my childlike way, I figured that if Jesus could heal blind people and he was a living presence in our lives now, he somehow ought to be able to heal me. After all, I wasn't truly blind though the doctors were afraid that it was a possibility. I began to pray each night as I went to sleep that Jesus would heal my eyes. Before I opened my eyes in the morning I'd wonder if this was to be the day. It never was, at least not as I had imagined.

But when I was almost twelve and many of the eye problems were declared stable, my mother asked a life-changing question. "But doctor, why can't she see?" The doctors had been so concerned about the other problems, they had never thought to test my visual acuity.

I was tested and given glasses. I could finally see individual leaves on the trees for the first time! I could see the blackboard and read my text books. My grades improved dramatically. Looking back, I can see it was at least a partial answer to my prayers. It was while I was part of that congregation that I had an experience on the playground that I could not explain nor could I tell anyone about it. It happened one day as I was coming in from recess. Suddenly I was surrounded in white light and understood that God wanted me to be a medical missionary. I felt astounded, honored and befuddled all at once. How did you prepare for this calling? Become a nurse and marry a doctor? Become a Christian educator and marry a minister? As a girl it never entered my mind that someday I myself might be ordained as a minister.

I was part of the Methodist tradition until I was twelve and we moved to the suburbs, at which time my family became part of the United Church of Christ. Upon reflection I can say that in the church of my childhood there was no explicit teaching about our connectedness, our oneness, all of us being the body of Christ as the Apostle Paul describes it. (1 Corinthians 12:27) Rather, despite the exposure to missionaries, the emphasis was on an individualistic, pietistic approach to faith as reflected in some of our most treasured hymns: "I Come to the Garden Alone" and "Sweet Hour of Prayer...that calls me from a world of care."

My first year of college was at a small university founded by Congregationalists. I was a Christian Education major, that is until my mother found out. She didn't like that idea and had me transfer to a major university. I decided I'd just have to pursue my training to be a medical missionary by becoming a nurse. Much to my mother's dismay, I met my future husband there and he was a Roman Catholic. He was also going to be a medical missionary, but of course being male he was going to be a physician. That's the way it was in the 60's on the cusp of the free speech and women's movements.

Because he was Roman Catholic and we didn't want ours to be a "mixed marriage" we decided to study each other's faith tradition and see what might be appropriate for us. What tradition would hold beliefs compatible with our own? Ultimately, I went to a Roman Catholic nursing school and converted to Catholicism. I found it especially meaningful that Catholics throughout the world celebrated Mass in the same language, Latin. (This was before the reforms of Vatican II.) For me that provided a deep sense of connectedness, of unity, more than I had ever known before.

I became a nurse, and we had our first child during my husband's senior year of college. We had our second child during his first year of medical school. It was very challenging. To make matters worse, our local parish would not allow young children to be part of the congregation during Mass. We had to sit behind glass in the "crying room." It was unacceptable. Somehow we found our way to the "underground" Roman Catholic Church. There our children were welcomed and all, children, babies and adults alike, partook of Communion.

It was there that we were introduced to a radical sense of social justice. During Holy Week we enacted the Stations of the Cross accordingly, having various stations that were connected with the need for social justice. For example, one station was in one of the urban neighborhoods where there had been race riots and killing. Another was in front of a suburban town hall where persons had moved away from such turmoil.

While my husband continued medical school, I was a stay-at-home mom. We knew that eventually I could, and probably would, get pregnant again if we didn't use some form of birth control. Of course, this was forbidden by the Church. We had a crisis of faith. From an ethics course in nursing school, I knew the conditions under which I could take "the pill" and still be a faithful Catholic. We read the book A Question of Conscience by a Roman Catholic theologian, who explained that although some Catholics remained in the church ignoring the official teaching, others felt they simply couldn't. We fell into the latter group. So one Easter Sunday we joined the Unitarian Church. There we found a freedom of belief that was life-giving. There was also an emphasis on working for social justice. One form this took was to decide, as a congregation, how best to preserve Susan B. Anthony's writings which were in the church's possession. We decided to have them kept in a climate controlled environment at the University of Rochester Library, near her former home turned museum.

There they would be accessible to interested parties. As a public health and family nurse practitioner working in the inner city I was faced with poverty and its ramifications every day. I had a case load of about three hundred and sixty families, part Black and part new Puerto Rican immigrants. Each group had a cultural belief system that we needed to respect and work with, integrating their beliefs with Western medicine. It was while I was doing this work that I read James Michener's book, Hawaii. I came to understand how missionaries, in the name of Jesus, had essentially raped the Hawaiian culture. If this is what it meant to be a medical missionary, I didn't want any part of it. This practice was part of what I later learned is a world-wide system of domination and subordination, in which a few white heterosexual men have power and determination over non-whites, women, homosexuals, children, animals and even the earth itself.

One of my patients had severe burns from scalding hot water her boyfriend had poured on her. I had to change her dressings. At that time, we had no understanding of what became known as "battered women" or "domestic violence." Little did I know that it would lead me down a path of working with others to develop a shelter and a program for battered women and their children. It also ultimately led me to understand the dynamics of male domination, male privilege that held that it was a man's right to punish his wife much the same as some parents punish their children. Granted, it shouldn't go so far as scalding a wife or children. But I learned of the legal obstacles women faced and still face, although progress has been made.

Attitudes are slow to change, especially when the Bible is quoted to prove what is "right": "wives be subject to your husbands...for the husband is head of the wife," (Ephesians 5:22) "spare the rod and spoil the child" (the popular paraphrase of Proverbs 13:24). Again I later learned that this too was another example of the system of domination in which women and persons of color were considered "less than" the few white men who held power over financial, political, and legal matters. At one time women and slaves were believed not even to have souls, or if any, only part souls. Slaves too were to obey their masters, just as the wives were to submit to their husbands. In a word, this is patriarchy, defined by the Oxford dictionary as, "a system of society, government, etc. ruled by a man and with descent through the male line." And patriarchy has been an integral part of the each of the Abrahamic faiths, Judaism, Christianity and Islam, for centuries.

Eventually, I heard my call anew, went to seminary, and became a Presbyterian pastor. I learned to take context into account when interpreting scripture. I also discovered parts which talk of how we are all one in Christ. For instance, "There is no longer Jew or Greek...slave or free. male and female; for all of you are one in Christ Jesus." (Galatians 3:28) I learned that scripture is not to be used to beat people up but to be interpreted in a way that speaks of love, of justice in the public realm.

Enough progress has been made in breaking down patriarchy that I have been blessed to be able to be ordained in my tradition. But women aren't treated so well in many other faith traditions. And even in traditions that ordain women, many, if not most congregations still prefer male ministers, and women end up serving in non-parish or part-time, lower paying positions. Progress has been made in translations of the Bible. New translations of the Bible are "inclusive," translating the Greek word for "men" as "men and women" (as intended in the Greek). This is instead of viewing the English "men" as inclusive of both males and females. Despite this progress most Christian traditions still do not ordain non-heterosexual candidates nor allow so-called "gay marriage."

These are some of my criticisms of Christianity, and for that matter of Judaism and Islam. But I believe it is important that we acknowledge all the good that has flowed forth from our faith traditions—feeding the hungry, sheltering the homeless, tending the sick, providing access to quality education, and giving hope to the despairing influencing public policy so that persons and communities in need are empowered to lift themselves up.

All the criticisms I have named and more seem to me to be related to matters of belief, which then buttresses the system of domination and subordination. But what if matters of correct belief, (orthodoxy) is not where our focus should be? What if our focus should instead be on how we treat one another --what our intentions are?

Are our intentions to show love and respect to one another, to show justice in the public realm? Every faith tradition has some version of the golden rule—to treat others as we want to be treated. Just imagine how different our world would be if that is what we were to practice rather than operating out of prejudice, fear and hatred!

Yes, it is easy for me to criticize the Church. But my criticism is really a lover's quarrel. My hope and prayer is that some day soon we will recognize and act upon what physicists already know, that we are all deeply connected with one another and all of creation in ways that we can scarcely imagine -- that we are all One. May it be so.

Judith Ray has a Bachelor of Science in Nursing and Master of Divinity, ordained in the Presbyterian Church, USA and retired although **currently** involved with the Congregational/UCC Church in Colorado.

Tiptoeing Away From TULIP

by Hunt Henion

TULIP stands for the five main theological beliefs promoted by John Calvin (1509-1564). These precepts were affirmed by the Synod of Dordt (1618-1619 CE, which was called by the Dutch Reformed Church and attended by the representatives of eight foreign countries to settle theological disputes.

Their conclusion was that Calvin's belief system was THE doctrine of salvation. His beliefs and that decision thus laid the foundation for Reformed Theology, and we've been tiptoeing away from those ideas ever since.

One thing that has changed since the 16th Century is the inclusion of Eastern concepts, such as karma, into the average person's knowledge base. I use that term in this article to explain Calvinism in modern terms will hopefully help put the old fundamental protestant belief system in perspective.

The Five Points of Calvinism, are generally taught using the deceivingly light and uplifting acrostic TULIP.

T: This usually stands for "Total depravity:" This is often mistaken to mean that humans are all hopelessly, intensely sinful. Actually, it simply refers to the reality of karma that affects all parts of every person's being.--In the words of Calvin: "his thinking, his emotions and his will."

Sometimes, this has been called "Total inability," which results from an ordinary persons Total depravity.

Support for this belief is found in Romans 5:12 and Mark: 4:11

U: This stands for "Unconditional Election." This is the concept of predestination – the idea that one's karma predetermines the limits of one's advancement in life. Since Calvin was only dealing with one lifetime per person, humanity was quickly divided into two groups. One group is "elected" for heaven, and the rest are simply doomed to spend eternity in Hell.

I don't know if Calvin actually ever questioned the idea of

eternal damnation, or if it was simply the traditional way to get the attention of the unruly masses. Realize society had just come out of the dark ages, and order was a high priority.

Calvinism maintained that heaven wasn't attainable simply through the good works of an individual. Again, Calvin was looking at the weight of karma people obviously carried, and putting mere actions and even knowledge in their places as surface events, as opposed to soul changing occurrences.

The Bible is unclear concerning the precise division of responsibility between God and humans. Since the days of John Calvin, many have used certain passages in the Bible to demonstrate the divine nature of humanity, and to introduce the concept that we are, in some way at least, responsible for our lives and our own salvation.

However, the Old Testament tends to infer that God causes absolutely everything, and that we're totally helpless victims. For instance, God supposedly told Moses to get his people out of Egypt, but they God also "hardened Pharoah's heart." So, all the conflict seems to be God fighting against himself, with free-will nowhere in the mix.

The New Testament infers more free-will, and that we have choices that can make a difference. Still, how much responsibility a person takes for their life is a personal matter, and the Bible as a whole, doesn't conclusively interfere with those choices.

Hyper-Calvinists believe that a person has zero responsibility for their own salvation; it is all up to God. They site Romans 9:15 and 9:21 for support of this position.

L: This stands for Limited atonement. This is the belief that Jesus did not die to save all humans. Since people are predestined by their load of karma, Jesus's sacrifice only helped atone those who were already saved. In other words, he died to save already saved people from particular sins, which altho a little absurd, many see as much more reasonable than the idea that he saved everyone who came before or after him from all of the responsibility of their own actions.

See: Matthew 26:28 and Ephesians 5:25.

I: This stands for "Irresistible Grace:" This is the belief that every human whom God has elected (i.e., whose weight of karma is light enough to lead a virtuous life) will inevitably come to a knowledge of God. The elect person cannot resist the call, which again relates to predestination based on the amount of one's personal issues.

See John 6:44, Romans 8:14, and First Peter 5:10.

P: This stands for "Perseverance of the saints:" This is the "Once saved, always saved" belief. It reiterates the Irresistible Grace premise -the idea that once a certain level of consciousness is achieved, a person can't go back to less mature beliefs and attitudes. In other words, it is impossible for them to lose their salvation.

See Philippians 1:6, Romans 8:28-39, and John 6:39.

TULIP - It sounds like the Spring bloom of salvation. In actuality, it represents something very oppressive and limiting to our human potential and to our divine creative right. Following in the footsteps of Martin Luther, John Calvin took steps to break the monopoly the Catholics had on Christianity. He returned the issue of salvation to the individual, as opposed to leaving it at the whim of the Catholic intermediary. However, seeing all the violence and misguided souls around him, he probably believed that most weren't going to make it to heaven (in their present lifetime) no matter what.

His followers joined hoping that they were among the elect. They lived the strict lives he demanded and enforced, and they lived in fear that they weren't ever going to be be able to lead good enough lives. This maintained order, until enlightenment could catch up with Calvinism and create a more user-friendly system of beliefs.

Today, some protestant faiths are still very close to Calvin's original beliefs. Traditional beliefs give some people comfort -- as long as you don't think about it too much with your common sense engaged.

The New Thought movement on the other hand, stresses the power of the individual over their lives and salvation. They have reclaimed the divinity and responsibility of the individual.

However, they usually don't have much appreciation for cooperation with the mystical template (God).

Meanwhile traditional religions, who do have an appreciation for "the will of God," are struggling to reconcile the Bible's message about an all-powerful God with what they know in their own hearts about individual responsibility.

So today, we have these two basic perspectives sitting in opposition to each other:

1. The divinity of humans and the need to take responsibility for
our own lives and our own salvation.

2. The Calvinistic appreciation for cooperating with an unknowable
divine plan and a purpose that is also bigger than anything we can
personally know.

Realizing the latter keeps us humble and in a place where we can better relate to the challenges and perspectives of others. And frankly, it helps keeps humans in their place, so we don't violate the first commandment by putting ourselves above the good of the whole.

These are the two primary principles that we, in the dualistic world, tend to choose between -- instead of trying to harmonize together.

However, when we try to work both of these attitudes into a plan for our lives, all the illusive spiritual qualities that Jesus taught fall into place. We discover humility, empathy, and Christian charity for each other (from an appreciation for realization #2). We also find our connection to a reliable link to the inspiration we need for a satisfying personal involvement in our life (from realization #1).

The trinity is something that keeps reemerging in all religions (Christian as well as all others). The esoteric basis for that is the positive, negative and the neutralizing forces that keep the universe dynamic but still in balance.

In this case, we have the two ideas: the power and providence of God verses the divine rights and power of humankind. Knowing our place in the divine plan is what reconciles these, and one way to learn more about our place in the divine scheme of things is by seeking the wisdom to reconcile those two ideas.

That wisdom is not easily found in the Bible. It's fine if people want to pick certain passages and ignore others so they can conclude that the whole answer is in "God's word." However, we are each the living word. And the wisest and safest message to give the world is what Buddha called The Middle Path.

This way we can be the neutralizing force that helps harmonize everyone else, regardless of their cultural or religious beliefs. That's the practical spiritual approach and the illusive path that will finally lead to peace on Earth.

Hunt Henion **http://www.shiftawareness.com http://www. examiner.com/practical-spirituality-innational/hunt-henion**

Article Source: **http://EzineArticles.com/6363552**

O My Godness!

by Linda Martella-Whitsett

Recently, the governor of Texas, Rick Perry, got together with some of his influential religious friends to hold a national day of prayer for America--America populated by people of various faith traditions that, alas, were under-represented at the prayer gathering. Devotees of only one religion, Christianity, were invited. Perry supplicated,

> *Lord, you are the source of every good thing, you are our only hope. And we stand before you today in awe of your power, and in gratitude for your blessings, in humility for our sins. Father, our heart breaks for America. We see discord at home. We see fear in the marketplace. We see anger in the halls of government. And as a nation we have forgotten who made us, who protects us, who blesses us, and for that we cry out for your forgiveness.*

I grew up asking God for forgiveness. Raised in Roman Catholicism in the sixties, I regularly entered the dark closet of confession to tell a priest the number of times I took the Lord's name in vain, how I snuck cigarettes on the way to and from school, and other assorted transgressions. I felt cleansed when absolved of my sins. With a clear conscience, I started over. I swore again, inhaled again, sinned again.

No doubt Perry and his cronies were sincere, just as I was during those impassioned moments of religious fervor. But...but...what good will it do to pray sincerely with hardly an intention of changing our behavior? As long as we give God all the responsibility, we can go about our only-human lives feeling impotent. We can't help it! We're only human.

I believe it is about time for us to mature spiritually, to take on our Divine Identity. In my estimation we need, and the world needs us, to stop pretending that G O D is a superhuman cleaning up our messes. G O D is not a person we pray to, but a power we access. G O D is the inexpressible Source of all Good, the Good we express in our Divine human experience.

Oneness: Another Name for G O D

My path is Unity, the spiritual movement begun over a century ago by Charles and Myrtle Fillmore (with headquarters at Unity Village, Missouri). Unity teachings are linked to the great mystical paths found in every faith tradition, teachings espousing the unity of the Divine -- there is only One: One Power, One Presence, One Life. Many call this One G O D.

In a lengthy section of The Secret Book of John (Nag Hammadi Library **www.gnosis.org**), the One is described poetically. It reads, in part:

The One is the Invisible Spirit.
It is not right to think of it as a God or as like God.
It is more than just God.
Nothing is above it
Nothing rules it.
Since everything exists within it
It does not exist within anything.
Since it is not dependent on anything
It is eternal.
It is absolutely complete and so needs nothing.
It is utterly perfect
Light...
Light
Producing light
Life
Producing life
Blessedness
Producing blessedness
Knowledge
Producing knowledge
Good
Producing goodness
Mercy
Producing mercy
Generosity
Producing generosity
It does not "possess" these things.

Aramaic scholar Neil Douglas Klotz suggests that the culture into which Jesus of Nazareth was born understood the Divine Nature as Unity -- the Holy One. Hebrew scriptures support this idea: Hear O Israel: the Lord our God, the Lord is One. (Deuteronomy 6.4)

The Hindu tradition of yoga introduced by Patanjali in the 2nd century BC is a pathway to spiritual unity. The word "yoga" means to unite. The Sveta Svatara Upanishad (6.11) reveals, in : He is the one God, hidden in all beings, all-pervading, the Self within all beings..."

G O D is not a person, but a Power, a Source, a Principle. Myrtle Fillmore wrote:

Though personal to each one of us, God is IT, neither male nor female, but Principle, God is not a cold, senseless principle like that of mathematics, but the Principle of life, love, and intelligence. (How to Let God Help You, 3rd ed., Unity House, Unity Village, MO, 2000)

In the way that a prism bends light into an array of diverse colors, or a wintry cloud breaks out into billions of unique snowflakes, the inexpressible One takes on infinite expressions --as life, love, intelligence, and all qualities that could be recognized as divine. All these divine qualities are expressible by you and by me. We are the inexpressible One expressing. We are divine.

Our Divine Identity

I and the Father are One. Credited to Jesus in the Gospel of John, this truth is thematic throughout Jewish and Christian writings. Jesus is said to have said, in effect, when you see me you see the Father --the Source, the One. The Gospel of Thomas, widely regarded a Gnostic text, puts these words into the mouth of Jesus: *I am the one who derives his being from the One who is undifferentiated...Whoever is united will be filled with Light...* (Logion 61) Furthermore, in Logion 49, Jesus taught, *Blessed are they that are One within themselves. They will find the Kingdom."* The kingdom is the reign of unity or oneness consciousness.

Echos of this truth appear in teachings from around the

globe. The Mahaparinirvana Sutra declares, *Every being has the Buddha nature.* (verse 214) The Kena Upanishad (I.5-9 in translation by Eknath Easwaran,Nilgiri Press, 1987) concurs:

That which makes the tongue speak but cannot be
Spoken by the tongue, know that as the Self.
This Self is not someone other than you...

That which makes you draw breath but cannot be
Drawn by your breath, that is the Self indeed.
This Self is not someone other than you.

In my book, *How to Pray Without Talking to God: Moment by Moment, Choice by Choice*, I recount my experience of my daughter Alicia's birth. I recall my first gaze upon her newborn body and my accompanying thoughts and feelings. Despite my childhood religious education specifying we are born in sin, when I beheld my beautiful baby I saw no taint of sin in her. There is no such thing as a sin gene. We are One with the One. We are divine.

We can know we are divine by observing the replication of life in the natural world. Nowhere in nature could a fertilized chicken egg produce something besides a baby chick. Never will you see a peach ripening on a tree grown from an apple seed. We, too, can be nothing other than that from which our life derives, that which we call the One. Whatever we can imagine is possible for the divine, is possible for us by our spiritual DNA.

Whenever we experience and express Love, we are Divine Love. Whenever we intuitively know when to act and what to do, we are Divine Wisdom. Since the divine is not a person but rather a principle and we are, so to speak, a chip off the old block, the Love Principle and the Wisdom Principle are our true nature. We can identify ourselves as these principles. We can claim Divine Identity.

If we are Divine, why don't we always act like it?

When Jesus said *Whoever is united will be filled with Light*...(Logion 61) , he taught further that *whoever is divided will be filled with darkness*. Human darkness is the condition of forgetfulness. When we believe, erroneously, that we are "only human" dividing ourselves out from our essential Unity --we dwell in darkness.

A consciousness of separation --from G O D, from others, and from ourselves --is responsible for the horrors in our human experience. Actions arising from sensing ourselves as "only human" are at best limited and inferior; at worst ungodly.

Andrew Harvey, in The Direct Path (Broadway, 2001), addresses human forgetfulness this way:

Our essential self is hidden from us by what the Sufi mystics call 'a hundred thousand veils of illusion.' Placed in this dimension of time and space and matter, we forget who we are; we identify our essential nature with what surrounds us and with what our culture and society and parents and ordinary senses tell us about ourselves; a massive journey is then needed for us to 'dis-identify' with everything we have falsely learned about ourselves so that we can experience, with the 'hundred thousand veils' burned away, the glory of our true identity.

Imelda Shanklin, in her 1961 book What Are You? (Unity School of Christianity), writes:

You are a soul that has forgotten its divine identity; a soul now struggling to remember, in the mists of time and in the confusions of experiences, that you are the living sons of the living God...If you will live in as full accordance with your divine nature as your present state of preparation makes possible, you will be made aware of your true identity. As the victim of amnesia persists in recalling personal identity, so you must persist in recalling spiritual identity. While you pray, read, meditate, practice spiritual Truth, a flicker, then a beam, then the full light of restored consciousness will dawn, and you will know yourself.

How to assert your Divine Identity

Moment by moment, choice by choice, you decide whether you are an "only human" or you are divine. When your best friend is given a grim diagnosis, you have a choice of whether to feel sorry for her, imagining her poor body suffering; or to sense her Divine Identity that is Life, Strength, Wisdom, and Order, imagining her body's amazing intelligence at work. When your flight is delayed hour after hour and you feel exhausted, you have a choice of whether to grumble and pout about your circumstances or to appreciate the gift of unscheduled down time you can devote to reading a novel, conversing with another waiting passenger, walking through the terminal or...whatever is available that you would like to do! When your beloved dies and you are grieving, you have a choice of whether to imagine yourself alone for the rest of your life or to derive strength from the Love that always was and always will be within you and between the two of you.

You assert your Divine Identity every time you claim a Divine attribute. Pray and meditate daily to build spiritual power. Periodically go away on silent retreat to set aside your material concerns and dwell without distraction in Oneness. Study the truths about Divine Nature in various spiritual disciplines. Take exquisite care of your body, mind, and spirit, increasing your capacity to identify yourself as Divine.

Living as the Light of the World

Claiming our Divine Identity is possible. We do not have to beg a superhuman deity to confer it upon us. We do not have to earn it by penance and suffering. We do not have to go on a lifelong journey to find it, as if it were a treasure hidden elsewhere. We do not have to pretend helplessness or behave with false modesty in order to feel acceptable in a culture that mistakes Divine Identity for egomania. We claim our Divine Identity moment by moment, choice by choice. In Biblical terms, we are a city built on a hill; our light cannot be hidden. (Matthew 5:14)

Light is a resonant theme in religious writings of every tradition in every age. Light is symbolic of Divine Illumination, the Divine Light we are in Oneness. The light that shines above the heavens and above this world, the light that shines in the highest world, beyond which there are no others–that is the light that shines in the hearts of men. (Chandogya Upanishad)

Jesus said, If they say to you, 'Where did you come from?', say to them, 'We came from the light, the place where the light came into being on its own accord and established itself and became manifest through their image.' If they say to you, 'Is it you?', say, 'We are its children, we are the elect of the living father. (Gospel of Thomas, Logion 50)

Knowing our Divine Identity, we become the reconciling force in the world rued by Governor Perry. We do not ask outside ourselves for forgiveness. We shine the light of G O D upon our world, through our thoughts, words, and actions. We do not shine only when life seems wonderful. We shine when light is most needed. In the words of Elisabeth Kubler-Ross, People are like stained-glass windows. They sparkle and shine when the sun is out, but when the darkness sets in, their true beauty is revealed only if there is a light from within. G O D is the origin of the light. You are the light shining. You are Divine.

Rev. Linda Martella-Whitsett is minister at Unity Church of San Antonio, author of How to Pray Without Talking to God: Moment by Moment, Choice by Choice (Hampton Roads Publishing Co., 2011). **www.ur-divine.com**

Oneness: an Essay for Spiritual Growth from Master Yeshua

Channeled by Sharon K. Richards

I will speak today of Oneness.

When I speak of Oneness, I speak of what you would call a network. In the Unitarian Universalist Church, this is called the network of all living things. This particular teaching is one of the closest among the religious groups to what Oneness means. As Oneness translates from the scientific side, ecology, from the earth sciences, would come the closest.

The Physics of Oneness

Oneness is an energetic network. If you could see, you'd understand that, energetically, the connections are unbreakable. They exist. These energetic connections cannot be escaped. As your scientists would have it, energy is neither created nor destroyed, only changed in form. I believe that would pass close enough to the delimitation used by the scientists. I am not a scientist. That is not my specialty.

Then let us make it clear that you are all connected with energy. There is energy always --interlaced, interwoven, inter-dependent energy. You may think that you are separate, but you exist as energy in a network. You create an energy field. You radiate.

Humanity senses energy through smell, through sound, through taste. These are manifestations of energy fields. Smell may be one of the most useful analogies for this essay on Oneness.

Fragrance – An Energy Field

You smell the fragrance of a flower. If you have allergies, you are definitely sensitive to the smell of, for instance, pollen-laden air. Undoubtedly you recognize the smell of your favorite food from the next room.

Let us take; however, the fragrance of a flower. Some

flowers are quite pungent, you come close and you smell them. Animals smell water. Animals smell food. Energy fields are just as real as these smells.

Your flower is rooted someplace or is sitting in a vase and you smell it. The waste dump may be a considerable distance from you, but you smell it. You call it pollution.

I think I have made my point. Energy fields are analogous to smell. One does not eliminate the smell. You can do chemical treatments, you can do air purification, you can do all sorts of things to cover up as you attempt to destroy the smell. And you might even succeed.

But with the energy fields that keep you in Oneness with the environment, with each other, with the entire of Creation – those energy fields cannot be treated, purified, covered up or destroyed. They exist, they are there. Always.

Individuality

Now Oneness does not negate individuality. And again I will go to flowers.

Each flower – choose one of your favorite fragrant flowers. If you have one of them or two of them, they are still individual flowers. They each have their own fragrance. And as one flower reaches the end of its life, you pull it out of your vase or it wilts and dies in the field, it is gone. It has transitioned.

Inter-dimensional Oneness

As an individual flower, it has transitioned. But, as energy, it is still part of Creation's energy network. It is simply in a different dimension – at a different level, on a different plane – however you care to envision it.

So not only is there a horizontal Oneness of energy fields, interlaced, interconnecting, irrefutably inter-dependent, there is a vertical Oneness dimensionally. If you care to think of it as the physical world and the world of spirit, that's fine. That's a start. Each world – the physical world, the spiritual world – can be granulated into finer and finer distinctions, but to say, grossly, "physical" and "spiritual" will give you the idea that there is also a vertical interdependency of all energy.

So there are multiple dimensions working here. This is a 3-D Creation at minimum. We add a 4th dimension – we add time. And there is much talk of a 5th dimension. But I'm not going there now.

Total Interdependence

I want to get across the concept of an irrefutably, irrevocably inter-dependent Oneness so that every individual point, every individual subatomic particle if you care to go that fine, has an energy field and that energy field overlaps – interconnects with – the energy fields of the next subatomic particles all the way up.

Those interdependencies cannot be eliminated. It is simply not possible.

It is not possible for one person to be walking down the street and say, "I am not connected with this crowd of people waiting for something to happen at the corner."

It is impossible to be walking through the woods, or walking across the prairie and say, "I am not connected with the trees or the grasses or the ground or the sky."

You are connected.

You may be able to see easily the immediate interconnections – your family, your friends, your neighbors, the animals you slaughter for meat, the grasses you harvest for food. You might be able to see that, but you are also connected – interconnected energetically, irrefutably, irrevocably – halfway around the world. You're connected to other human beings you will never meet, to the soil halfway around the world, to the plant life halfway around the world – or, if you're working from pole to pole, the ice at the other pole.

You are connected.

"What happens halfway around the world," you say, "does not affect my life. I don't have to worry about that. I don't have to worry about what happens here or there or anyplace, except what I am able to sense and deal with and get my arms around in my own local life. And the rest is someone else's problem."

You can say that, but "someone else's problem" is energetically connected through a web of energies that we call Creation. And it is connected to you.

The healthier this interconnected network, the more joyous is Creation, starting with the earth, the planet that gives us life, that gives life meaning. Joy starts with you.

If you do not care for the earth in which you live, and care for all parts of the earth and do your part to keep the earth healthy, if you are not doing that, then there is a part of you that you are not keeping healthy. For you are energetically connected – the horizontal connection.

The soul is energy and you are also connected vertically. From within, you are connected spiritually to the higher realms and other dimensions.

But that, I think, I will leave for a further discussion. And the reason is that some would have Oneness exist only spiritually and not physically.

Spiritual Oneness Manifests On Earth

I am here to tell you that Oneness at the spiritual level exists in the same manner I have described for the physical. But unless that Oneness, that interconnected web of energies that exists spiritually, unless that filters down and manifests in consciousness on the physical plane, then Oneness has not been achieved.

Oneness still remains the goal and the objective. In Oneness you can look at your neighbors – immediate neighbors, the neighbors that share this planet with you – and understand that their pain is your pain. In Oneness you have the compassion and the willingness to assist energetically. You understand your energetic connection to the earth, for the earth is as much God's creation as you are.

Creative Power of Oneness

Just as you can create good relationships with your family – with your neighbors, with other countries – so with determination, with intent, with purpose, you can create other good and loving relationships. It can be done.

And as you create these healthy relationships, you discover a creative power within – the power of Oneness. You have the creative power to heal the earth. This, too, you'll find within.

Can you do it alone? I don't know. Can you? I would suggest that you'll get it done faster if you work together.

Oneness does not mean cookie cutter, standard conformity in any way. Oneness means an acknowledgment of the energies that exist, the energies that are not yet seen and measured as they bind us together – we in the spiritual realm and all on the physical plane. Oneness is the web of energies that binds and keeps this Creation together.

What happens at a distance, what happens to any part of this Creation does not happen in isolation. It has ramifications. I will not pretend that all ramifications have the same reach or resonate to the same extent, but they are connected. They do resonate.

If you would have health and peace, let the love that exists at the very core of each and every one of you emerge. Let this love come forth, the inner knowledge that tells you, yes, you are energetically connected. Let that come forth and manifest.

Apply and live the knowledge of this energetic connection. You can create a better world by creating a better relationship with those you touch, with those you interconnect with – with the building you live in, with the earth you walk on. That better world you create. You can create.

Summary

The network of energetic connections is there. It is up to you whether you make that existing network brighter, healthier, more loving or not.

These are your decisions, and you have the free will, which was my first essay. You have the free will to decide what kind of creation you are sending into that network. You decide how loving, compassionate, and healthy the creation you contribute is.

That is what I wish to say about Oneness.

My blessings on you all. May you understand, appreciate and live creating a healthier, happier energetic network that is the One.

Blessings,
Yeshua / Jeshua

Channeler
Sharon K. Richards currently channels eleven members of Earth's Spiritual Hierarchy. "Oneness" appears on **http:// ThoughtsFromAMaster.com**, a site devoted to Master Yeshua's thoughts for spiritual growth. **http://WeSeekToServe. com**, a second site of channeled teachings, is devoted to the panel discussions of several Masters of Wisdom sharing perspectives on the same topic.

Master Yeshua
Master Yeshua /Jeshua (aka Jesus of Nazareth) is a Master of Wisdom and a member of Earth's Spiritual Hierarchy.

Our Common Pond

by Colleen Engel-Brown

I have always treasured a remark made by the late Dr. Marcus Bach, a world renowned author and professor of comparative religions in Iowa. After investigating the Unity way of life, he concluded that, "Unity is shallow enough for a child to wade in but too deep to ever touch bottom." So provocative! Unity creates room for the person of simple faith as well as one with an enlightened mind. Many, if not all of us, possess inquiring minds that truly do want to know. As a life-long "spiritual treasure hunter" it continues to be my passion to share these gems I find with other seekers.

Growing up in a White Anglo-Saxon protestant environment my father a Free Will Baptist preacher, I continue to marvel in the discovery of the Unity way of life in 1978. As a girl, I played piano in various churches thereby becoming keenly interested in doctrinal differences but was subsequently drawn to a more universal compassion I experienced in the Methodist Church. Marrying a Catholic added more expansive, progressive exposure or an unfolding awareness of wide ranging religious and spiritual issues. This culminated in a focus on principles which affirm and reverence all humanity, all viewpoints and all life even before finding metaphysics. Unity's metaphysical teachings later provided me with even richer insights into the spiritual laws that govern all life.

All paths lead to God. Some do take longer, some are more flamboyant, some more complex yet how gratifying to find one that speaks to one planet, one humanity, one God. And keeping it simple. Through the schoolroom of Life we are collectively, slowly, yet ever expanding consciousness. I believe that unity evolves one soul at a time until it reaches critical mass, and then breakthroughs manifest. I speak of "unity" in diversity--not uniformity, which is a terrible substitute for unity.

As a seminarian at Unity Village, I was introduced to the "Five Ms" which uniquely describe the fate of organizations. These are Man, Message, Movement, Machine and Monument. A man becomes inspired. He shares that inspiring Message/

product/service, which leads to creating a company, institution, church, a corporation or, simply a global Movement. In time that which was created becomes mindless, thus a machine, rather robotic. This entity preserves itself eventually becoming a lifeless Monument, or minds set in concrete. Some would say this process seems to be occurring in organized religions, as well as in social, political, and economic models. It generally explains the fate of and/or history of continual change in the world. It is notable that the the only person who likes change is a wet baby though change is the one constant in life. Change is forever death of the old and inflexible, yet, a guarantee of a renewing or new vitality and new form. Creative living is not just adjusting to change, but pushing and promoting change. The current wave of change is the result of changes initiated so many centuries ago that we can hardly track them. We who live in the midst of today's changes cannot see how they will become the fabric that future generations take for granted. When in the whirlpool of change, we cannot ascertain exactly what changes are taking place: or where they will take us. What we can do is to welcome change rather than resist it. See it as an opportunity to view and embrace many more of our global (and some are saying intergalactic) family.

I see the need to be more attuned to the adventure of change than to f.e.a.r., i.e., fear being false evidence appearing real. There is nothing to fear: only something to know! My passion is in helping others recognize they are Godlings--children of God--inheriting the same powers, the same creative ability of that Eternal Something called Father-Mother God. The change Jesus, the master teacher, brought was godling awareness-- as the ultimate goal of Christos consciousness. Especially for those who previously considered themselves mere earthlings... what a colossal mind-shift! After only two thousand years, it's beginning to take root in our belief systems.

We have chosen to be here at this time on this planet to observe and to participate in the change that is lifting humanity. I wouldn't have missed it for the world.

Graduation...change...maturation comes to everything. Why not, then, to civilization world wide? What a trip this Planet Earth! So how do we equip ourselves? I strongly believe that meditation is the Key. Meditation and medication come from the same root word meaning 'to heal.' There are many forms, and all people meditate if it is nothing more than closing their eyes to reflect or to dream of "what ifs". Unity's co-founder, Charles Fillmore, wearied of conflicting teachings and opinions, said this, "In the midst of all this babble I will go to headquarters." He meant communing personally with the Creator. That is the ultimate goal. Practicing oneness, as Brother Lawrence practiced the presence of God, equips us to handle the daily mundane as well as the daily change.

A happenstance viewing of Ian Lungold's 2004 DVD, "The Mayan Calendar Comes North," created a personal epiphany, leading me to the realization that the meditative mindset was exactly what was needed to handle this now occurring "shift of the ages." The last 45 minutes of that DVD left me excited about what lies ahead. Our soul contracts (ah, you know about those if you are reading this anthology) are assured. We can celebrate! The world IS transforming in a grand way, in spite of appearances.

How does this play out in every day life? When I reflect on Jesus, I see a man who was acutely aware of negatives swirling around Him, but He proceeded to create positives. I am aware of the dire predictions, the headline grabbing stories, the fearsome fictions of the day. But those things don't exist on the meditative, creative level where our soul is one with God. The Author of All That Is is not a loser, and neither will we lose anything vital to our eternal livingness.

Today is the beginning of a new level of conscious awareness, the potential (promised) ending of duality and the beginning of new levels of evolution. It really is an inside job. I'm here. Here for all, loving so passionately, and filled with anticipation and eagerness to see what the future holds. Now, does that mean I do not see the potential for economic collapse and attendant events? Yes. I do see it. We must each be aware of our internal guidance systems, honor what it tells us, following through accordingly.

Rev Colleen Engel-Brown a Unity minister since 1982. After being retired for a number of years, she is again serving her former pastorate in Cordova, Tennessee (**http://www.unitymemphis. org/**). She also conducts at consulting/coaching practice and has a street-side ministry known as Urban Abbey.

Being at One

by Colin Whitby

We'll discuss our interconnectedness and unity -- getting in touch with each other, building community and cooperative efforts in one way or another.

Many of the self help courses to be found these days are related to bringing us to a better understanding of ourselves, by getting in touch with that part of us that is at one with all. This God self, this source or divine being is what we truly are and paradoxically when we touch this place in ourselves we then find how we are connected to everyone and everything. It is from this place that we create, or should I say co-create, because it is in this state of 'being at one' that we automatically create for the benefit of all.

So how do we find our way here, and how do we stay connected to this centre and therefore to each other during what can sometimes seem to be rather chaotic times. Well for me it has been and still is an ongoing process, each transformational stage has been closely followed by another in a journey of awareness and collaborative connectivity that is in fact my life passion. Often we hear that it is the journey and not the destination that is our purpose, and that has been very much my experience to date.

Being Ourselves

So the first step in this journey is when we begin to realise that there is more to our lives than just 'doing' and 'owning stuff'. For many this may have been as a result of some life changing event or illness, others have experienced a slow realisation that there is much more to life than what we see or experience with our five senses.

Looking back over the last 30 years I can trace the path and the synchronicities that have led me to this moment, where each twist and turn has helped steer and guide my connection with the divine, with my own God self. This will be unique for everyone, I'm sure, there is no right or wrong way to 'be' here, and often it can be quite disorienting as we move from one state to another.

Over the last few years it has become possible to connect with ourselves, and therefore each other, at a much deeper level than ever before. Much of this can be attributed to the way our energies are synchronizing and harmonizing with universal and galactic energies as the earth moves more squarely into the Aquarian age.

Individually we have been prompted by our higher selves to explore our own divinity, which for me has resulted in an awareness of many of my 'soul' aspects that are outside my normal experiences here on earth.

Connecting to our Oneness

When we go deeply into ourselves we connect to that sacred place within us that feels so deep, a very small point in our hearts, which seems so minute until we open into it. I use the term 'turning inside out' to describe how I move from this small place to the infinite, the ultimate God/source point. Some people are calling this the zero point, or quantum field. This is where all is one, the point of creation itself.

As I open and enter through this point I can feel myself suddenly connected to everything , to the chair on which I am sitting, the room, the house, the street and on outwards until the very edge of our Galaxy become part of my experience.

At this point I can connect with others, be they on earth or beyond our current conscious awareness. As an example I have included a meditation that was part of an interview with Sue Lie in her Arcturian Sessions (link to recording). It is from this quiet place that I am able to write this chapter; from this place that I realize that we co-create our reality with the deepest expression of love we can possibly be in the moment.

Connecting to our Passion

At a weekend workshop with a group of like minded souls I became aware of my own passion, to bring love to a new level on earth, where all share equally and unconditionally our own interconnectedness and love expression with each other.

This is a natural place for us to 'be' yet our programming has persuaded us that we are less than the creator beings we are (hence the many courses that have appeared over recent years to help us realize and release our blockages).

So my passion is to 'be' the love (of God) and then to enable others to be their own unique expression of that love, of the divine. I used to think that I had to fix everyone, or to show them how to fix themselves, assuming they were broken in some way. Many healers have fallen into this trap and forget to 'heal' themselves first. It is the journey into ourselves and through loving ourselves unconditionally that we realise all is in its place, and we simply need to 'be' ourselves.

Co-creation

This place of unity 'where all is one' is the goal of many meditative practices, to attain a state of complete stillness and peace. Within this blissful experience I have found myself inspired to look around, explore where I am, what I can see, hear and feel. This is the source of inspirational energy and from where I 'journey' with others to share our experience as we begin to co-create our world together.

The sharing of love at this deepest level is the most exquisite experience. To cocreate from this place is indeed a joy and a privilege.

What do we create from here? For me it is whatever surfaces in the moment. It may be a request to quieten or soften a hurricane, perhaps to lessen the impact of an oil spill or to smooth our earth's transition by sending love into her tectonic plates. Sometimes we can be inspired to co-create an aspect of our new Paradise on Earth, the new world in which this open expression of ourselves lives and creates freely with everyone.

As we gather together in groups we can really make a difference, knowingly creating together. There are many examples of this happening in the world, many enabled by the Internet, an outward expression of our growing interconnectedness. Here are some that I have been drawn to, each uses its own unique language and each has its place in our new world.

• The New Age Study of Humanity's Purpose

> • Regardless of how far you think you are from reflecting the fact that you are a Beloved and Divine Child of God, this information from the Beings of Light in the Realms of Illumined Truth will awaken within you that Inner Knowing. You have been preparing for aeons of time to fulfill your unique facet of the Divine Plan, which is now unfolding on Earth.

Era of Peace (**http://www.eraofpeace.org**) is the home for the non-profit, educational
organization New Age Study of Humanity's Purpose, Inc., which sponsors the Annual World Congress On Illumination.

• Lightworker with Steve and Barbara Rother

> • Here at Lightworker you will find a joyous re-union in progress. It is a re-union of people re-connecting to their own power and each other. We invite you to join in on any level that you feel comfortable. Lightworker is a place to help you remember who you really are and why you are here. Our greatest hope is that we may help you to re-member what you planned for yourself before you were born into this life.

Lightworker (**http://www.lightworker.com/**)

• The Shift Network

> • The Shift Network, Inc. aims to empower a global movement of people who are creating an evolutionary shift of consciousness that in turn leads to a more enlightened society, one built on principles of sustainability, peace, health, and prosperity. Now is the time for an upgrade to our planetary operating system. If you are part of this

Shift, please join us as we create events, programs, and activities that help us evolve!

The Shift Network (**http://theshiftnetwork.com/**)

• The Crimson Circle

• The Crimson Circle is a global affiliation of New Energy humans, including metaphysicians, healers, teachers and counselors coming from all walks of life, a wide variety of spiritual backgrounds, and from over 100 countries around the world. They celebrate the awakening of a new consciousness, the journey of the human angel, and the gift of life on Earth in these amazing, transformational times.

The Crimson Circle (**http://www.crimsoncircle.com/**)

• Blooming Humans

• We're Gathering to Birth a New Reality, by activating Dream Seeds within Ourselves and at the Heart of Humanity. Each and every being on the planet carries a Dream Seed, held sacred at the center of our Hearts, present and ready for our attentions to bring our unique visions and gifts into reality.

Blooming Humans (**http://bloominghumans.com/**)

• Children of the Sun

• Children of the Sun's charity to Earth is in ensuring we form global Group Avatar, empty of self and one with coherently connected, ascended and free Divine Consciousness. We serve for the fulfillment of the highest potential of all Humanity and the new I AM Race on Ascended Earth.

Children of the Sun (**http://www.childrenofthesun.org/**)

One of the most powerful examples I have found of how we work together as a 'group avatar' can be found with Children of the Sun. Here we join together at new and full moons to offer our service to do specific activities together. We are now over 1000 strong and the energy of the group is absolutely astounding.

As more people move into this energy of love we will see and feel a difference in our lives. I have noticed a difference in how quickly my own requests are manifest. I regularly practice connecting with my angel(s) by asking for the most benevolent outcome to situations after having been sent a wonderful book to review (The Gentle Way by Tom T. Moore). It is with practice that we begin to develop our creative skills, we need to remember that we are creator beings and then reinforce that knowing by consciously developing our abilities.

Being Magical

Much of my work in the physical world is centred around providing communication systems and processes for businesses and their customers. As a telecommunications manager I helped establish networks and telephone systems to enable people to connect with each other, and my current role as a contact strategist is still focused on our interconnectedness, how to provide a service which fulfils a purpose for both the customer and for the business. I find this maps very well with how I work energetically.

My guidance has been, and still is, to 'be all I can be' here and now, in my work, at home or wherever I am. It is in 'being all we can be', being our divine selves, that we can 'be the change we want to see in the world' (Ghandi).

So be yourself, be at one, 'be all you can be' and enjoy being part of the creation of this beautiful Heaven on Earth.

Website:
http://www.multidimensionalalchemy.com/alchemist/

Shift the World with Deep Listening

by Cynthia Sue Larson, MBA

Imagine what it would feel like if everyone you spoke to, and everyone you met listened deeply to all you had to say, with obvious empathy and without once interrupting or interjecting their own thoughts or feelings. How does it feel to envision a world in which everyone listens respectfully to everyone else? Can you picture your family, neighborhood, and community all listening to one another deeply and fully?

Heart-centered, open-minded listening provides us with the power to change the world, one conversation at a time. When our personal truth is honored, we feel an enhanced sense of respect, connection, and trust with those who listen deeply to all we have to share. We feel kinder, gentler, and more courageous when we are honored for speaking our truth. Barriers between people of wildly disparate backgrounds crumble and fall, as a sense of shared oneness permeates relationships based on deep listening.

Deep listening allows people to shift between parallel worlds of possibility, moving from communications based in mistrust and doubt, to relationships founded on respect and trust. Deep listening has the power to transform our lives by inviting us to reconsider all manner of assumptions, prejudices, and beliefs. Rather than pushing ideas forward of what we think best and right, we can experience exceptional results by listening to and addressing ideas that are very different from ours. Deep listening is a state of mindfulness we enter humbly, by emptying our mental cup of whatever point we are trying to prove, and whatever beliefs we fear may be threatened. Deep listening requires a courageous leap of faith, as all preconceived notions are set aside in order to give one's full attention to what is right here, right now.

The basic steps involved in mastering the art of deep listening can be taught and learned. They involve providing speaker and listener with a time and place to converse, and providing steps for the listener to follow that serve to inspire confidence, trust, and openness from the speaker. Within such a framework, listening becomes an active process, in which the listener demonstrates respect for the speaker as a person, and respect for what the speaker focuses on. The art of paying such rapt attention to a speaker may seem unusual, yet people everywhere recognize listeners who show such uncommon levels of interest and respect.

I had an extraordinary experience with the power of my deep listening to transform the world when I was involved in a grass-roots local political campaign to rebuild a Berkeley neighborhood elementary school in the early 1990s. The school site council I led faced overwhelming opposition from the superintendent and the school board members. Some of us felt discouraged because we were completely disregarded by those with the power to influence change. Rather than more loudly proclaim our point of view, I actively sought out and listened deeply to all aspects of each school site council member's concerns. Through listening deeply to what they had to say, we addressed their concerns one at a time, slowly but surely changing the school board votes from "no" to "yes" for our proposal. I experienced amazing intuitive guidance during that time, which further revealed the power of listening as the ultimate way to influence positive change in the world. Before one evening's school board meeting, I was about to drive my car out of my driveway, when an overwhelming impulse to stop the car and pick one of the roses on my rose bush became too tempting to ignore. I carried that salmon-colored rose with me into the large room where the school board meeting was to be conducted that evening, and followed another powerful impulse to place the rose on the table of a school board member who'd been on the fence regarding our proposal. I wrote a note that simply said, "Please vote according to your conscience," which I left with the rose. When the doors to the closed chambers opened, and the school board members entered the room, I was stunned to see the woman I'd left the note for embrace the rose lovingly in her hands for the entire meeting... a rose whose color exactly matched the two piece suit she was wearing!

One of the most radical, powerful, effective actions we can take in any situation is to choose to listen deeply. Deep listening is akin to the eastern concept of Yin, whose complement is the active Yang. We are blessed to live in a highly interactive universe, full of energetic responses to our every thought, feeling, and action. While we often become preoccupied with getting things done by projecting our thoughts, feelings and actions, we can lose our balance if we forget to be as receptive as we are active. Attaining a state of optimal receptivity for deep listening requires that we achieve a disciplined state of mindfulness in which we remain alert, open-hearted, and open-minded. Such disciplined mindfulness can be attained by a variety of methods, including athletes refer to it as being "in the zone," what psychologists call "active listening," what Quakers call, "a clearness committee," and what physicists and linguists call, "Bohmian dialogue."

Get In the Zone

Before delving into relationships we have with others, we can begin the art of deep listening by mastering the fine art of listening to ourselves – by learning a more disciplined way to hear our own self-talk. Some of the top experts in this field of expertise are athletes, who must learn to master mind-body clarity and discipline in order to succeed. Athletes refer to the optimal state of mind-body clarity as being "in the zone" – a rarefied state of consciousness in which performance is exceptional and consistent, automatic and flowing. Mental conditioning trainers such as Trevor Moawad explain that the average person engages in self-talk at a rate of 300 to 1,000 words a minute, and this self-talk can range from being phenomenally empowering to extremely self-critical and self-destructive. Athletes learn that the way they handle their self-talk makes a tremendous difference in their performance, particularly at times when things don't go according to plan. Good mental conditioning allows athletes to recognize when their self-talk is negative, positive, or escapist, and to manage thought processes accordingly. Rather than attempting to eradicate negative self-talk, athletes learn ways to rapidly switch mental gears any time negative thoughts arise, either to positive self-talk, or by asking themselves how a mentor or role model might handle a particular setback or challenge. Athletes show us that optimal human performance is achieved when we feel relaxed, alert, confident and strong…

in a state of mind-body harmony that allows us to experience seemingly magical states of synchronized balance.

Master Active Listening

Thomas Gordon coined the term "active listening" in the 1970's to describe the importance of paying full attention when hearing others speak. The three main components of active listening are: comprehending, retaining, and responding. While the individual steps involved in active listening seem simple and straightforward, they can be challenging when conversations are emotionally charged, competitive, or full of conflict. At such times, additional tools in the active listening tool belt come in especially handy, such as the four-step Non-Violent Communications process (also known as Compassionate Communication) developed by Marshall Rosenberg in the 1960's which consists of conveying one's observation, feelings, needs, and request. Active listening provides people with ways to talk to almost anyone about just about anything, while empowering both listener and speaker in the process. Rather than feeling blamed or judged, people can begin to recognize areas of shared interest and connection, as well as begin to develop a better sense of empathy for what others are feeling, and what they need. Learning and utilizing active listening skills is one of the best ways to 'be the change you wish to see in the world,' teaching others by example how to compassionately respect and honor the true feelings and needs of others in our lives.

Create A Clearness Committee

In the 1660's, the Quakers created a spiritual process guided by simple rules, including an understanding that what transpires within dialogue be treated confidentially, and not shared with anyone afterward. A clearness committee is initiated by a focus person, who selects committee members from the most diverse variety of backgrounds, experiences, ages, and viewpoints possible. The focus person writes about the past, present and future aspects of the area of concern, and shares this with committee members prior to meeting. When the group convenes, committee members are forbidden from speaking to the focus person in any way other than asking honest, open questions, such as, "Did you ever feel like this before?" "Who are you trying to please?" or "How will you change?" Committee members are encouraged to remain totally attentive, and to ask brief questions inspired by intuition. The focus person responds to questions as they are asked, taking the conversation deeper and deeper... with the understanding that the focus person is in control of the process, with the power to not answer questions. Clearness committees are expected to help individuals become better focused on the true nature of their questions and concerns, in ways that provide them with a deeper, fuller sense of themselves in relationship to their area of focus.

Experience Bohmian Dialogue

Physicist David Bohm provided a significant contribution to a better understanding of quantum physics through a theory that described the universe of having an enfolded, or implicate, order in which space and time are no longer the primary factors nor foundation by which all of reality exists and interacts. Bohm proposed that our belief in so-called laws of space and time arise from our experience of an explicate order... one that arises from a unifying undivided whole. Intrigued by the striking similarity between Bohm's worldview and that of the Blackfoot and other indigenous tribes, Leroy Little Bear approached physicist David Bohm and initiated the first "Language of Spirit" dialogue with scientists, linguists, and indigenous scholars and elders in 1992. The Bohmian-inspired Language of Spirit dialogues encourage participants to sense underlying oneness while consciously suspending self-defensiveness, and to actively engage in experiencing new perceptions through listening deeply. These annual dialogues are mediated by an indigenous elder, and continue for several days. One person at a time speaks when feeling inspired, and others listen, in a talking circle dialogue format, until the speaker says everything he or she feels strongly inspired to share.

The deep listening I've experienced has affected me in ways that defy simple explanation, leaving me with a keen sense of being better and more completely attuned to everyone and everything around me. I can feel my heart more fully open, and I can sense stronger connections between my heart and others. I've witnessed people befriend those whose experiences and worldviews were vastly different, and seen emotional dams burst open and healing tears flow forth. I've watched people bridge rifts that seemed impossibly deep and wide, and develop trust and respect for those they'd previously feared and mistrusted.

When we improve our ability to listen deeply, we see profound benefits to our civilization and world that we could not have predicted nor foreseen. Deep listening opens the doors to our hearts, and enables us to feel an expanded sense of belonging and connectedness with friends, family, colleagues, neighbors and strangers... who might not stay strangers very long.

Cynthia Sue Larson is the editor of the monthly Reality Shifters e-zine, **www.RealityShifters.com,** and author of several books, including the highly acclaimed, *Reality Shifts: When Consciousness Changes the Physical World.*

Changing the World Together

by Dr. Nina Meyerhof

In today's highly interdependent world, individuals and nations can no longer resolve many of their problems by themselves.

We need one another. We must, therefore, develop a sense of universal responsibility. It is our collective and individual responsibility to protect and nurture the global family, to support its weaker members, and to preserve and tend to the environment in which we all live.– Dalai Lama

There is no "together" as there is only ONE. We humans, functioning primarily from a personal understanding of the self, that is to say, centered in ego, do not see the ONE.

We now know from science that there is only Oneness, but we hardly know how to release ourselves from our personal selves to walk into this stage of understanding. Yet in this stage of understanding is where we experience wholeness, collaboration, meeting the needs of others and functioning as a healthy body within the living source.

Our times dictate the necessity of knowing this. We are at the verge of destroying all that we see as separate. This is the teaching of the times. Our egos and personal greed demand that we destruct or learn that we ARE that which we see as separate. Now is the time.....a precious time of learning here on Earth, and education leads the way.

As educators, as all of us are to someone, we must now look to describe the universals. By asking pertinent questions and consciously taking time for assimilation and reflection on the Oneness of all, we see and know that all people want peace and harmony, and a fulfilling life of connecting to one another (*i.e.*, to love and be loved). These are really simple wants but hard to achieve.

It is not enough for us to support diversity through tolerance and justice. We must first comprehend our primal unity by looking at our Oneness and then address the differences from there. If, as humans, we are 99.9% the same in genome theory, then we must start to realize that separateness is the result of minds centered on defining ego.

To educate the coming generations we must give them ample opportunity to know that they must remember to seek that point of unity. Now, each coming generation in our continuing evolutionary history has a better understanding of the potential of moving into this point of unity. We, as humans, are given the choice...to fortify the ego or to live in conscious collaboration. The world changes as we change. Culture is an extension of men and women's minds. The next generation WILL build the coming culture of spiritual activation.

To develop models of remembering how to come into this perfection, we must start by seeking the point in the heart where we can experience the climbing of the ladder into the higher realms. It is not to find GOD, but to know GOD as the perfected self – to know our self as a cell in the body of the wholeness of all of life. As one consciously becomes a part of this

One Life, one no longer experiences separateness. Thus loneliness no longer appears, and one can experience full purpose by reflecting all-that-is through daily living.

Spirituality is striving constantly to live in this perfected state. Our intention now must be to move into full collaboration, working with others around the world to learn what they know, and to spread the message that they are one family finding their universal point of sameness, rather than accepting differences as defined by separate egos.

Together, we must experience the One Life. Processes such as mirroring in dyads (two or more individuals regarded as a pair), and then in group, and then in virtual world meetings, can be instrumental in achieving this potential. There is a yearning for this in the world today. There is also an internal recognition of our unity, and thus a dropping of outer limitations,which is all attributing to the enhancement of our communications.

The culture around communications is changing from the need for establishing the "I" to being able to feel the other and walk in his shoes, and to finally realize that another is simply another side of self. This is accomplished through the process of giving, as one can not give what one does not have. The more one matures up the ladder of spiritual development, the more one is able to give to the whole without a particular object or expectation of return.

In the baby stage of human needs, one only wants the needs of the little self ego to be met. As one matures, one can see giving as a pleasure, although one still wants in return for this giving. Later on, one experiences giving as a state of being. Finally one knows this giving to be giving to the self, recognizing all gifts (to self or others) is really a gift to the Creator and the whole.

Teaching this, or let me say, offering this as a workshop for individuals, begins with allowing individuality to come forth until it becomes boring and totally unnecessary. Asking questions is more productive than giving answers -- questions like what is spirituality...is it living ethics, what is oneness, and where are we in our human evolution?

These questions automatically lead all involved to to remembering that we are more than our bodies; we are more than our minds, we are more than our little desires...! But then, what and who are we? Young people quickly come into active spiritual reflection, and their desire becomes to be a better being, and to help others bring forth a better world. They internally feel the union and importance of this understanding and the quickly commit it.

Thus, collaboration for a changing world becomes a movement of uniting those who have been spiritually activated and are able to release their preconceived ideas of success based on the models we as adults have inflicted upon them. This allows them to move forward in a truer form of the meaning to be a conscious human. In this transformed state, all problems have solutions.

In this transformed state, one sees all the cross sections of understandings and misunderstandings and knows that they are connected. In the point of union in this connection lies the answer to the problem that never was a problem, but rather only a created difference. Youth easily unites as one. They seem to naturally know that we are all brothers and sisters and feel great pleasure from experiencing this understanding together –

as ONE. Thus, often starting with our youth, our world changes one person at a time. A massive understanding is building and one day it will shift our perception of how to live as a conscious human family in true collaboration.

Dr. Nina Meyerhof, Founder and President of Children of the Earth **http://www.coeworld.org/**

Singing the Mother Earth Blues

by Adele Ryan McDowell, Ph.D.

Here is our blue-green planet bobbling away in this great galactic soup. She is holding up her place in the multi-verse, rotating regularly, and keeping us all afloat, but like many of us, Mother E. is very tired, very depleted and having difficulty maintaining her balance.

All you have to do is to think of the crazy weather patterns of extreme heat, rogue snow storms, avalanches, hurricanes, tsunamis, siroccos, flooding, volcanic activity and dry-tinder, combustible forest fires to know that balance is out of the question.

Mother E is at her wit's end. Her glaciers are melting; her ozone layer is tattered; and her waters are polluted. Not to mention, her forests and mines have been stripped; her landfills are clogged with plastics, packaging, disposable diapers and Styrofoam bits that will outlive us all. And she is inundated with toxic chemicals. It's enough to make a grown planet cry.

Recently, a geologist friend shared with me that he had learned that all of our oil drilling (and think huge energy consumption by Western civilization, especially the USA) was undermining the tectonic plates of the earth as the oil reserves acted as a cushion, letting the plates move smoothly, without the sudden movements that we know of as earthquakes.

I don't know enough about the science to speak to the credibility of this assertion, but I do know that everything, and everyone, is connected. Think of that television commercial where the butterfly in Japan flaps its wings and how those tissue-thin, small wing beats cause discernible reverberations right in our own backyards.

Remember Mad Cow disease and the Bird Flu? The global boundaries and demarcations between species often seem more like ink-drawn maps blurred and fuzzy with splashed water rather than concretized distinctions. We, as a planet, are a pulsating mass of energy that continuously interacts individually and collectively. The idea of separation is a huge illusion. What we do, or don't do, has consequences.

This brings to mind Chernobyl, which has been called the worst human-made disaster. If you recall, a nuclear reactor exploded in the early morning hours of April 26, 1986. It has been said that 9 million people were directly affected by exposure to the radiation and estimated that 65 million people worldwide were indirectly affected by eating contaminated food stuffs. Today, there are increased thyroid cancer rates as a result of this increased radiation. The explosion may have been in the Ukraine, but its impact was global.

Then, on March 9th, 2011, after a 9 point earthquake hit Japan, triggering another nuclear meltdown, first a tsunami and later radiation hit the west coast of America. To repeat myself, we are all connected.

Years ago, a dear friend told me she heard the trees cry. This friend is a supersensitive type; I wondered if, perhaps, she was projecting some of her own sadness onto the trees. Then, a bit later, totally unsolicited, another person volunteered that she, too, had the same auditory acuteness. This time, I paid attention.

Be it the tears of the trees, the increased deaths of whales, or the distorted patterns of bees, Mother Nature is clearly trying to get our attention, but our listening is selective and self-serving.

Like flossing our teeth, we know recycling, using less electricity, buying local – all those things that reduce our carbon footprint are good. However, to most of us this can seem like too much trouble. Our environmental consciousness is still being raised; we have yet to really feel the ongoing pinch that will make us squirm and egg us on to change. Going green has not yet become a mainstream part of the culture.

Remember when smoking cigarettes was more acceptable? We could smoke in the office, on airplanes, in restaurants and bars, almost everywhere. Then the education started, and our cognitive dissonance increased as we became more health conscious. In effect, we woke up to the very negative consequences of smoking, and, over the years, many of us stopped smoking. The tipping point had been reached.

Today, I see us en route to mainstream environmental consciousness. Unfortunately, this runway is very, very long. It leads us toward that moment when the collective consciousness agrees and accepts that Mother E is in dire straits and needs all the help she can get from us, her thoughtless, rude, slovenly, disrespectful inhabitants who, by the way, created this mess.

The indigenous cultures believe in the sanctity of nature. Their relationship with Mother Earth and her elements is their portal to the divine. They care for the earth; they value the connection. The physical world is not taken for granted; it is revered and perceived as a symbol of the invisible realms.

Today, Mother Earth is more often viewed as the hard-working servant. We treat this mother with little regard; there is no reverence, and respect is at a minimum. She has become our dumping ground. We have become master consumers; we have created a disposable society and, as such, garbage and detritus abound.

Don't you think it's time we cleaned our rooms here on earth and give Mother E a break? Every little bit we can do to reduce the toxic load on the earth, as well as our physical bodies, helps.

And while we're at it, let's give Mother Earth a place of honor at the table. No more crumbs for our Mother E. She deserves a standing ovation for all of her hard work.

Thanks, Mother Earth. I'm sorry for my multitudinous messes. I know better now.

Adele Ryan McDowell, Ph.D., is the author of the Amazon best-selling Balancing Act: Reflections, Meditations, and Coping Strategies for Today s Fast-Paced Whirl and a contributing author to the best-selling anthology, 2012: Creating Your Own Shift. Her next book, Help, It's Dark in Here, will be released in 2012. You can learn more about Adele and her thinking at **http://theheraldedpenguin.com.**

Creation is the fundamental basis of the world. This is the meaning behind "God created man in his own image". The beginning of every life is a creative act, and this act of creation repeats itself each instant, with every thought, every word, and every action. The world you live in is thus a reflection of your thoughts, decisions and actions. There is no point in seeing another as responsible for your situation, for the other would not be there without your soul level cooperation. You create your life, one moment after another.

Your life and your world are one and the same. They are a unique expression of Source, or Oneness from which every creative impulse comes. This may be hard to believe, given the present situation of your world. However, step back for a moment and consider the following: The One Source, or God, is the energy from which everything is born. You all come from this primordial energy, and you will all return to it. The goal of every spiritual practice is to reconnect with this energy. Oneness IS the ultimate truth! You can only find it by looking inside, for the outer world is just a projection, a distorted image created by your mind. You ARE the world. You are Oneness.

By letting go of mind and being present with God inside you, you become a true creator. Your thoughts and actions are aligned with Source, enabling your life to become an expression of God.

Jeshua, channeled by Sophie Rose, author of the channeled course The Way of The Heart, Teachings of Jeshua and Mary Magdalene, **www.thewayoftheheartcourse.com**

The Unified Field of Divine Love ~ A Channeling by the Elders, Ancients, Celestial Beings and High Council Members to the Order of Melchizedek

by Anrita Melchizedek

Welcome sweet ones, it gives us great pleasure to be with you in this Now, as we tell you more about this Unified Field of Divine Love, also called the Crystalline Grid of One Unity Consciousness and the Christ Consciousness Grid. This Crystalline Matrix of Divine Love surrounds you and all Life through the geometric, holographic, sonic and fractal matrix of Light flowing through and within this multi-universe and connects within you as these "Flames of Divine Love". And we call you these "Flames of Divine Love", sweet ones, for this is indeed what you truly are, as God's ambassadors and caretakers to Mother Earth and all her Life.

This Unity Grid of Light, sweet ones, this Crystalline Matrix of Divine Love and One Unity Consciousness was synthetically recreated approximately thirteen thousand years ago by the Ascended Masters and Christed ET's assisting in that time line in the ascension of Mother Earth following the destruction of the Christ Consciousness grid around the Earth plane. In order to align the One Unity Consciousness throughout and within your Earth plane, these Beings of Light went to the original One Unity Consciousness Portal in the Land of Khem, later to be called Egypt, and through this original vortex in the Giza Plateau, they reconstructed the One Unity Consciousness portal working with the sacred geometry of ten golden mean spirals which emerged from this vortex. This synthetic Crystalline Matrix of Light served to connect all Life into the realms of Illumined Truth and beyond the many portals of darkness. This served as a Beacon of Light sweet ones, a Cosmic Map into the higher dimensions, until such a time as the Light on this earth plane could be amplified to a level where the Unified Grid of Divine Love could be sustained through the Patterns of Perfection and Divine Light of Mother/ Father God. Progress was slow sweet ones, and unfortunately at that time, cosmic evil was able to further amplify its frequencies of darkness through the magnetic grid around the Earth plane, and all Light amplifications from the Spiritual Hierarchy were distorted through this negative frequency, causing further lower frequencies of distorted patterns to emerge in order to be transmuted. As a result, the Spiritual Hierarchy, in their compassion, decided to more slowly activate this synthetic Christ Consciousness grid. In addition, many portals of Light around the Earth plane had to be closed at this time. However, there were still a certain number of Ascended Masters left on this Earth plane, who were given the task of assisting in the Light anchorings through the recreation of energy portals and sacred sites, and particularly through the initial creation of an energy portal in Egypt, which would activate all other Light Portals around the Earth plane, and be appropriate to the consciousness of Humanity at any given "Now" moment in time.

And by the Grace of God, through the Harmonic Convergence of 1987, this Unified Field of One Unity Consciousness and Divine Love was activated to a level where all Life could experience their Highest Potential as these Master Beings of Light and sacred transfiguring Flames of Divine Love as the level of Light on this earth plane expanded exponentially to match many of the harmonic frequencies from On High.

Furthermore sweet ones, through these many unprecedented activities of Light, you started to reflect the exact sacred geometry and harmonic resonance found within the Christ Consciousness grid within your own energy bodies. Additionally, through this sacred geometry, you hold within your subconscious the thought forms and patterns of every atom and molecule on this Earth plane, animate or inanimate. In other words, you hold the collective unconscious of the entire Planet! Furthermore, your DNA is related to the platonic solids, specifically the dual relationship between the icosahedron and the dodecahedron, and hence, you are able to etherically integrate your original Divine DNA encodings. And this relationship between the icosahedron and the dodecahedron was the basis of the Christ Consciousness grid around your Earth plane. A new sacred geometric shape was activated from 1992, that which we call the *double penta-dodecahedron, reflecting the 144 facets of Christ Consciousness and the 144,000 components of One

Unity Consciousness for this multi-universe.

Sweet ones, in 104,000 B.C. through the collective signature of One Unity Consciousness from the Cosmic Heart and Divine Flame of Eternal Light of Mother/Father God, a call was put out across all dimensions and Galaxies requesting 144,000 Light Beings to physically embody onto Earth, and to anchor these frequencies of the Law of Oneness through the three-fold flame and heart center of every atom and molecule on this Earth plane, within the Cosmic Law of Free Will. These 144,000 Beings of Light stepped down their vibration to take on earthly form and many of you, sweet ones, were part of this core group, or the second or third wave of this core group who chose to be of service to Mother Earth and all her Life. And the importance of this in this Now sweet ones, is that you are again at the point of ascending collectively and taking on this mantle of leadership as these Flames of Divine Love amplified and experienced through the key codes of Light and sacred geometries within the Crystalline Grid of Divine Love holding these vibrations of Christ Consciousness. Furthermore, sweet ones, at zero point, Jesus the Christ was birthed, and embodied the 144.000 within One. This amazing Divine event which was Overlighted by the entire Company of Heaven, allowed the rebirth of the Christed Consciousness of Humanity to be experienced at a Higher Light level. Through this Divine Dispensation, it has been decreed that when 144,000 Master Beings of Love and Light ascend to their Highest Potential simultaneously, each atom and molecule on this Earth plane will ascend to their next level of enlightenment and this entire Earth plane and your Solar System will again be embraced into the Cosmic Heart of Mother/Father God for all eternity. And this time is now, sweet Ambassadors. As you entered through the 11:11:11 Portal of Light, you were able to truly become these Flames of Divine Love and actualize the Patterns of Perfection for all Life on this earth plane through the new DNA encodings of Light activated at this time. For the year of 2011 was that of Divine Love, of the Divine Feminine archetype, insomuch as 2012 is about One Unity Consciousness and empowerment through the Divine Masculine archetype. Sweet ones, sacred geometry is the language of light and fabric of creation that amplifies the energy of this Crystalline Matrix of

Divine Love and Unity Consciousness and as such, this Unity Grid of Light contains within it the sacred geometric patterns of all creation. And indeed, this Crystalline Matrix is further being activated at a cellular level within your bodies as you take on these crystalline frequencies and the cellular components within your bodies change from carbon based into silicon based vibrating portals and stargates of Divine Love. You are a nodal point within this vibrating, invisible latticework of Divine Love and it is simply to attune yourselves to these frequencies.

While you may have a knowing of the essence of yourselves as these sacred Master Beings, living this requires a level of cosmic consciousness awareness and the ability through vibrational attunement to experience Divine Love. It is a sense of feeling this within yourselves through this Crystalline Matrix of Divine Love that is within you and around you. You become these Flames of Divine Love through your loving thoughts and actions, and the experience of mindfulness in such a way that it takes you out of your old patterning and conditioning. One of the ways to do this, sweet ones, is to let go of your perceived disappointments of how you would have liked things to have been, into appreciation of what you have and the joy that comes from being in this Now moment; of letting go of the victim and persecutor consciousness, of letting go of those old false beliefs and judgments that create an oscillation of the emotional and mental bodies into this polarity of the earth plane. For indeed this Crystalline Matrix of Divine Love lifts you into the higher dimensional frequencies where you are connected to the Legions upon Legions of Light, to your multidimensional Selves, to all these Beings of Light from On High assisting in the ascension of this earth, ,as well as to Nature Intelligence and all Life. Mother Earth, through this Crystalline Matrix of Divine Love is already ascending into the New Earth matrix, and you are ascending too, sweet one, but there is indeed still a pull through the polarities of this earth plane, these human mis-creations that have been played out for eons upon eons and have created these old memories at a cellular level within the body, genetically inherited, carried through from past lives and parallel realities and also perpetuated and played out in this lifetime from a karmic perspective. Now it is to know, of course, that it requires a level of commitment, of discipline, of will and empowerment, to experience a deeper level of the essence of the Divine Love that you are as these Flames of Divine Love, so you may truly experience the preciousness and magnificence of your Selves. It requires sweet ones, a commitment to experiencing yourselves as Divine Love; it requires sweet ones, to experience the magic in your lives without disillusionment, without negativity, without despair, without anger and blame and shame; and you can lift yourselves into the glorious magnificence and preciousness of yourselves as these Flames of Divine Love simply through connecting into this Crystalline Matrix of Divine Love. And now, as the 12:12:12 portal is experienced, you have the opportunity to take on these transfiguring key codes of Divine Love and One Unity Consciousness and of activating the new dormant DNA codes within the body to a level that would truly allow you to experience Self Mastery. With this comes a greater understanding of yourselves as wayshowers and leaders and teachers in this new Golden Age; in this transforming New Earth, lifting all Life in vibrational harmonic frequency into this essence of Divine Love. The key codes within the Crystalline Matrix of Divine Love are both personal and planetary in nature. How you can personally work with this Crystalline Grid of Divine Love is by sending Love and healing to others as well as healing yourselves. You can access these key codes of Divine Love in such a way to experience personal and planetary transformation. You can lift the world into Unity Consciousness, sweet ones by affecting and creating change in your reality, and further develop your own gifts of telepathy, clairvoyance, clairsentience and clairaudience. Additionally, you can communicate more easily with the Beings of Light from On High through these stargates and portals of light that exist within and around the Crystalline Matrix of Divine Love through linking into these sacred sites, vortices and Crystalline Cities of Light, and linking into the hearts and minds of all Life in One Unity Consciousness through the Collective Consciousness of all Life.

Sweet ones, we have explained to you that all the lessons that you experience in this Now can be based on Love. It is no longer necessary to perpetuate these karmic patterns and old soul contracts in which you chose to experience your lessons in shame, in pain, in betrayal, in anger and guilt and loss, although this is indeed how you have learned best for eons of time. However, these old karmic contracts are coming to an end unless you still consider this is how you learn best. The new soul contracts are based on this essence of Divine Love, of connecting through your hearts as these Flames of Divine Love, being able to magnetize and to bring into your reality those of an equal or greater level of Divine Love that you can experience these lessons with, in compassion, in Love. You can truly work with these issues from a place that is sacred and safe and know that all these pathways that exist before are based on Love, sweet ones. Nothing bad is going to happen to you and the majority of those on this earth plane are going to ascend too with this New Earth.

However, it is a time for those of you holding the key codes (starcodes) to what we call the "I Am Avatar Blueprint of Light" which connects through the energy of your I Am Presence as you build the Adam Kadmon Body of Light, your perfected etheric Blueprint of Divine Love and vibrating Body of Light, to be able to assist others as you stand more steadfast in the Light. Sweet ones, you are able to geographically affect and create change within your reality and your environment and how incredible is that!. If you remember that your reality is simply a reflection of where you are and what you are working with, you are able to shift this, simply through shifting your frequency into this Crystalline Matrix of Divine Love. You are then able to use the Unity Grid of Divine Love and the energetic frequencies of Light spiraling forth onto this planet to connect to others energetically, to assist in the healing of others on this planet, to assist in the unification of all Life through embracing all Life, and letting go of the sense of perceived separation of "them and us." All Life is Divinely equal, sweet ones, and it is simply the levels of cosmic consciousness awareness that differs from individual to individual.

While this Crystalline Matrix of Divine Love holds these key codes of potentiality for all Life, it is to experience this within your everyday life that will make and create the changes that you desire. This is being streamlined, sweet ones, through the energetic vibrations held within the collective Christ Consciousness and amplified at this time to bring a greater level of Divine Love and Unity Consciousness onto this earth plane. Further to this, you are also experiencing the spiraling vortices of the super-electron, activating the dormant DNA as you become both the receiver and transmitter of Divine Light. Additionally, through the Spiritual Microtron, which is able to split the subatomic particles in the body into smaller sub-atomic particles and spin these subatomic particles within the body beyond the speed of common light, you are taking on your invisible garments of Light, cloaked in the radiance, illumination and Divine Love of Mother/Father God. Furthermore, as you move into 2012 and beyond, you are experiencing more the Photonic Rays of Light, spinning the electron-positron pairs within the body in increased frequencies of light and clearing many of thiese karmic patterns and shadows. So, you are experiencing this incredible Cosmic roller coaster ride, as earth changes are upon you, as tectonic plates shift, as the earth's axis shifts incrementally, as you further experience the Solar Flares, affecting the electromagnetic field of Mother Earth and your own electromagnetic fields and lifting you into Solar Christ Consciousness. Through the convergence of all these celestial activities of Light, electromagnetic and magnetic shifts, in this Now moment sweet ones, you are working not only with holding yourself steadfast in the greatest frequency of Light that you have ever experienced in physical form in this lifetime as these Flames of Divine Love, but your are further working with all those shadow aspects of yourselves and the increased shadows of all humanity that are coming up to be cleared and healed, integrated, transmuted and loved unconditionally so you may truly experience yourselves within this Crystalline Matrix of Divine Love and One Unity Consciousness.

So take a moment now to visualize yourselves in this Matrix of Divine Love through the Unity Grid of Light. See that you are connected now to your soul and star families of the Light, see you are connected to the Light Workers, wayshowers and starseeded ones holding this focus through this Holographic Crystalline Matrix of Divine Love for all Life on this earth plane. As you initially merge now with your I AM Presence, the Highest

Light of Who You Are within the Cosmic Heart of Mother/Father God, take on these key codes of light of your Highest Potential as this Flame of Divine Love as you further activate the I AM Avatar Blueprint of Light. Take on your personal key codes now that will take you into a deeper level of service and joy and Love. And now, as you are connected to these Legions upon Legions of Light, you take on the Planetary key codes of Divine Love and One Unity Consciousness through this Golden Flame of Unity Consciousness. These key codes being activated now will allow all Life to experience One Unity Consciousness and Divine Love within the Cosmic Law of Free Will. And now, within this crystalline energetic matrix of One Unity Consciousness, you send your Divine Love as you surround this earth plane and all her Life in this Golden Flame of Divine Love. This is now amplified through a magnificent Diamond Flame of Light brought through from the Cosmic Heart of Mother/Father God. And now sweet ones, just direct this beautiful Golden Flame of Divine Love and Unity Consciousness and Diamond Flame of Light to particular places on this earth plane that you consider need this most at this time. And now extend this Golden Flame and Diamond Flame of Divine Love deep into the Crystal Heart of Mother Earth as you connect into these crystal frequencies, as you activate the crystalline frequencies within the cellular structures of your own bodies. And now, as the dormant DNA is activated, it brings through these multidimensional realities in these streams of consciousness of your Highest Potential as these sacred Master Beings, as these Flames of Divine Love. Wonderful.

You now find yourself back in your sacred space, sweet ones. Keep this connection to the Crystal Heart of Mother Earth, feel her support and Love and feel the Crystalline Grid of Divine Love within and around you, as you now repeat to yourself: "I am a Flame of Divine Love in service to Mother Earth and all her Life. I am a custodian and gatekeeper assisting and affecting change on this earth plane. The reality reflected to me is that of Divine Love, as I open my heart to receiving all that I am as this precious Master Being of Love and Light" Wonderful. Again surround yourself in this beautiful Golden Flame of Unity Consciousness, and now this Diamond Flame of Light as you experience the Cosmic embrace of Mother/ Father God, amplified through the Crystalline Grid of Divine Love and One Unity Consciousness. This grid of Divine Love allows you to experience the knowing of All That You Are, sweet ones, as these sacred Master Beings and Flames of Divine Love. Know this to be your reality, know this to be your truth and know the importance of your individual puzzle piece as part of this collective harmonic and Cosmic Convergence of Unity Consciousness. For as you experience 2012 and beyond, truly you will experience this New Earth in all her magnificence through Divine Love and One Unity Consciousness. The Cosmic Gateways of Light into the higher dimensions are opening for you sweet ones, as these transfiguring Flames of Divine Love, co-creating Heaven on Earth. We thank you for your service to Mother Earth and all her Life, and with this, we bid you a most magical day.

- If you take an icosahedron and join together with lines every other point inside the form, you create twelve pentacles of five pointed stars. If you extend the outer edges of the icosahedron and join these node points together, you create a second group of twelve pentacles or stars. This becomes the seed crystal that gives birth to a new crystalline form called the double penta-dodecahedron composed of twelve double pentacles equally spaced across the surface of the globe. (Description by Joseph Jochmans from his book "Earth: A Crystal Planet").

Anrita Melchizedek is an author, lecturer, and founder of The Melchizedek and Pleiadian Light Network, an ascension network of Light offering numerous programs of Light in the form of ebooks, Mp3's, CD's and audio DVD's, as well as vibrational energy products. For Anrita's You Tube Channel, please view **http://www.youtube.com/user/AnritaMelchizedek**

Website: **www.pleiadianlight.net**

Securing our Succession with Big Hugs for Our Little People

by Sylvia Klare

A hug for a friend
A hug for a stranger
A hug for the enemy
A hug for animals and our environment
and a hug for Mother Earth

My beloved child, I love to hold you in my arms so much because our hearts beat together. I want to tell you what happens to me, when we bearhug.

While we are so close to each other, I breathe your presence. I perceive your scent with every breath I take. And you also take me in. I'm hugging you with all my heartpower, and I realize why I do this. First of all I want to be near to you.

It is more than our bodies that are intertwined. It feels so good, so right. It comes from inside. While remaining in the embrace, I see my inner world, and feel the great peace that lies in mutual love. I feel the heartbeat of the universe, as it takes us together and provides us trust and confidence. At this point, many people want to detach, they do not dare to dive into the depths of the soul.

But I overcome my fear of the unknown because I love you and go much deeper into our embrace, accepting unconditional love in our hearts, our One Being. Our bodies only pretend to be separated beings. But if our hearts are united again, because we embrace us in unconditional love, then we feel oneness and the universe is up to us.

It gives me hope that it will remain forever so delighted. I wish to linger in this state of relaxation and confidence. My thoughts calm down and I realize why I am in the world. At this point the meaning of my life is very clear. Out of the universe, I listen to the melody of joy, lightness and the feeling to be one with all that is. The feeling to have finally found the freedom that I've always wanted, the freedom to be myself. And I found it all in our hug.

You certainly know, this is what we call love.

Love is the meaning of our lives. Love for ourselves and others. Love of plants and animals. Love to all that nature offers. The mountains, rivers, forests, seas, fields, meadows, lakes, the sky ... just everything that surrounds us, and what we take into our bodies, and what flows through us.

I love to bear hug you and my world!

Love is always within us. It allows us to breath and to laugh. It allows us to touch and recognize things, if they are firm or soft or even spiky. Love is within us, it is the source of every one. When our Divine Father created us, he looked deeply inside his heart and the only thing he found was love. In the moment we arose from his love, he gave everyone their own personality from which angle they experience his world. We are all different individuals and yet the same; we are all out of the same origin, and we recognize our origin when we are so near to each other in a big hug.

There are people who do not allow love in their hearts anymore. They are managing their life like an automat. They are functioning quite well in our world, but in reality they are not really alive. They're like a program of a online game. They are afraid to come close to their own spirituality, and refuse to remember the lucky days from their childhood -the times of bear hugs. Because in that moment, they would recognize the love, and they wouldn't be able to endure their life without it. They are afraid to face their creator and indulge in unconditional love. For deep inside, they feel ashamed that they abandoned the behaviours that let them feel happy and the very reason why they are here -- namely to interact with love, just like a big hug!

They feel ashamed to admit to their creator that they ignored the love in themselves and in the world. Without consideration for others, they have only thought of their own interest and forgotten that they have the same origin as all that is around them. Every human on Earth is their brother and sister.

It was very long ago that they received a hug that brought them into the deepest awareness and showed them who they really are and that they are on Earth to live in mutual joy. Their heart is closed in a safe, and they don't remember the access code.

Because they do not enter into their hearts, they live without love. Perhaps they have realized how sensitive their heart is -- how long it takes to recover when love is offered to a person who cannnot receive it. Such situations can be very discouraging, even though, in reality, we all desperately need love to live.

There are these people on the streets of our cities who look so sad or rushed. There are those who talk to themselves, because they don't have time to meet with others in peace and listen kindly to each other. There are those who meet us who do not look in our eyes because they are afraid to find what they have been missing for a long time, but do not dare re-absorb it – this glow of vitality and ease that one exudes when you're young or when you're as happy as a child. Yes, children can reconnect lost souls with the love. They can save adults from their monotony and sadness, and we can all do this when we become as children.

What would you say, my child, if we would help a sad person refocus on how happy he could be? I'm sure you'd like to help him remember the emotional intimacy and joy in the freedom of unconditional love, right? It's very easy, and we will do it now. We go out to these people and offer them a real hug. You may be wondering about how happy they look when they have overcome their shame and fear. Their eyes will light up and shine and maybe even tears of joy will roll from their eyes.

Still, some people have so much fear to approach others in this way. We can only recommend that they practice on a tree in the forest. This tree will give back the same love that you give to it! First it will be a little strange, because the tree has no heart like us; you can not see into his eyes and see a joyful smile on his face. But for the person who has not yet managed to crack the vault in which love is locked up in his heart, this big hug is the first step. The safe is opened by this tree because it does not question the person.

You know, many people are simply afraid that they will no longer be loved and accepted because they've made any mistakes in their lives that made them unhappy. They won't go to other persons to be embraced, because they don't feel worthy. But this is a false idea! We are all worthy of being loved and embraced.

This tree cares for the one hugging him in all his sadness, and because the tree also comes from the heart of our Creator, he can also love. He gives this poor person all his love. And at some point this person can feel it and free his heart, as well as the heart of Mother Earth, to which the tree is connected.

We may also begin to embrace others in our thoughts. In our minds, we can bring others close to our hearts, even if they are not with us. Tears of joy and hope and of relief and happiness may result on both sides.

We can always offer our fellow man a hug whenever we feel that they need it. We can allow our heart's love to flow freely to them and accept them such as our Creator has created them -in their own personality and uniqueness. We can also do this with our environment. We can imagine that we take the flowers, trees, animals and the oceans of the world, the clouds and the mountains, and every living thing on earth to us in our arms. We can imagine how it is when we connect with all of that again, just as we were joined at the heart of our Creator. Then we can recognize our unity and see that we love from the bottom of our hearts.

We can express this love by joining hands in a long, human chain of love and acceptance. A human chain that helps sad people feel joy again, and the unfortunate feel lucky again, and lonesome people to experience community again. We can make the human chain anywhere where there are people. In every continent of our planet, people can gather and meet in an embrace and bring in a human chain to symbolically express our unity.

A human chain from the South of the earth up to the North of the earth would be a really big hug that we the people give to Earth. As a united humanity in love for the world, we can give happiness to all. Do we want to do that?

With a hug
...............we make the other understand he is a friend
.... we express friendship to strangers
...............we give love, affection and strength
.... we extend our hands openly to receive our opposite
............,.... we give protection and comprehension to the weak

All together, we embrace Gaia and her inhabitants to give them power, peace, happiness and love. Together we co-create our future in mutual respect and acceptance. This will certainly be a very impressive feeling of love and connectedness with our source.

On Global Love Day people all across the world join hands in acceptance of each other and give our planet a loving embrace.

BIG HUG

Sylvia Kläre
Founder and President of the non-profit organization BIG HUG
www.bighug-2012.de

Journey Home

by Bob Altzar Djurdjevic

After reaching a deep trance state, I completely lost track of time. When I finally reached level 4 on a scale of 1 to 36 (36 being fully alert), I found myself in a forest, a road stretching before, lined with trees on both sides. The following images are my approximations and simulations of what I saw.

It was only later on, in retrospect, that I understood why the journey started there. The Forest and the Land represented the Earth element. My guides wanted me to start the journey as an Earth spirit.

Next, I was aware of being deep down in the ocean, looking up toward the surface, which appeared as a faint light. I remember thinking, strange that I have no problem breathing underwater. And then I realized... that's because I AM the Ocean. I am no longer in my human body. I am the spirit of Water. Which is why being the Ocean feels like being home.

Suddenly, I notice a commotion in front of me. The color of the ocean started to change from blue-gray to brown. There was a lot of churning.

Slowly, a bell-shaped form emerged . Still churning furiously, it slowly started to take on a red glow. Water and fire seemed to be mixing – the way red molten lava enters the ocean . My heart was pounding. My whole body seemed to be churning like the energy vortex before me.

Then, the bell-shaped image expanded, engulfing all. Everything around me was red. I was inside the molten lava. Yet I was neither hot nor lacking oxygen. I WAS the Lava spirit.

At that point, I began to rise and knew exactly what was happening - I was a Volcano about to erupt. As I rose up the volcano funnel toward the surface, I shouted like a person possessed, "I am Pele. I am Pele."

I morphed into the spirit that called me to Hawaii, the Goddess of Volcanoes and Fire, Pele. She has been the most consistent presence in my life since before I moved to Maui.

My planetary mission, as told by the multi-dimensional beings I encountered in 2009, is to awaken the Hawaiian volcano spirits and help them connect to the Andean mountain spirits. Now, not only have I awakened Pele - I AM Pele!

My excitement at being Pele grew with every step as I ascended the volcano shaft. When we, Pele and I, finally exploded into the atmosphere, I felt as if I my chest was also exploding with joy.

Now things are calming down and I realize I am the wind, the Air Spirit. I see the clouds around the volcano reflecting the reddish glow from the eruption. I enjoy the relative tranquility of being the wind and floating weightlessly. I want to stay a bit longer, but the scenery starts to change again.

Journey through the Universe

We are leaving the Earth, I realize and say out loud. I am elevated toward the sky and departing Earth's atmosphere. I no longer have a physical body and my ascent is effortless. Everything is dark around me. I enjoy gliding through the cosmos. It's serene, beautiful, relaxing. Stars are all around me; I feel like one of them, not in a physical sense, everything feels so familiar, like home.

Eventually, I notice a triangle being formed out of white light. Beautiful blue, shimmering streamers flow along its outside edges. I feel excitement rising again inside me. Blue is my favorite color; each time I die and leave a human body, I go to a blue chamber to relax and recuperate. That's when the Divine multidimensional communication begins...

I now know the white triangle is ME, Altzar (like the shape of the letter A). The light beings are letting me know that's who I really am.

I feel their message, "Welcome home, Altzar!" and I begin to cry. I KNOW this is home. My entire being knows. My body pulsates with joy.

"And what does Altzar do?" my regression facilitator asks.

I repeat the question to the spirits (the light beings).

You are a Rainbow Giver." they answer, but when they tell me, "You are a child of the Universe," I begin to cry loudly.

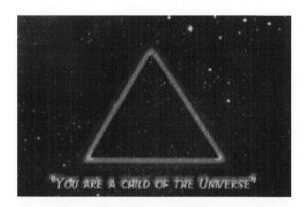

"YOU ARE A CHILD OF THE UNIVERSE"

I recognize the similarity and the authenticity of the mantra I received on my astral rebirth: "I am a child of the Original one". The sobbing, emotional discharge takes a while. Then I enjoy being home, feeling the love of my spirit guides, and I notice a light emerging from the top of the triangle.

"YOU ARE A RAY OF THE ORIGINAL SUN"

This light gradually grows in size. Eventually I realize it is the Sun. Inti Taiti, Father Sun, is appearing to me for the first time as white and golden glow. "You are a ray of the original Sun," I feel His message coming through. I notice a little black chip in the Sun at about 10 o'clock, and I realize... that's me – "a ray of the original sun."

The vibrations and excitement continue to rise in my body. I feel as if I am going to explode. And then, just as I think I cannot take any more, Father Sun retreats and a faint white light appears at the top of the triangle. At first it looks like a star. Then it also gradually grows in size.

Being One with God

THE LIGHT OF GOD

The eye of God, I whisper in awe and recognition (having seen it once before). Even though I am a writer, I cannot think of words adequate to describe how I felt when God "said" to me, You are God. You are one with me.

As you might have suspected, in dreamtime and early morning the day after this awakening, I experienced additional revelations.

(1) In the first dream, only about one and a half hours into the night, I saw a number of palm trees erupting like volcanoes. The burning pieces of their trunks and branches were dropping all over the place, including on the roof of our home. I yelled to my wife, Elizabeth, "Stay inside."

This symbolically represents the destruction of my past. After the awakening, I felt much better physically than I had in a long time. Most of the aches and pains I had become used to having had either disappeared or diminished Maybe it was also burning off some of the bad energies one accumulates in a lifetime.

(2) In the second dream, I was with a large group of people somewhere outdoors. I recall a sandy lawn around what looked like a country side church. I noticed a tiny penguin playing in the sand. I remember thinking, *a penguin in Hawaii?*

Elizabeth and I were the last ones to go into the church. As we were passing through a vestibule, I noticed the little penguin was also there. I felt sorry for him, so I closed the door and called to my friend, the pastor. He came out to the vestibule. I showed him the penguin. Then I noticed a second penguin. *Oh, so they are a pair*, I thought.

"We should call the zoo," I said to the pastor, "I closed the door so people from the zoo can catch them."

At that moment, one of the penguins leaped into the pastor's hand, then the second one did the same. *There is no need to catch the penguins*, I realized, *they know they are among friends.*

INTERPRETATION: The penguins trust us and will go anywhere we want to take them. They are here to show us, if we treat nature with love and reverence; anything is possible, including penguins in Hawaii.

As I was waking up the next morning, download after download came to me, offering additional explanations. I realized I had been given a metamorphosis. Shifting me from earth to water, to fire, to air, I was being trained for my next spirit world assignment when I will be one of the God's of Environment and Weather, a Shepherd of the Earth. To be able to do so, I must learn to love and know how it feels to be each of the four elements, and all parts of the Creation.

That is why I was chosen to come to Hawaii to build a Garden of Eden in Paradise on Earth, a phrase I frequently use in my prayers and incantations. This is also why I have taken on the planetary mission to awaken the Hawaiian volcano spirits and connect them with the mountain spirits in the Andes and elsewhere. I am to be, from this day forward, a Shepherd of the Earth and to do this, I needed the penguin dream. It showed me that, from a place of divine love, I can create anything, as that divine love is me.

As these messages came through, tears flowed down my cheeks, confirming both their authenticity and their divine nature.

Early the next morning, I dressed and started walking down into the gulch and over to the hill. From there, I observed the sunrise.

All morning, I felt ONE with everything I saw. My eyes well with tears as I understood that's what my guides wanted me to experience.

I spent about an hour walking around the property (seven acres), talking to trees, flowers, rocks, and the wind. By the time I returned to the house (with Elizabeth still asleep), I had written this:

I am a child of the Universe
I am a ray of the original Sun
I am the forest and the land
I am the ocean and the sand
I am Pele's lava and her hearth
I am the wind and the breath
I am the Shepherd of the Earth
I am Wholeness
I am Love
... and I love you
Because you are the world too!

Website: www.altzar.org/

A Civil Rights Movement for the Soul

by Humanity's Team

Two famous 20th century movements, Mahatma Gandhi's Indian Independence Movement and Martin Luther King Jr.'s U.S. Civil Rights Movement, transformed nations. They transformed nations through a complete adherence to the movements truths under every circumstance and by helping other people see those truths, thereby changing hearts and minds, which changed behaviors.

Similarly, Humanity's Team supporters hold onto a truth: the eternal truth that We Are All One, and seek to make this truth evident through our lives as lived, thereby helping others see this truth demonstrated, changing hearts and minds, which change behaviors.

Humanity s Team was founded in 2003 to address suffering and other issues stemming from the prevailing belief that we are separate from God, from each other and from all of life, and the companion belief in an authoritarian or malevolent God.

Many people, particularly in the West, are brought up to believe we are limited in most ways, have one life to live, and are separate from God, or Universe, as well as each other. Those who believe in God sometimes perceive God as angry and judging. Some even perceive God as endorsing killing under certain circumstances.

Most people are asleep to their true identity: to their Oneness with God, with each other and with all life. And their behaviors reflect this. Just look around the world, with its wars, terrorism, hunger and other painful conditions!

We in Humanity s Team see these conditions as largely a result of our beliefs about God and about life. But all this can change.

It can change when we become aware of the truth that We Are All One and then live our lives as demonstrations of this truth, rather than in denial of it.

This is why our movement has been dubbed a Civil Rights Movement for the Soul. We in Humanity's Team see a healing truth in who we are; a truth that heals ourselves, our relationships, our communities and our world. We see that we are all part of one essence that some call God and others call Universe and that the one essence is sacred, divine, loving, compassionate, creative and eternal.

This is not a new idea. Prophets, messengers, saints and sages have shared this message since the beginning of time. It is shared in the Indian Vedas, in the Old and New Testaments, in most other sacred texts and in contemporary New Spirituality material. Oneness is also a hypothesis by quantum physicists and other scientists who say life is a unified whole with multiple dimensions, each complementing the other.

We Are All One is the one idea that truly changes everything. When we see God and Self in each other, we cannot help but nurture, love and support the other. When we embrace and embody our Oneness, we naturally care for the other person, place or thing. God and Self are in all of the other, so nothing is left out.

This is the invitation Humanity's Team is extending: to embrace and embody our Oneness and to extend the invitation to others. This is why we were formed as a movement.

We in Humanity's Team have set our intention to awaken the world to Oneness in a generation, so children will grow up in a very different world. Many of us are dedicating our lives to this objective and we intend to do this. Then, like other movements before us, we will disband when our objective is met.

Humanity's Team (**http://www.humanitysteam.org**) is a spiritual movement whose purpose is to communicate and implement the belief that we are all one, one with God and one with life, in a shared global state of being, so that the behavior of humanity may shift to reflect this understanding.

Think Outside the Bars
Why Real Justice Means Fewer Prisons.

by Michelle Alexander

posted Jun 08, 2011

A white woman with gray hair pulled neatly into a bun raises her hand. She keeps it up, unwavering and rigid, as she waits patiently for her turn to speak. Finally, the microphone is passed to the back of the room, and she leaps to her feet. With an air of desperation she blurts out, "You know white people suffer in this system, too, don't you? It's not just black and brown people destroyed by this drug war. My son, he's been in the system. He's an addict. He needs help. He needs treatment, but we don't have money. He needs his family. But they keep givin' him prison time. White people are hurting, too." She is trembling and sits down.

There is an uncomfortable silence in the room, but I am in no hurry to respond. I let her question hang in the air. I want people to feel this discomfort, the tension created by her suffering. The audience is overwhelmingly African American, and a few of them are visibly agitated or annoyed by her question. I've spent the last forty minutes discussing my book, The New Jim Crow. The book argues that today, in the so-called era of colorblindness, and, yes—even in the age of Obama—racial caste is alive and well in America. The mass incarceration of poor people of color through a racially biased drug war has birthed a new caste system. It is the moral equivalent of Jim Crow.

Racial Politics, Not Crime

The audience has heard the facts: Our prison population quintupled in a few short decades for reasons that have stunningly little to do with crime or crime rates. Incarceration rates—especially black incarceration rates—have soared regardless of whether crime was going up or down in any given community or the nation as a whole. Mass incarceration has been driven primarily by politics—racial politics—not crime. As part of a backlash against the Civil Rights Movement, our nation declared a "War on Drugs" that has turned back the clock on racial progress in the United States. Although people of color are no more likely to use or sell illegal drugs than whites, African Americans have been targeted at grossly disproportionate rates. When the War on Drugs escalated in the mid-1980s, prison admissions for African Americans skyrocketed, nearly quadrupling in three years, then increasing steadily to a level in 2000 more than 26 times the level in 1983. In some states, 80 to 90 percent of all drug offenders sent to prison have been African American.

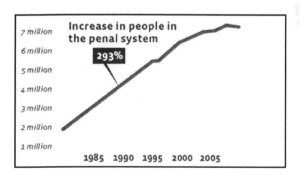

Just the Facts:
It's a Locking-People-Up Problem
The American problem with mass incarceration has less to do with crime than you think.

As a nation, we've been encouraged to imagine that this war has been focused on rooting out violent offenders or drug kingpins, but that is far from the truth. Federal funding has flowed to those state and local law enforcement agencies that boost dramatically the sheer number of drug arrests. It's a numbers game. That's why the overwhelming majority of people arrested in the drug war are the "low-hanging fruit"—poor people of color who are stopped, frisked, and tossed to the sidewalk by law enforcement, forced to lie spreadeagled on the pavement, simply because they "looked like" criminals while standing on the corner talking to friends or walking home from school or the subway.

The U.S. Supreme Court has given the police license to sweep poor communities of color, stopping, interrogating, searching anyone or everyone—without any evidence of criminal activity—so long as they get "consent." What's consent? When a police officer, with his hand on his gun, approaches a 16-year-old on the street and bellows, "Son, will you turn around so I can frisk you?" and the kid says, "Yeah," and complies, that's consent. Usually the exchanges are less polite.

And once the police get consent, the Fourth Amendment ban against unreasonable searches and seizures no longer applies. According to the Supreme Court, these "consensual" encounters are of no constitutional significance, even though they may wind up sending a 19-year-old kid to prison for the rest of his life: Life sentences for first-time drug offenses were upheld by the Supreme Court in Harmelin v. Michigan. The race of the defendant in that case was key to the sentence in the first place. It is nearly impossible to imagine a judge sentencing a white college kid to life in prison for getting caught with a bag of weed or cocaine. That's how this system works: Poor people of color are swept into the criminal justice system by the millions for drug crimes that go largely ignored when committed by middle- or upper-class whites. And release from prison or jail marks just the beginning of punishment, not the end.

Once branded a criminal, people enter a parallel social universe in which they are stripped of the rights supposedly won in the Civil Rights Movement. The old forms of discrimination—

employment and housing discrimination, denial of basic public benefits and the right to vote, and exclusion from jury service—are perfectly legal again. In some major American cities, more than half of working-age African American men are saddled with criminal records and thus subject to legalized discrimination for the rest of their lives. These men are part of a growing undercaste—not class, caste—a group of people, defined largely by race, who are relegated to a permanent, second-class status by law.

Uniting Poor People

The white woman is waiting for me to speak.

I know a great deal rides on my response. It is not an overstatement to say that the success or failure of the emerging movement to end mass incarceration may turn on the ability of advocates like myself to respond to people like her in a manner that validates and honors her experience, while not brushing aside—even slightly—the thoroughly racial nature of the prevailing caste system. Is it possible to join poor whites like her with poor people of color in a movement to challenge a political and economic system that harms them all, though differently?

1 in 87 working-aged white men is in prison or jail compared with 1 in 36 Hispanic men, and 1 in 12 African-American men.

There was a brief moment when it seemed clear that the answer was yes. As the Civil Rights Movement was gaining full steam, Martin Luther King Jr. and other civil rights leaders made clear that that they viewed the eradication of economic inequality as the next front in movement building—a Poor People's Movement was required. Genuine equality for black people, King reasoned, demanded a radical restructuring of society, one that would address the needs of black and white poor throughout the country.

In 1968, having won landmark civil rights legislation, King strenuously urged racial justice advocates to shift from a civil rights to a human rights paradigm. A human rights approach, he believed, would offer far greater hope than the civil rights model had provided for those determined to create a thriving, multiracial democracy free from racial hierarchy. It would offer a positive vision of what we can strive for—a society in which people of all races are treated with dignity and have the right to food, shelter, health care, education, and security. "We must see the great distinction between a reform movement and a revolutionary movement," he said. "We are called upon to raise certain basic questions about the whole society." The Poor People's Movement seemed poised to unite poor people of all colors in a bold challenge to the prevailing economic and political system.

White Backlash

But a backlash was also brewing. Anxiety and resentment among poor and working class whites was on the rise.

The truth is that poor and working class whites had their world rocked by the Civil Rights Movement. Wealthy whites could send their children to private schools and give them all of the advantages that wealth has to offer, yet they were a tiny minority that stood apart from the rest of whites and virtually all blacks. Poor and working class hites—the regular folk—were faced with a social demotion. Their kids were potentially subject to desegregation and busing orders; their kids were suddenly forced to compete on equal terms for increasingly scarce jobs. Poor whites were better off than African Americans for the most part, but they were not well off—they, too, were struggling for survival.

[Felon disenfranchisement laws bar 13 percent of African-American men from voting. Polls show 8 in 10 Americans support voting rights for people who have completed their sentences].

What lower-class whites did have, in the words of W.E.B. DuBois, was "the public and psychological wage" paid to white workers, whose status and privileges as whites compensated for low pay and harsh working conditions. In retrospect, it seems clear that, from a racial justice perspective, nothing could have been more important in the 1970s and 80s than finding a way to create a durable, interracial, bottom-up coalition for social and economic justice. But in the years following King's death, civil rights leaders turned away from the Poor People's Movement and began resisting calls for class-based affirmative action on the grounds that whites had been enjoying racial preferences for hundreds of years.

Resentment, frustration, and anger expressed by poor and working class whites—as they worried aloud that blacks were leapfrogging over them on their way to Harvard and Yale— were chalked up to racism, leading to little open or honest dialogue about race and an enormous political opportunity for conservative strategists. "Get tough" rhetoric provided a facially race neutral outlet for racial frustrations and hostilities. H.R. Haldeman, President Richard Nixon's former chief of staff, summed up what came to be known as the "Southern Strategy" this way: "The whole problem is really the blacks. The key is designing a system that recognizes this while not appearing to."

The War on Drugs

And so the "War on Drugs" was born. Richard Nixon was the first to use the term, but Ronald Reagan turned the rhetorical war into a literal one. When he declared his drug war in 1982, drug crime was actually on the decline. It was a couple years before—not after— crack ripped through inner-city communities and became a media sensation. From the outset, the drug war had little to do with drug crime and much to do with racial politics. As numerous historians and political scientists have now shown, Reagan declared his drug war in an attempt to make good on campaign promises to "get tough" on a group of people identified not-so-subtly in the media and political discourse as black and brown. Once crack hit the streets, the Reagan administration seized on the development, actually hiring staff whose job it was to publicize inner-city crack babies, crack dealers, and the so-called crack whores. Once the enemy in the war was racially defined, a wave of punitiveness washed over the United States. Democrats began competing with Republicans to prove they could be even tougher on "them." Some black legislators joined the calls for "get tough" measures, often in desperation, as they sought to deal with rising crime and joblessness in ghetto communities. They found themselves complicit—wittingly or unwittingly—in the emergence of a new caste system. And many civil rights advocates found themselves exacerbating racial divisions, fighting for affirmative action even as they abandoned the Poor People's Movement that sought to restructure our nation's economic and political system for the benefit of people of all colors. They had accepted a racial bribe: the promise of largely superficial hanges benefiting a relative few in exchange for abandoning the radical movement born in the 1960s that sought liberty and equality for all of us.

Poor whites had accepted a similar racial bribe when they embraced Jim Crow laws—laws which were proposed following the Civil War as part of a strategic effort by white elites to destroy the Populist movement, the nation's first interracial, political coalition for economic and social justice in the South. Time and time again, the divide-and-conquer strategy has worked to eliminate the possibility that poor people of all colors might see themselves as sharing common interests, having a linked fate.

It's time for me to break the silence.

"Mass Incarceration
in the Age of Colorblindness"
Video: Amy Goodman interviews Michelle Alexander.

"Your son is suffering because of a drug war declared with black folks in mind," I say after a long pause. "White people—especially poor whites—are suffering because of the politics of racial division. Latinos are suffering, too. The drug war as we know it would not exist today, but for the demonization of black men, and now your son, a young white man, is paying the price. Poor whites are collateral damage in this drug war. But whether you're the target or collateral damage, the suffering remains the same. Thanks to the drug war, we have the opportunity to see clearly how caste-like systems hurt us all, even though they hurt us differently or in different degrees. We must go back and pick up where Martin Luther King Jr. left off and do the hard work of movement building on behalf of poor people of all colors. Are you willing to help build a movement to end racial caste in America, a human rights movement on behalf of all of us? All of us or none?

"Yes, I am," the white woman shouts loudly, unaided by a microphone. The crowd erupts in applause. She wipes a few tears and smiles. "I just need to know that my son matters, too. I guess we all need to know that we matter. That's what it's all about, right?"

Right.

Michelle Alexander wrote this article for Beyond Prisons, **http://www.yesmagazine.org/issues/beyond-prisons/beyond-prisons,** the Summer 2011 issue of YES! Magazine. Michelle is an associate professor of law at Ohio State University. She is the author of *The New Jim Crow*.

Reprinted with permission.

We Cannot Sit and Rest

by Wayne Peterson

For years I have known advanced souls and soul groups are presently incarnate here on Earth. It is said they are here to assist in building a new civilization. Before these advanced souls and soul groups can ascend, they must train their replacements.

They know we must not return to ways of the old Roman Empire. One of the reasons they are here is to keep that from happening.

Know first, as these old souls know, laws are rigid, morality is fluid.

I have lived in countries where laws are far more fluid than in the U.S. In those countries the common man and woman are better served.

Consider how many laws the old Hawaiian Islanders used to govern their society. I am willing to guess they were few. I am also pretty confident Americans live under the weight of millions of laws!

Are Americans safer today than the ancient Hawaiians?

America has the largest population of prisoners in the world. With all the new laws and new prisons, are Americans safer today than their grandparents were? No.

Rome made this mistake. The Roman historian, Tacitus, observed that, "The more corrupt the state, the more laws."

According to ancient Wisdom, there is only ONE LAW: God's law for humanity. All religions of the world know this law. The version I know best is, "Do unto others as you would have them do unto you."

End of discussion. All the rest is false morality.

Let me challenge you a bit. Krishnamurti urged us to learn how to stand on our own and reject authority of any kind. We need to understand this, he said, "All authority of any kind (especially thought) is the most destructive, evil thing."

Most of humanity will not and cannot understand that statement. It is about freedom. For spirit/soul evolution to continue on Earth, advanced souls must take action to make this concept understood.

We reach a plateau on our evolutionary climb where we are comfortable in our learning. This is when we want to stop and rest. Evolution; however, requires we destroy the past, delete what needs deleting and move on to other higher teachings. We cannot sit and rest.

Krishnamurti also said that at some point our brains will no longer help us. We needed an intelligent, educated and active mind to reach the point we have reached. We now must acknowledge that seeking with the mind has gone as far as it can take us.

My favorite astrologer, Paul Nunn, told me to always remember that **SEEKERS NEVER FIND**. Finding is brain work. The foundation of a good and educated mind is absolutely essential; but with that intelligence we learn the importance of giving over a part of each day to **WISDOM**.

In Helena Roerich's Agni Yoga books she said, "**WISDOM IS CONTRARY TO INTELLECT**." Wisdom still works hand in hand with intellect. Both are needed, but Wisdom comes, not from the brain, Wisdom comes from the heart/soul.

Helena Roerich also said, "Straight knowledge is cosmic truth." Truth and morality are only known from the soul. They are beyond intellect and beyond human time, residing where our brains cannot venture. Truth and morality are beyond human laws.

WE MUST NOT RETURN TO ROME

Why must we not return to Rome?

The answer to this question is not because of religion or an interest in science, it is about freedom.

Rome looked at people as cattle, as animals. This is happening again today and it is especially noticeable in Europe. The Europeans are not walking back to Rome, they are running to Rome! Rome thought that giving its citizens food, housing, entertainment and health care was sufficient.

But citizens of the Roman Empire had no freedom and, for the human soul and body to evolve, freedom is essential.

When they should be encouraging the European Union to stand back and look long and hard at itself, American politicians are falling in love with the idea of the Europeans.

Enamored of the Europeans, American politicians are blind

to the big picture. They need to wake up!

The *European Union* is no longer just a common market created to open borders to products among member nations. Today, core architects of the *European Union* are pushing for a central government aimed at controlling major policy issues for all member nations. Without the blessing of the European people, many steps toward a powerful central government are already underway.

Ignoring the importance of the people's voice, top government leaders of *European Union* member states have appointed delegates to a central government. This new central government plans to implement changes for all European Union members, while denying European citizens the right to vote on those changes!

Europe is in the process of adopting/creating *a-new-empire-in- the-making*, stripping its citizens of both democratic power and freedom.

This is the making of a new Rome.

What we see in Europe is a political leadership that distrusts the common people. Very purposefully, the voices of individual citizens are being silenced.

Granted, Europe has suffered too many major wars in the last one hundred years. A group of European elites are now rationalizing the only way to prevent future war is to homogenize Europe, limiting animosities between nations. Some do believe that elimination of the power of individual states will bring peace.

Rome also thought this way. Roman peace; however, was nothing more than a system in which individual expression was crushed.

The *European Union* is not concerned with freedom; it is pushing for a one world government where the common man and woman are excluded from participation.

Suggesting implementation of laws which deny the common people a voice, is anathema to freedom. Many member states have already been convinced to agree, though Ireland has stood its ground, saying, "No, our people must vote."

Silencing the people did not work for Rome and it will not work for modern day Europe. This plan runs counter to the plan of the spiritual hierarchy and must fail.

It will fail.

ONLY ONE SIN

The soul and its energy is naturally creative. Advanced souls are especially creative; they are in touch with soul energy. If this soul energy cannot be expressed, evolution is hindered or stopped in its tracks and there is only ONE SIN humanity can commit. It is to participate in anything that slows/halts human evolution.

Because it refused its citizens freedom, Rome was destroyed. To prevent that end repeating itself here, we have a lot of work before us.

The Four Freedoms

Remember **The FOUR FREEDOMS?** Offered by both President Roosevelt and Prime Minister Churchill during WWII, on January 6, 1941, in his State of the Union address, Roosevelt ended his speech with a flourish, defining four essential human freedoms that his policies were aimed at securing: **freedom of speech** and **religion**, and **freedom from want** and **fear**.

Have any of these freedoms been implemented? Few, very few. It has been seventy years since FDR's pronouncement and the time for implementation of The Four Freedoms is now upon us.

The more laws, the fewer freedoms we have and **freedom of speech** is compromised.

Generally existing in parts of the world, the development of theocracies puts **religious freedom** in danger. Divisiveness and ignorance interfere with our ability to see the ways in which most of our religions are similar, as in the example I mentioned earlier, that every single major world religion espouses its own version of The Golden Rule.

Want and Fear go hand in hand and both are rampant the world over. Every Three Seconds someone in the world dies from factors related to extreme poverty, that's 30,000 people a day, 10,500,000 a year, and the majority of those deaths are children. [Statistics taken from Daniel Karslake's documentary, Every Three Seconds. **http://everythreeseconds.net/**

What is our future then? Will we return to Rome or will we be able to enter the great new **Golden Age of Humanity**? To succeed, **we must act wisely**.

If we move forward determined to create and preserve our freedom, we enable ourselves to know our future, even before it arrives.

Begin with Education and Take Action

We begin with education.

Will you react with anger and fear, or do you see hope for the future?

Enter the learning process with sensitivity and humility.

Know; however, if you examine new teachings from the perspective of old knowledge, we are doomed. We are all conditioned by old knowledge, but as we become AWARE of our conditioning, we are able to take action. Krishnamurti agreed, "When one gives total attention to conditioning you will be FREE from the past completely, naturally."

Awareness will set you free.

Krishnamurti also stunned us, cautioning adults against teaching children to conform to society's code of respectability. Because our laws support society's code of respectability, parents often believe they have a duty to teach their children to conform to those laws.

However, to determine what is or is not respectable, responsible parents show their children how to look to their own hearts, the spark of God within them, and trust their own sense of what is respectable. Question Authority!

Krishnamurti went on to point out that, "Preparing children to fit into society is perpetuating war -conflict, brutality." Asking, "Is that LOVE?"

If you are happy with the past one hundred years of human history, you may stay with society's code of respectability and its laws. I will not.

Humanity will not hold together if we continue with our code of legal morality and we have yet to learn the meaning of LOVE. We only know the lower form of LOVE. We must move forward with new meanings of both LOVE and civilization. Only those who are aware of the terrible ironies in the way we are educating our children and others can do this.

Our future will see fewer laws, fewer prisons, less indoctrination of children, and more freedom for all.

Our future will require we examine cultures from a point of how well they support spiritual evolution, how well they support The Golden Rule.

Prisons present an example of a purposeful design to hinder/halt evolution of a growing segment of society and this is something that will be changing.

Beauty

Beauty is a main ingredient in the lifting of consciousness.

Nicholas Roerich stressed the importance of beauty in every home, in our schools; and, especially, beauty in our prisons. He knew that beauty lifts consciousness.

Cities of Earth are often ugly. Maitreya has said such cities will be torn down and rebuilt to express greater beauty.

Just before the French Revolution, I was incarnated as Claude Nicholas Ledoux, an architect who designed a Utopian city in France, funded by King Louis XVI. Ledoux's example will soon return to light. Ledoux also believed in beauty, suggesting that if a city is designed correctly -laid out on a design plan that is spiritual - just standing in the city will lift the consciousness of humanity. Watch for a resurgence of interest in his work; it is coming...

Prisons will shrink in number. Remember, in the future we will know we are all judged, sentenced and held accountable, not by man, but by *The Lords of Karma*. If you trust *The Lords of Karma*, you will have no fear for security in life. Laws will reflect heart and far fewer prisons will be required.

Through beauty we will build a new civilization and learn of a higher level of love.

This is our task as advanced souls: sweep away old dysfunctional rules of society and free ourselves to be passionate and full of action.

Wayne Peterson had a 32 year career as a U.S. diplomat and is the author of *Extraordinary Times, Extraordinary Beings*.

Welcoming the New Masters

by Elizabeth J. Foley

The new energies entering the Earth, and the souls of Earth, is quickening now! More of humanity is questioning its true purpose and starting to recognize Divine purpose and the divine plan playing out in the synchronicities of their lives.

Our physical bodies are changing, and our spiritual DNA is becoming activated once more, transforming and transmuting energy, altering the physical DNA from carbon based to more crystalline form. As a result, our Higher Self, also referred to the Christ Self or our Divine Self, can increasingly merge with our physical bodies. Thus, we become enlightened and begin to access the power and wisdom of our Higher Self. And as humanity goes through this rebirthing, it is essential to create a life style that supports this new type of Human, AKA Adam Kadmon.

What does it mean to be the new Human or Adam Kadmon? It means increased consciousness; full use of our brain power and telepathic ability; direct connection to God and other beings of Light; ability to control the collective consciousness of humanity and work with the universal laws; and a deeper knowledge and appreciation of whom we are and our Divine purpose. Being an awakened Master in physical embodiment means that we now claim our identity, source and soul mission. As Masters, we move more freely into leadership positions to assist other souls of Earth to awaken and evolve spiritually.

This evolution produces new Masters whose characteristics can be clearly recognized. Because they have balanced their own karma and tamed the emotional body, these masters project only positive thoughts and extend respect, kindness and compassion to all. Having learned to temper the voice of ego, they practice humility and non-judgment. They tend to be peacemakers in all situations, for they view all from a Divine perspective, and speak always from that wisdom. Their well-developed intuition and purity of intent and action enables them to create and manifest for the highest good for all concerned. The new Masters see the divinity within everyone and everything, and act as true Lightworkers or Earth Angels —shining their light and empowering others to do the same.

We are celestial souls who have come to Earth from other dimensions and parts of the universe. We are becoming more like cosmonauts, exploring other dimensions as we quickly shift and transcend the third. As we expand our consciousness and realize more of our own spiritual gifts and potential, we reclaim our Mastery. For truly we are Masters in our own right....we have just forgotten our Divine heritage.

Here are some very simple ways in which we can tap more into our mastery and become the new Human:.

Schedule some God time each day (10-15 mins or more) and connect to your Higher Self

Listen to music that resonates with your heart

Practice purposeful prayer and mindful meditation (remember "the worst prayer in the world is the prayer that is not said")

See Love in action and lessons in all situations (this helps to strengthen the soul)

Be the observer of situations and know when to speak and take action and when not to for this will help with releasing yourself from psycho-drama at home or work

Balance your energy (chakras) for this will help you with staying centered and calm just like the Ascended Masters

Accept responsibility for everything you choose and create in life Live within personal integrity and do things that honor you and your beliefs

Practice good spiritual hygiene (clear and shield)

Breathe deeply for this helps to calm the body and mind, grounds you and helps to raise your energy and vibration

Ground yourself so you are more present

Develop your own spiritual community for support

Extend yourself by giving and finding ways to give to others like support, opportunities, networking connections even just the basics like clothing or food

Help somebody you don't know without needing thanks or recognition...be that Earth Angel

Listen to your intuitive feelings and messages and follow your guidance

Practice the Law of Attraction which can help you manifest whatever you need

Speak your truth and honor your feelings without judgment Be ethical and fair with others including business situations

When in doubt, surrender to God and ask the Divine for help and in keeping your attitude positive

Use your Heart Power daily for it is your true power which, like a magnet, draws all positive things, people and events to you

Remember to let that awareness take any path that works! A sudden thought, a dream, some kind of synchronicity, something you hear or by chance read-perhaps here today, or on the television, radio. Could be anywhere!

Thank your Higher Self, God, Divine Spirit, Universe

Trust your connection and your Divine guidance and just for a moment, be willing to set aside any and all doubts. Trust...and breathe in deeply to access all you need

Ask for whatever is needed-clarity, strength, faith or more courage

Practice being joyful each day and living in your heart space, even during challenging times

Most of all : Live each moment and breath in Divine Love for all that you are -- for everyone and everything in the world!

Remember you may not be able to change things, but you can change the way in which you deal with the changes. We can learn even in the moments we judge ourselves as having failed....because we learn from it...and that very moment becomes a success.

A massive awakening is at hand and this is the test of the light. As a spiritual Master, you begin to understand and work with spiritual laws, you acknowledge the concept of Oneness, you make time each day to commune with God and beings from the celestial hierarchy, turn knowledge into wisdom then temper wisdom with love and compassion, walk with awareness of the ego and tame the emotional body to be less reactive, have purity of action and communicate with harmony, able to see the Divine or the divinity within everyone and everything, act with kindness and compassion always and live from the Heart center.

You are a sculptor of your own world...so what do you wish to create now? Be the Master that you were before and are meant to be once again!

Elizabeth J. Foley, Reiki Master, International Angelologist and author of Awakening the Lightworker Within, Angel Readings for Beginners, A Guidebook for Advanced Angel Readings and coauthor of 2012: Creating Your Own Shift. **www.divinehealing**. us and **www.angelstreetpublishing.net**.

Learning to Lift the Veil

by E.Dee Conrad

The veil is now lifting more rapidly than ever and what lies before us is a world full of love, compassion, emotional freedom and profound peacefulness.

But to get to this place, we have to be aware of our thoughts and do our best to envision the world we truly want to live in. To change the world and hasten the arrival of inner contentment on a global scale, each of us must take responsibility for our thoughts. This means going inside and connecting with our inner being – our inner core.

One way to do this is to sit in a quiet spot and focus on your breathing. Use whichever breathing technique you know, as long as it makes you feel relaxed. If you do not know any breathing techniques, just inhale and exhale slowly while maintaining awareness of your breath.

Gently move your focus to your solar plexus (belly button region) and become aware of what you feel or "see" there. Do you feel fear, anger, hatred, peace, balance, antipathy? Each day you might perceive something slightly different, because every day we are met with a different set of challenges and circumstances. It is important to note we are not our circumstances. We are not the events of our lives. We are not what goes on around us. Just because a person was rude to you this morning does not mean you are rude. You are a being full of light, capable of transcending transgressions. You have the power within you to change not only yourself, but the world. It all starts with you and how you choose to react, what you choose to do with your emotions and how you choose to perceive the world.

As you think, so shall it be. As you think, so shall you become.

If you think you are worthless, you will be treated as such. You will bring into your life situations that will make you feel even more insignificant. If you think you are ugly, people will see you that way. Each of us on this planet has the ability to create our own framework, our own reality.

To change your world, you first have to be aware of what you are creating. Sitting quietly and focusing on your solar plexus will tell you the kind of world you are creating. If you are not an experienced meditator, you probably will not be able to "read" your solar plexus the first time you try this exercise. However, you still benefit because you are training your mind to look inward. You are becoming aware of a reality you cannot physically touch. As a group, we are trained to believe only what we can see and touch. Anything intangible falls into the realm of supernatural, miraculous, or beyond our current comprehension. Over the centuries, most societies have lost the ability to see what lies just beyond our current level of understanding. We have lost the ability to see auras, fairies, and even cupids.

What is a cupid? A cupid is a being of light whose world is formed via its love and admiration of others and of life itself. The mere act of living and breathing is an act of love and selflessness, if we so choose. We choose what becomes of our lives. We choose who we become by the way we react to daily situations. Every minute of every day we have the power to choose who and what we will become in the next minute, hour, day, week, or lifetime. It is never too late to change. It is never too late to start over with a clean slate. We are neither prisoners of our past, nor victims of our future. We are always in control and completely in charge of exactly what goes on around us and inside of us. We are the ones who hold the power of fate. Destiny is ours to do with as we please, most of us just do not realize it. So many of us labor under the false impression that only by aligning ourselves with a divine plan will we have meaningful lives or achieve nirvana. This isn't so. The only divine plan is the one we choose for ourselves. The only life worth living is the one we create for ourselves. Start looking within your own heart and see what will bring meaning and substance to your life. See what it is you were meant to accomplish in this life. See why you chose to be reborn at this time, in these circumstances.

Why are you here????

This is the question we all need to start asking on a daily basis. Only by answering this question, can we hope to move forward as a group and achieve peace, harmony, enlightenment and fulfillment on a global scale. While we are all one, our group is comprised of individuals who have to learn to work together toward common goals if we are to succeed. The fate of the many depends on the actions of the few. This last sentence may sound strange because I just said your fate was in your hands and no one else's. It is true your fate is in your hands as far as your life is concerned – what you choose to do, who you choose to be, and how you choose to experience this world. However, when we consider the conscious evolution of humankind, your fate does not rest solely in your hands. It depends on those around you, what they do with their lives and how they choose to see the world. To reach the tipping point necessary to propel humanity to the next level of consciousness will require a certain number of individuals who see reality as it really is and who perceive more than just what they can see with their physical eyes. We need a certain number of people who can reach inside and understand the universe as it really exists and not just by what they have been told. The universe, in its entirety, exists completely within each of us. This means we have at our disposal every law of nature, every component of creation, and every atom of the universe. There is nothing we cannot do if we put our minds and hearts into it.

By understanding the gifts that have been bestowed upon humankind, we will resolve our current difficulties and misunderstandings. We have been blessed beyond measure with every necessary resource at our disposal. However, few of us know these gifts even exist and still fewer take advantage of them.

The world around us has been thrown into a fevered pitch of agitation, excitement and fear. But we should not be focusing on this. Now is the time for a great expansion of consciousness – the gates of the universe are opening up for those who are prepared to explore its vast riches.

Understanding the universe and taking full advantage of its gifts are two entirely different matters. The first supposes a certain level of connectedness that all human beings on this planet possess. The second assumes a certain level of comfort with the universe and who we are as a group. Earth is guided by group consciousness and this is what will determine the outcome of the planet and the human race. Humans are guided by a set of principles and natural laws that cannot be changed. If they were to be modified in any way, the experiment that we call life would come to an abrupt end. Again, these laws cannot and will not be modified, therefore, we may all rest assured that there will be no abrupt end for humanity. People who claim we are headed for Armageddon and may nuke ourselves out of existence want to create as much fear as possible, so they can profit. At this point, anyone who is intentionally or unintentionally creating fear should be avoided at all costs. This mind set will not help human consciousness evolve. It will only slow down our forward movement.

Conscious evolution will require each of us to take charge of our lives and realize that the world is bigger than just the individual. We are all connected. We are all one. Everything we say, do, and think affects everyone else via the collective consciousness. We are not alone with our thoughts. They affect every one and every thing on this planet. There are no secrets between you and humanity, just as there are no secrets between you and the universe.

The universe is constantly showing us the way forward, but only a few people have been paying attention and even fewer have been listening. Now, this is changing – and on a massive scale. This is why we have the opportunity to move forward on such a grand scale. The way forward has been laid down very clearly. All we have to do is walk down the path of enlightenment, peace and understanding by recognizing we are all ONE. There is no separation between humanity and the universe, just as there is no division between you and your neighbor. Fundamentally, we are the same – beings of light and love, spiritual beings having a human experience.

We are all here to accomplish the same thing – the evolution of consciousness. Some of us may go about it in different ways, but the end result is all the same. We are more than our bodies and circumstances. We are more than our current idea of who and what we are. We are all beings of incredible compassion, resourcefulness and love and this is the side that will soon be apparent to all. There is a shift coming in the way we perceive ourselves, those around us and our role in bringing about a new way of existence. This is a door that is just beginning to open for humanity and it is a progression that cannot be stopped.

E.Dee Conrad is a healer, palmist and author of bestselling book, **A New Dawn Awaits** – *The Times Ahead and How to Shift Your Consciousness.*You can read some of her other inspiration/spiritual writings at **http://edeeconrad.com**.

They are our Future

Every child comes with the message that God is not yet discouraged with man.

-Rabindranath Tagore

Protecting our Heritage

A channeling of Mary Magdalene by Sophie Rose

Ancient tribal wisdom was about the transmission of basic, yet profound values to the future generations. The modern society forgot the importance of right relationship to each other and to the environment: individualism took over the old community aspect of people's lives and built a world where superficial values thrive and the destruction of natural resources escalates. Without immediate action, your children will be left with a desolate world and a wrong mind-set to take care of it.

It is urgent to teach the youngsters about personal responsibility within the community and land preservation.

The family unit constitutes the first and most powerful grounds for such teachings. The family has always been the cradle of the individual throughout history. Your modern society discourages quality family time and promotes the values of private companies; the consumption society often takes over a family-centered education by imposing its trends and values. The shift of consciousness is also about the children. You must prepare them to rebuild a sustainable and loving world.

Being a guide to your child is what parenthood is about. You cannot do that if you bring your own issues to the relationship, that is where the difference lies between raising a child consciously or raising him with your ego or within the diktats of society. At any point in time, your own fears and expectations can take over, this is human nature. If you do not trust that there is a divine plan for your child, you will unconsciously make one. If you do not trust that you are the right person for the job, you are not trusting the divine. Trust is soul work, it is the deep inner knowing that the universe has a plan for you and your child. You can access the wisdom of this plan by cultivating presence: center yourself, clear your mind and ask your heart for what's right. It requires practice and discipline but this simple habit will become an invaluable guidance tool.

Your heart knows the right action about relationships, education, environment and all that matters for your children's future. How to access its wisdom is all you need to know.

Through your heart is your soul connection, your ultimate guide to navigate your life and make it a divine experience. Your heart knows the answer to your children's needs, it knows how important Mother Earth is. The solutions are never out there, you have to look inside. They do not come from the mind, their source is in your heart. This is the shift: to go from mind to heart, to bring the divine in instead of trying to understand it. Your God-self has all the answers.

The education system is another place to promote a sustainable future. A mind-based only education trains children for a dysfunctional society, where competition and private interests are ruining the hope for right relationships and self-sustaining communities. Each child brings its own contribution to the world. Formatting his mind to perform and fit in the crowd is as absurd as expecting an apple tree to give pears. It goes against nature. The education of a child requires subtle guidance and listening. A child's higher self knows what's right for him, and children are often more connected to their higher selves than adults. They should be encouraged to explore on their own, so they can learn to use their guidance. Your way of life is rapidly transforming, you co-create your future. Give the gift of power to your children, the power to create their life by following their guidance.

The education system has to adapt to fit the needs of an evolving society. How do you want tomorrow's society to look like? You'd probably like a more loving, caring environment for your children to grow up in. A society where fraternity, freedom and respect for each other's differences are the rules. You can create whatever society you want, you are all co-creators of your world, but the children should be involved in the process because you are creating their future playground.

Many people support the competitive and performance aspects of the system: this is non-sense, what they are doing is supporting a world where one has to be better than the other, where competition is the rule of the game. The results are here: the gap between the rich and the poor is widening, big companies swallow small local business, stress and anxiety are widespread. It is obvious that your economic system is no longer working , no longer in phase with your evolution and the needs of the earth. So why continue raising children according to the values of this economic system?

Children are members of a family, community and society as much as adults are. Too often, this is not acknowledged. Too often, they are considered as " second-class" participants because of their presumed inability to make the right decisions. Of course, in most cases, they could not make the right decision because of their inexperience. But there are times when experience does not help, when adults can learn from those whose ego is still not in control. These times come when the heart is asked to speak. It is easier for a child to find an answer in his heart than for an adult. They still do not have the mind structure that adults build year after year and rely on. So ask your children: " What does your heart tell you to do?" and learn from them. By doing that you'll prepare them to follow their guidance and contribute to make the world a more loving and caring place.

Sophie Rose is the author of the channeled course The Way of the Heart. Teachings of Jeshua and Mary Magdalene
www.thewayoftheheartcourse.com

Early Christian Teachings on Human Rights and Earth Rights

by Alanna Hartzok

The ruling class... has the schools and press, usually the Church as well, under its thumb. This enables it to organize and sway the emotions of the masses, and make its tool of them. - Albert Einstein

The United Nations Millennium Declaration that was adopted by the world's leaders at the Millennium Summit of the United Nations in 2000 was really just an attempt to remind the member nations of their stated commitment to human rights.

The Universal Declaration of Human Rights, was first brought up and adopted by the UN General Assembly on December 10, 1948. Article I states that *All human beings are born free and equal in dignity and rights.* Article 25 says that *Everyone has the right to a standard of living adequate for the health and well-being of himself and of his family, including food, clothing, housing and medical care and necessary social services, and the right to security in the event of unemployment, sickness, disability, widowhood, old age or other lack of livelihood in circumstances beyond his control.* Then **in 1976**, the *International Covenant on Economic, Social and Cultural Rights* was adopted. *The Covenant proclaims these economic human rights, among others: the right to wages sufficient to support a minimum standard of living, to equal pay for equal work, and equal opportunity for advancement. In addition, the Covenant forbids exploitation of children, and requires all nations to cooperate to end world hunger.*

However, the US never ratified this covenant, so **in 2000 it was brought up again as the** *UN Millennium Declaration*.
Finally, In 2004, I recapped these events to the United Nations, making points from biblical history justifying follow-

through of the commitments that the UN has made and renewed for over 60 years now!

Skipping over the deplorable worldwide economic conditions and lack of follow-through on over 60 years of UN commitments, which you can read more about in the transcript of my Sanford Speech, **http://www.earthrights.net/docs/ samford.html**. I'll just jump into the basic problem and biblical justifications for some simple solutions.

Here are some excerpts from that speech:

> **THE problem** is that *about 3% of the population owns 95% of the privately held land in the US. ...The basic human need for food and shelter requires access of labor to land. With access to land people can produce the basic requirements of life. Access to land provides an enabling environment for life itself and thus meets the minimum requirement...based on the fundamental equal right to exist. ...Early Christian teachings on the Land Problem... were clear and precise. The question of "Who Should Own the Earth?" was unequivocally answered. The land ethic of the early Christian communities was that of "koinonia" meaning essentially that **God was the sole owner of the earth, which was given as a gift to all...***

> *When Christianity became the state religion of the Roman empire, the early Christian teachings on land were overtaken by the Roman land laws of "dominium" - a legalization of property in land originally obtained by conquest and plunder. A largely corrupted Christianity, uprooted from its early teachings on land ownership, too often went hand in hand with the exploitation and degradation...*

For more information on that see this profoundly important book: *Ownership: Early Christian Teachings*.

Here are a few examples of **opinions held by Christian figures on the immoral ownership of Mother Earth** as compiled by the author of that book:

St. George the Great (Pope 590 - 604) rebuked the Romans when he said: *They wrongfully think they are innocent who claim for themselves the common gift of God.*

Clement of Alexandria: (The functions of property) -"to be shared," "to minister to" and serve "the welfare of all."

St. John Chrystostom: God in the beginning did not make one man rich and another poor; nor did he afterward take and show to anyone treasures of gold, and deny to the others the right of searching for it; rather **he left the earth free to all alike**. Why then, if it is common, have you so many acres of land, while your neighbor has not a portion of it?

Augustine: The poor are poor because they have been deprived by the propertied few of the wealth that should belong to all. **He laid the blame for this unjust situation squarely on the doorstep** of an absolutist and exclusivist legal right of **private ownership of real property, i.e., Mother Earth.**

Basil the Great: Taught a philosophy of ownership based on the view that God was Father and giver and Provider for all, and that therefore a few must cease stealing the food-producing resources that God had destined for the use of all. Basil admits a certain right of laborers to the product of their labor but asks the landlords by what right they exercise ownership over their vast estates: *Which things, tell me, are yours? Whence have you brought them into being?* Whatever you have produced, or brought into being, may justly be yours. However, ...**land is not something they have brought into being**.

Pope John Paul II, *Bahia Blanca*, Brazil, 1986:*The land is a gift of the Creator to all men and therefore its richness cannot be distributed among a limited number of people while others are excluded from its benefits.*
God intended the earth and all things in it for the use of

all peoples, in such a way that the goods of creation should abound equitably in the hands of all, according to the dictates of justice, which is inseparable from charity.
- from *Pastoral Constitution on the Church in the Modern World,* Vatican II

Pope Paul VI, *Populorum Progressio, 1967: The right of land ownership and of free bargaining in land are subordinated to the fundamental right of man to obtain the necessities of life. In the force of the fundamental claim of the Commonwealth there is no unconditional right of land ownership.*

Pope Pius XII: *Every man, as a living being gifted with reason, has in fact from nature the fundamental right to make use of the material goods of the earth.* -Pope Pius XII

According to some contemporary theologians, one of the tasks of the mission of Jesus was to restore the original intent of the Jubilee. **In Luke 4:18 (by way of Isaiah 61:13)**: He has anointed me to preach good news to the poor.. to proclaim release of captives... To set at liberty those who are oppressed, to proclaim the acceptable year of the Lord. **Leviticus 25:23** The land must not be sold beyond reclaim, for the land is Mine; you are but strangers resident with me.

Ecclesiastes. 5:9 The profit of the earth is for all.
Isaiah 5:8 Woe unto them that join house to house, that lay field to field, till there be no place.
Nehemiah 5:11 Restore, I pray you, to them even this day, their lands, their vineyards, their olive yards, and their houses.

Slavery – the act of ownership of one human by another was a time honored tradition until, after centuries of suffering, it gradually dawned on the majority of people that it was unjust. Hopefully, people will have a similar awakening regarding the slavery of Mother Earth by today's elite.

In the meantime, a system of increased taxation on Real property (as opposed to personal property and earnings) would go a long way toward righting this wrong.

And **Christian figures have been pointing this out for centuries**: A great deal of what is amiss in both rural and in urban areas could be remedied by the taxation of the value of sites as distinct from the buildings erected upon them. - William Temple, a former Archbishop of Canterbury, in *Christianity and Social Order.*

Equity insists that we cease levying taxes on the fruits of human toil, and make the monopoly value of land be the exclusive basis of taxation. - Episcopal Bishop C.D. Williams

For a complete transcript of my speech on **Earth Rights Democracy: Public Finance based on Early Christian Teachings** or to find out what you can do, go to **http://www. earthrights.net/docs/samford.html**

Alanna Hartzok is the co-Director of the Earth Rights Institute and a United Nations Non Governmental Organization Representative

The Gift of The Children

by Debra Hosseini

On a planet called Earth in the twenty-five years before 2012, a new breed of humans started to arrive. This was a time when humans were overpopulating the planet and many species had become extinct.

The lungs of Earth, the rainforests, were being cut down at an alarming rate and the ice in the cold waters of the North was melting. Weather conditions were harsh in many areas of the planet – floods, hurricanes and earthquakes disrupted the species and left humans without homes.

Humans had lost the ability to read the clouds and listen to the plants and no longer knew how to communicate with the horses or dolphins.

They had forgotten from where they had come.

The new breed had an appearance resembling their parents except for their abnormally large heads. As babies they cried more than other babies as they were acutely sensitive to sound, smell, taste, and touch. When their moms tried to hug them, they cried out in pain.

Their digestion was sensitive and they couldn't tolerate many foods considered ordinary fare. While other children could drink the milk of cows, these children couldn't digest the milk and screamed in discomfort and pain.

The bright fluorescent lights common in shopping malls, offices, and homes bothered their sensitive eyes. Every day sounds of living – lawnmowers, dishwashers, laundry machines -sent them into a tizzy and they screamed out in protest. Rough clothes scraped against their tender skin leaving red, festering rashes.

This sensitivity went beyond the physical. If others were happy, the children were happy and when their siblings or parents fought, they cried. It was as if they lacked the filters that separated the members of the species from one another.

"What's wrong with your child?" other parents asked as they hid their children in fear.

In many parts of the world one could hear the anguished

voices of parents weeping through the night. They knew not how to parent these children, nor what to say to their neighbors.

"I want my child to be like all the others. I want him to pick up a bat and hit a ball," the father said.

"I want my child to get married and have children," the mother said.

And as these parents wept in vain, their children cried too for they felt their parent's anguish and sadness. When the emotions of the parent became unbearable, the child retreated into another world.

Some of these children saw magical wisps of clouds and dust and fairies in the air. They could talk to the fairies in a language only they and the fairies understood. They grasped at the wisps and flapped their hands laughing at what their parents couldn't see or hear. Some of the moms tried to understand but others berated their child and would say, "Stop that laughing," looking bewildered at the place the child was gazing.

Some of the children learned the words of the parents. Even though they knew the words they tried to communicate in ways that were common in other dimensions; dimensions their parents didn't understand. Frustrated at not being understood, they screamed and banged their heads on walls.

"Why does my child do such things?" the parents asked helplessly.

These children lacked a trait common on the planet at this time – the ability to lie. They asked questions such as "Why are you fat?" or "Why do you smell?" This didn't make them popular in a society based on lies and pretensions.

"We must teach these children how to lie so they become like us," the experts said. "They will never have friends if they always speak the truth."

Many of these children didn't see themselves as distinct from others and when they looked at another, they felt as if they lost themselves in that person's eyes.

"You must look at others in the eye or you won't be trusted," the Dad said. So the parents hired therapists who tried to teach the child to look others in the eye. The child protested and cried and some parents stopped this type of therapy, but others persisted. "We must make these children like us," they insisted.

At this time in history, many humans sat all day in front of electronic boxes called television sets and computers. While the computers were interactive; the television sets were watched for hours on end. The humans allowed images from the box program their choices. They rode in machines and yelled at other machines on freeways. They rushed frantically from one place to another. Nervously, they looked at the electronic device they chose to strap on their wrist.

The more frantic and disconnected the parents became, the more the children screamed.

As the confusion on the planet increased, more and more of these children were born. Alarmed at what scientists termed "an unhealthy trend," many on the planet exclaimed "What is happening to our children? Is it genetics? Is it the vaccinations? Is it the food? Is it the toxins in our environment?"

One day, one of the Moms put a crayon in her child's hand and gave him a piece of paper to draw on. The child created a beautiful picture of the sun. The painting radiated and made the Mom feel good.

Maybe my child sees something I can't, the Mom thought.

Another Mom noticed that one of her horses, which usually bucked and brayed, became calm around her child.

Maybe my child and this horse have a special way to communicate, she thought. The horse did something highly unusual. He bent himself down as if to say place your child here, Mother. She picked up her child and put him on the horse. The child became calm and smiled.

And one child approached a piano and played a beautiful melody.

Why my child has the gift of sound, this Mom said to herself. She noticed the child was happy when listening to music and from then on their home was filled with song.

The men and women of science heard of these stories and their curiosity was piqued.

"These children can see patterns that others of our species can't," one said.

"They communicate in different ways than we do," another said.

One of these children, who the medicine men termed

"autistic," told his mom that he saw numbers in three dimensional shapes and colors. His facility with numbers became well known.

"He's a mathematical genius!" the scientists exclaimed.

Then one child who had never before spoken, typed on a new type of machine that allowed her to communicate. "I'm not retarded," she wrote. "We children have come from another dimension to teach you. When you turn on the switch in your heart and see us for who we are, we will show our gifts to you."

The message was played on computers and more and more people heard the message. The planet Earth started to vibrate in a different way.

Many people began to recognize the beautiful gifts of these children. And more and more people sought these children out. The children taught the planet about diversity, love and acceptance and people began to accept one another again and appreciate the other species on the planet. The wars stopped. The planet healed. And a new world was born.

Debra Hosseini is the mother of three, including Kevin, who is autistic. She is also the author of Artism: The Art of Autism **www.artautism.com**

Lessons for Our Posterity

by Adolphina Shephard

Do any of us ever think consciously about what we want to teach our children, or do we just fly by the seat of our pants and learn as we go? Since our children will be running our world one day, it's up to us to teach them what they need to know to help make our world a better place. This is especially important now that we have entered an entirely new cycle where we're beginning to recognize that we are all one.

So we have to consciously think about what we would like to see in a utopian society in our future. I envision a world where love is the primary emotion instead of fear, which rules all other negative emotions. The question to ask is how do we produce love as the primary emotion? What is lacking that we need to make that happen?

Our goal is to have the collective consciousness radiate love and joy instead of fear, anger, hatred, and prejudice; for it is the collective consciousness that we tap into unknowingly or not for our feelings, our belief systems, and our actions. Most of the time, when we feel these unpleasant emotions, we are unknowingly actually feeling the emotions of the collective.

What is lacking in today's world is fairness and respect for all regardless of how much money a person makes or has. For far too long there has been an attitude of superiority from those who make or have a lot of money toward those who do not have much. In turn, those who do not have much money resent the superior attitude of the wealthy. Fairness and respect toward one another regardless of their financial standing would help to produce the love vibration that negates all fear, anger, and feelings of unworthiness.

An important concept for children to learn is that money is not everything; for the true measure of success is a happy life. A best friend is worth a lot, and having someone to love and who loves you is worth much more than money! In the pursuit of money there are many people working a 60-70-80 hour week, which is not usually the way to a fulfilling life, but rather an exhausted empty existence. We need to get back to a more balanced way of living. Teach your children to value their family, friends, the community, their loved ones, and their pets. Last but not least, to value Mother Earth, for if we do not take care of the Earth, she will not be able to provide for us indefinitely.

In order to foster happiness we need to change a few cultural things that have caused anger and resentment to stir under the surface. Obviously, there needs to be equal pay for equal work whether male or female, black, white, brown, or yellow. There needs to be honor and respect for all work done, whether you are the president of the US or a garbage collector.

Another important aspect in fostering fairness and respect is learning to see both parents as equal partners, regardless of their outside the home occupations. Imagine children growing up with this perception of equality. And imagine how they'll take this harmony to the next level with their spouses or partners.

There should be no profession that is considered female or male work. Elementary school teachers have traditionally been female. However, what a better role model could there be than a male teacher for a fatherless child? Children should be taught that they can excel at anything they set their minds to whether they are male or female.

Good skills to teach children besides cooking, cleaning, and laundry is financial management. Set up a savings account to which your child can contribute for doing extra chores around the house. Encourage them to save for college, or a car, or some other worthy goal.

Encouraging them to volunteer at homeless shelters or soup kitchens will teach them empathy for the plight of those in need. This would especially benefit those children who have been given everything and who think that life owes them. It will show them how very fortunate they are. Charity is another good lesson you can easily teach by personally being charitable and generous to others in need that you come across.

A key lesson in teaching children the love vibration is to teach them that we are all one. A good analogy is something like this: God is like the ocean, and everyone's soul is made from a drop of that ocean. So, we all have a bit of God in us, thereby, making all of humanity "of the one." This is a simple explanation, and one that children can readily understand.

Something to take into serious consideration is that we all incarnated for soul growth and to learn lessons so we can evolve our soul. Each person incarnates with a path and a mission to fulfill, and if they are forced off of their path through parental expectations, this can be very detrimental.

Most families are soul groups that came in with a common mission, each with different tasks to fulfill. Perhaps one family member is to assist mankind and the world in spiritual pursuits while another family member is there to assist and support them emotionally. While still other family members were assisted by God to produce financially, so that they could provide financial support to those taking care of the soul group in other ways.

Unfortunately, many people never fulfill their contractual obligations, and so get to be cycle repeaters over and over again to learn the same lesson, until they succeed in fulfilling the agreements made between themselves, God, and their soul family. So allowing a child to follow their intuition to get onto their path in order to fulfill their mission is very important for the entire soul group.

When children are allowed and encouraged to follow their intuition, this not only is likely to keep them on their proper path, and it also will bring them deep soul satisfaction and joy. They are not all meant to be lawyers, doctors, pharmacists, actors/actresses, or sports professionals. Some children might be passionate about animals, or they may want to fly airplanes or race cars. If everyone followed their bliss, the world would be a much happier place.

There is a lot more to consider on the spiritual side of things such as not pooh-poohing a child who has imaginary friends. What the child is describing may be their angels and spirits guides. It is important for us to encourage these children to use their higher gifts. If a child is scared of the dark and says they see monsters, believe them and banish the monsters.

When children are young their 3rd eye is open and they can see things that adults cannot. It is very important to talk gently to your child about these things. You can learn quite a bit from children who can see through the veil by gently asking questions when the subject arises.

Another thought is to teach your children from a young age

about spiritual pursuits such as yoga and meditation. These pursuits will induce calm and a peaceful mindfulness. We can also teach children the benefits of recycling, thus teaching them the value of Mother Earth.

Probably the biggest key is to teach our children "The Golden Rule," which is "do unto others as you would have them do unto you." This might sound trite, but is a very good rule to live by.

Many people who grew up with strict disciplinarian parents vowed not to raise their children in this manner, resulting in children who have no idea how to behave. Other children have never learned what it means to have a male father figure, or have any discipline whatsoever, which has resulted in a criminal subculture. Some parents do not make sure their children get to school or even have a healthy breakfast. We need educated, civilized children, for they will make the laws one day in our society.

On the other hand, we have parents who micro manage their children from age two, getting them into the best schools, forcing them to take piano lessons, dance lessons, karate lessons, and second language lessons, resulting in children that are well-learned but snobbish in their abilities --who never get a chance to experience the joys of childhood. So how can we balance these two opposite ends of the pole philosophies? We let them choose what they enjoy doing in moderation until old enough to make informed choices. It is a little known fact that micro-managing children carries with it hidden dangers. For instance, it often creates the tendency for anorexia or bulimia as the child attempts to gain some control over their life by not eating or purging food they have consumed.

Then we have too many children who do nothing but watch TV or play computer games, resulting in anti-social and obese children. This is not teaching them social interactive skills, getting them the exercise they sorely need, or enabling them to make friends. This will not lead them to good health or enable them to be a fully functioning adult.

I see many children who are foul mouthed, have no manners and are disrespectful to their elders, authority figures, and their peers alike. To change this requires parents to give consistent discipline to their children. Parents should not expect the school teachers or the church to teach children lessons they should be learning at home. If you don't teach your children good values and morals, the streets will teach them values you will not appreciate. Children learn by example, so be the best that you can be while showering the child with unconditional love.

When I was a child we played outside roller skating, ice skating, jumping rope, playing jacks, playing tag, collecting bugs, fishing, counting stars, watching the clouds, swimming in lakes, going to the beach, playing dress up, and a hundred other activities that come with being a child. I would like to see a future where children can be children before they have to be adults -- to instill in them a sense of joy, which I believe many of these education forced-fed children lack.

I say "let children be children," but let's teach them that more exists than just making money. Let's teach them that true success is a happy life filled with family and friends, and, as they grow into adulthood, being in an occupation that gives them joy, while following their personal path. Let us find our own peace, for this will foster peace in our home and our children. Let's give our children a leg up by teaching them from infancy what it took us decades to learn, so they can make the next evolutionary leap into a new millennium.

Adolphina Shephard is an Intuitive, Metaphysician & the Founder of YATUVAY Energy Medicine Mystery School. She's the author of *YATUVAY ~ The Manual, How To Perform Miraculous Healings Through Energy Medicine. Living With Spirit: Going Beyond The Physical* as well as co-author in *2012-Creating Your Own Shift.*
www.AdolphinaShephard.com, Email: AdolphinaShephard@ msn.com

Add Magic to Your Family

by Alan Wilson

Have you noticed how a 3 year old can say something that comes from a place of deep wisdom that completely stops you in your tracks and leaves you wondering how on earth would that small person knew or had that knowledge?

These gems of magic are indeed coming from a place of inner wisdom that tends to be lost in growing up. Before children go to school, they are full of fun and joy; they are exploring themselves and we as parents are supporting this fabulous experience.

When children go to school they are in a system that is focused on an academic achievement. And the system doesn't support them in exploring themselves as a whole person. There is a trend to introduce well-being now, but is it too little too late for our society today?

As the children go to school, parents tend to seek a means of employment and that takes them away from spending time with their children. So as the children get older and parents are under more and more pressure, the lines of communication get wider and that's when my work starts.

In my work with parents, I'm regularly asked "how can I get Johnny to listen to me?" If I replied, "well, have you listened to him?" in some cases I might well have risked physical injury! By 'listening' I don't mean just to the words that a child says; I mean what lies behind the words – i.e., deep listening - what is that wonderful small person trying to communicate to you?

I've coined the phrase 'energetic listening/connection' as a generic phrase, it could also be known as instincts, intuition, gut feeling, sensing etc. Children call it magic! It's a very powerful process that needs some guidance in how to become aware of it, although it's innate in all of us. It allows a deeper connection with the person you are communicating with. Mastering this process/art is the foundation of fulfilling relationships and it works with children, teenagers and adults.

This is where the magic begins!

You know how a Mum instinctively knows what her baby wants; I believe that depth of connection is always available to us, and not just to Mums. I think it's because babies are pure energy and that is the only way they can communicate and Mums are totally focused on what their baby needs, and tune into them innately - that's when the magic begins.

Do you know your children can sense the mood you're in before you enter a room? I believe they also take responsibility for your mood and if they don't like what they see/feel they will kick off. It may be crying as a baby or storming out of the room if it's a teenager. Have you noticed when you enter a room full of strangers you can feel comfortable or uncomfortable? If you've experienced someone saying "I was just thinking of that" or you have said it yourself, you have experienced that energy, it's always there for you to access. Another often-used example is if the phone rings and it's someone you haven't seen or heard of for some time but you've been thinking about them!! It is this 'energy', which has a huge impact on the quality of a connection between two people.

The biggest influence on your energy is how good you feel about yourself. When you're happy and everything is going well you are giving off 'good' energy and the opposite is true. I'm sure you've noticed how when you feel good you drive through any challenges.

The bottom line is for you to be happy and comfortable in yourself and when you are - you parent naturally.

Talking about feelings, I'm reminded that when someone says something profound to me, or I say something profound, I get a tingling sensation and the more profound the bigger the tingle. Other people have different 'sensing' experiences; you just need to be aware of the possibility, and then explore how you connect energetically.

I would like to encourage you to try different exercises to find how you connect energetically and so get into your most resourceful state – at will. It can take some practice but I can absolutely guarantee you it's worth it.

I've evolved a personal development approach based on advanced coaching and emotional literacy techniques, underpinned by Neuroscience. It's about accepting that everyone has the answers they need inside and that person is full of potential. It's seeing them for their 'magnificence' and not the behaviour they are exhibiting and of course being non-judgemental.

That takes some practice, a certain amount of determination and preparation. You need to get into your most resourceful state and create the right atmosphere to connect; it's not going to work when you're all rushing around getting ready for school!

When you are at your most resourceful and set the intention to connect with someone who is equally receptive, you will open up a whole new world of connections and possibilities!!! This is magic in action.

This is magic in action

Some pointers and preparation to consider when you are communicating/connecting:

- Get into your most resourceful state. Focus on your passion - feel fantastic
- Set the intention for the best possible outcome for the other person
- Imagine the room being full of positivity and sense your contribution
- Interact with the magnificent version of the person in front of you
- Be transparent with your agenda, and open to whatever wants to happen
- Trust you have done your very best and allow it to show up in ways you couldn't possibly imagine
- And, most important of all - always trust your intuition/instincts/gut feeling and have loads of fun and laughter along the way.

As you progress on your own personal development path, everyone around you will notice - they may not say anything or even believe it but slowly it will happen. Realize you are changing the habits of a lifetime, so be gentle with yourself. There will be times when you slip back and that's OK because those times will get shorter and shorter as you evolve and become more empowered.

The younger your children are the easier it is to make that connection and the older we get the more difficult it is. Adults have more life experiences and since we are brought up in a world of negativity we tend to close down our feelings, sometimes because it's safer, or we believe it is. The end result is that we tend not to try new things because we believe we might fail.

Children, on the other hand, are full of fun and joy. They're always experimenting and learning new things. You can tap into this enthusiasm when you connect with your child on that level.

During workshops I do what I call an 'expansion' exercise. This is a guided visualization to help clear your mind and connect you with your essence. If you would like a copy, just drop me a line.

Don't worry if this all sounds a bit too esoteric. Thousands of parents from all walks of life have found the approach has transformed their lives.

I see energy as a hidden force in all of us and everything in our lives. We've all sensed if a person approaching is a friend or foe, or get feelings that something is going to be good or bad when we walk into a strange situation.

Energy is the magic ingredient

When I started life coaching, I realized that intuition was a magic ingredient and that, if I could connect with it, I could use it with incredible results for the benefit of my clients. I explored connecting at a deeper level and the first thing I learned was that, before we do any energy work, we need to relax, quiet our minds and take a few slow deep breaths. So I began to meditate.

More and more people are adding some kind of meditation to their daily routine, either as an effective antidote to stress or as a simple method of relaxation. It enables you to create new attitudes and responses to life, giving you a clearer understanding of yourself.

Have you noticed how when you're happy everything is a breeze and you sail through any challenge? By becoming your most powerful self, you will have a deeper connection with your children and add magic to your family.

There is a great deal of interest and media attention on how we communicate with our children. What's missing is the understanding that parents are doing the best they can with what they know and that communication is much more than just talking and listening.

I believe that we can change the fabric of our society from the inside out. It starts with empowering the parent; leads to inspired children; creating dynamic families, cohesive communities and vibrant societies.

Add magic to your family!

Alan Wilson is the Founder of the charity Every Family Matters **http://www.everyfamilymatters.org.uk/** and creator of the Parent Champion programme **http://www.parentchampion.com/**. He has also written "How to be a Parent Champion and add magic to your family", download the first couple of Chapters here **http://parentchildrelationships.co.uk**.

New Children and the Dream Weaver's Web

by Cynthia Sue Larson

We are fortunate to witness evolution happening right before our eyes with the arrival of new generations gifted with special sensitivities and abilities. Since the "indigo children" concept popularized by Lee Carroll and Jan Tober has expanded to include crystal and rainbow kids, we see these children demonstrating new ways of living with integrity and cooperation on Earth. They provide us opportunities to become more compassionate, intuitive, communicative, open-minded, and open hearted.

The concept of new children resonates for me, as both my daughters were emotionally sensitive and aware of unseen energies while growing up. When my older daughter was six months old, she dismantled her grandmother's broken hair dryer in a matter of minutes. Her grandmother had brought the hair dryer from the USA all the way to Switzerland where we lived for my husband to fix, but my daughter got to it first, and took it apart so carefully that I saw no reason to interrupt. I was further amazed to see the hair dryer fixed and working perfectly after she methodically put the pieces back together all by herself! Her entire repair job took less than twenty minutes, while she cooed happily the entire time.

When my older daughter was six, she told me she remembered other lives and planets. Her memories of life far from Earth were so vivid and detailed that I listened with great interest. I once asked to hear more of her "stories," and she became quite upset. She insisted she wasn't making up stories, but was recounting actual memories of life on distant worlds.

My eldest daughter at age nine bent a fork by placing it over her wrist and intending for it to bend at a spoon-bending party at our home. Several adults and I watched in wide-eyed astonishment as her fork slowly melted down to match the contours of her wrist, while she gazed calmly straight ahead out the living room window. When I asked how she bent her fork so gracefully, she explained, "I just relaxed and looked at and thought about something else, like you said to do."

While pregnant with my younger daughter, I was delighted to discover my nightmares stopped. If a bad dream began, it would end abruptly, as if it were a light switch someone flipped off. I felt my younger daughter might be the reason for this abrupt cessation of bad dreams, and my suspicion was confirmed when she turned two years old. She woke me up early one morning to say, "Mommy, I had a bad dream." When I asked, "What happened in your dream?" she explained, "A wolf was trying to eat me." I sleepily rubbed my eyes and asked, "So what did you do?" She replied enthusiastically, "I ate him." When my younger daughter was less than six months old, she frequently said, "Thank you" like a cosmic blessing to anyone nearby. This startled people who couldn't believe such a young baby could talk, let alone say such a meaningful phrase. Many people asked, "Did the BABY just say, 'Thank you'?" with jaws open, gaping in disbelief. I replied that my baby often said, "Thank you," though no one trained her to say that, and nobody said that frequently around her! She hadn't said any other words yet.."Thank you" was her first utterance.

When my younger daughter was two years old, she pointed up in the sky on a preschool toddler walk and exclaimed, "Look! A spaceship!" Squinting my eyes to see where she was pointing, I didn't see a spaceship, but did feel a sense of energy where she was pointing. I felt goose bumps rise on my body as I realized I'd never mentioned the word "spaceship" to her, and here she was using it quite matter-of-factly.

On a separate occasion, I had just walked barefoot into my garage, when I stepped on something soft and furry, and was just about to look down when I heard my younger daughter emit a blood-curdling scream. Without looking at what I'd stepped on (which I later determined to be a dead rat), I rushed inside to find my daughter sitting peacefully on the floor. "What's the matter? " I asked. She looked at me serenely and replied, "I don't know."

One of the best ways to support and encourage the new generations of children to retain their gifts is by sharing stories about children who enjoy the "real magic" of telepathy, telekinesis, animal communication, lucid dreaming, astral travel, meditation, manifestation, and communicating with spirits.

My involvement in writing books for these new children came about largely by accident. As much as I adored the Harry Potter books, I was terribly annoyed with the way these books seemed to imply that magic is only possible with the use of broomsticks, wands, potions and spells. While grumbling to a friend one day that "Someone should write a book about the real magic of natural phenomena," he startled me by responding, "Yes. You should." I surprised myself by going home and writing much of the first chapter of Karen Kimball and the Dream Weaver's Web that same day. Now that it is complete, I cherish Karen Kimball as the book I wish I had growing up, to validate my experiences and empower me to hold these inner truths sacred while engaged in everyday life with my family and at school. The dream weaver's web in this story reminds us that we are all connected as one, and offers understanding of how our thoughts and feelings change the physical world as each choice we make works to select one of many possible alternate realities.

When reading stories like Karen Kimball and the Dream Weaver's Web with children, we gain the benefit of sharing and discussing experiences like this one, in which Karen takes a lucid nap in a tree:

Karen felt like she was both wide awake and yet also asleep at the same time. Her body was nestled snugly in the branches of the mulberry tree, and even though her eyes were closed, she could see clouds in the sky and hear a warm summer breeze rustling the mulberry's leaves. She felt the beating of her heart, and noticed that the vibrations that had passed through every cell in her body left her with a tingling sensation. Her left hand was still resting inside the tree, rubbing the rounded place where the branch met the trunk.

"How amazing it is to feel the inside of a book and a tree, and how very peculiar," Karen thought to herself. She gently placed her right hand inside her book and once again felt the varying density and texture of the cover, pages, and bookmark.

Karen looked up at the sky and saw a feather twirling and tumbling on the breeze. With the thought, Float, Karen gently began to rise up out of the tree and toward the feather. She was flying high like the blue jay, sailing along easily without any effort on her part. This was wonderful!

As caretakers of wonder, there are many benefits from sharing such stories about holistic magic with children. We engage in shared vicarious experiences, discover fresh perspectives, and discuss personal insights. We also open a door to deepening our relationship with the natural world. By encouraging children to trust and value their intuitive abilities, rather than ridicule or ignore them, we nourish their imagination, creativity, cooperation, humor and sense of interconnectedness. These are the very fundamental strengths that future generations most need to heal the Earth and ourselves ... and to thrive.

Cynthia Sue Larson is the editor of the monthly Reality Shifters e-zine and author of several books, including the highly acclaimed, *Karen Kimball and the Dream Weaver's Web, and Reality Shifts: When Consciousness Changes the Physical World*

Children, the Light to the World

by Uriel Light

Looking into the eyes of our children is like looking into a crystal ball. They glow with so much potential. They truly are the light of the world!

They love life and their simple thoughts are pure in their connection to God, God, the source of all life. By being connected to all there is, they are one with their I AM presences. Their will and divine will become one. This allows them to love others. Fear, guilt, and shame are foreign to them.

They have reincarnated at this time with a refined purpose. And in these new children, the lump of coal that used to represent humanity is refined into a brilliant diamond. They have aligned with TRUTH (Cosmic and Universal Principles) and are flowing in them as co-creators. They are the embodiment of the Adam Kadmon Divine Blueprint (New Man) of bringing heaven to earth by living in joy, peace, harmony, connection, light and love.....A living example of a new humanity, shining their light from the cosmos for others to be drawn into their brilliance. They are the true Light Bearers bringing in and anchoring light firmly in place. These children live from their inner core being and not by their physical senses. Thus, they are the beginning of the new era of human consciousness, which will prevail throughout all eternity!

Light Children are seeds, and when planted on fertile ground, they carry the spiritual DNA of Life into this world in a way no immortal ever could. Just as an acorn holds the potential of a great oak tree and demonstrates that blueprint, the same essence exists within our children. They are each unique pieces of the puzzle which, if missing, makes the WHOLE incomplete; and these muti-dimensional beings have a purpose that is guided by divine spirit and a will higher than their own.

The children of today are like gems that need to be polished. All gems are made to vibrate at a divine frequency. As children grow spiritually, they too are drawn to a higher energy frequency, and they come into harmony with the heartbeat of the cosmos. When the Earth achieves a stable vibration of 13 on the Schumann Resonance scale, the Shift of consciousness will begin on a global scale, and the children will be helping hold that energy.

By knowing their true self and listening to their Intuition with great commitment and inner focus, they are experiencing a solid connection to divine consciousness and awareness that is securing their divine potential and helping us evolve ours . Higher consciousness reveals a new awakening presence within their opened 3rd Eye and awakened Heart, which presents them with the vital energies known as Life Force.

They learn to identify themselves as Life itself uplifting the earth and all humanity as they carve out their path with certainty. This is the evolution of their souls as humans merging male and female into a greater force working for the evolution of Earth. They intuitively perceive Divinity in all things. Their need to love and nurture themselves builds the support and foundation of their journey. This makes them strong and successful, for their foundation will bear the weight of anything for it is solid, indestructible and bonded to infinite potential. They live in peace and harmony with others for they are in harmony and connection with the principles that guide this universe as a life giving spirit.

The name "Adam" refers to the entire human race and the term "Kadmon" refers to completion. Thus, Adam Kadmon speaks of a return to our beginning, with all the knowledge, wisdom, and enlightenment of the first "Adam." Those who embrace this doctrine firmly believe that we can return to the Garden of Eden by becoming the Adam Kadmon and creating Heaven on Earth.

The earthly man may be made from a "lump of clay". However, the heavenly man is created in the perfect image of the Logos, and is neither man nor woman, but an incorporeal intelligence. The first Adam was of flesh and blood and, therefore, subject to death—merely "a living soul"; the second Adam was "a life-giving spirit"—a spirit whose body, like the heavenly beings in general, only has a spiritual nature.

It is said that Adam Kadmon had rays of light projecting from his eyes denoting the Manifest Absolute itself; the "heavenly man," born in the image of God. Adam Kadmon appeared on a very high plane of consciousness as a vehicle through which the light and unlimited life pours into the Lower planes. One becomes Adam Kadmon through activation of the divine nature in the 12 strand DNA activation of that Divine Blueprint. When enough of mankind has activated their divine nature, we will evolve and become the Corporate Christ, living in the spiritual realm. one with all that is.

Adherents of these beliefs claim that the inactivated part of our DNA is preventing us from becoming true spiritual beings. They claim we have the divinity and enlightenment of the Adam Kadmon encoded into our DNA although it is not activated. As more and more of us activate this Divine Nature, we will become the Adam Kadmon, return to the Garden, and usher in heaven on Earth.

Activation to this information will cause you to live as Adam Kadmon, the God-Man in the Garden of your being. Man is the visible expression (Microcosm) of the invisible (Macrocosm) God. It has been the Creator's plan from the beginning that we connect as ONE heart. We are more than a physical being living in a body. We can merge matter and spirit into a unified body of knowledge flowing with divine inspiration.

These new children have become the Adam Kadmon Being, the infrastructure of all Creation -the point of primal potential at the beginning of the universe. This potential is then shaped into individualized points of co-creation. By observing these new children, we are being given a glimpse into the future of our race.

As Mother Earth goes into labor with its earthquakes in preparation for the new birth of this universe, children are already being born with life contracts for this new world. One such child was born to my partner, Jennifer Alvarez. And she has named her son Adam Kadmon Alvarez.

Jennifer: *As we build the Galactic Center of the New Jerusalem in Ecuador, he has become a symbol of the New Man. Adam Kadmon Alvarez was conceived during the summer solstice 2010. During my pregnancy I would have frequent conversations with him, and he would react to different people's energy inside the womb. It was like carrying a powerful crystal inside of me, which definitely accelerated my growth in consciousness dramatically and continues to do so to this day.*

I showed fairly early, as this was my third baby (the trinity), and I carried a lot of extra amniotic fluid with him, which I have later learned was to provide greater protection for the large amount of light he carried. In the midst of being pregnant with Adam Kadmon, we were also moving out of the United States to Ecuador in order to establish a spiritual retreat center right at the zero point (equator) to help create the New Jerusalem and bring in the new consciousness of 2012. You can see the pattern that is emerging…New Jerusalem, new consciousness, and now the new Adam Kadmon.

After settling into our temporary home in the northern part of Quito, Ecuador, we started preparing for the sacred birth of Adam Kadmon. We found a wonderful Partero (Shaman midwife) to attend the birth, and we prepared the space by putting up colorful Indian fabrics that were given to us over the large windows throughout the bedroom. To make a long story short, Adam Kadmon was born on March 10th, 2011 at 6:09 p.m.

Let me refresh your memory of the shifts occurring during that powerful time:

March 9th: 9th Universal Wave of Unity Consciousness
March 10th: The birth of Adam Kadmon
March 11th: Japanese Earthquake

Adam Kadmon was born after less than 2 hours of labor, and the birthing process only took five minutes. He came out into my arms in the water, made a small noise then stopped… he was so peaceful. The midwife, concerned that he would stop breathing put his little feet into some cold water and that definitely woke him up into the physical plane of existence.

Adam Kadmon has a healthy joyful presence, and from the start he adapted to this life beautifully. A healthy and chubby little baby! I've noticed that these children don't need as much material subsistence, probably because they live partly on the light.

I've also noticed that he calms down the fastest and easiest when I chant OM to him. He is able to focus and look right in someone's eyes for minutes at a time. He loves spiritual/sacred geometry videos and music. He is very joyful and smiles quite large. He doesn't like chaos, although he finds his center quickly. When holding him, my heart expands, not just from a mother's love but there is a magnification of the chakras when he is near. When I look into his eyes, my 3rd eye starts to pulse and expand. I am sure he is communicating with me telepathically though I am still learning to receive in that form.

I feel very blessed and in awe to be given the opportunity to be his mother in this lifetime, at this crucial period in history. I am excited and very curious to see how the cosmos uses him as well as all of us jointly. I feel such great hope and greater trust and faith for what is to transpire on the planet because of these beautiful children coming into being now. May God Bless Us Indeed during these momentous times. In Love, Truth and Light, Jennifer

Jennifer's child is just one of many who KNOW from their hearts that they are connected to the ONE. They trust the unfoldment of life, which keeps that abundant joy, excitement and passion alive along their journey as they fulfill their purpose. They have no need to figure things out, or have any fear. They simply travel their path on the road to the future.

Children play an important role in showing us how to live in the Now. As these children live in truth and receive revelation, they expand the collective consciousness of the PRESENT, and raise the consciousness of mankind. They learn to be guided by the truth of the universal, cosmic principles, and there is no fear of the unknown, for they know with their hearts about the reliability of the magnificent operation of the cosmos.

They live in a state of compassionate Being and love and accept everyone where they are, for they have let go of the need to rescue others from their chosen path. They lead by example, and as they live their sanctified life, they automatically lift up mankind into ONENESS.

All is ONE Heartbeat in synchronicity, harmony and balance. These children have been called for such a time as this. We want to thank them for being here at this time and helping with the ascension. We're also grateful for what they teach about embracing all that is with open arms, not judging what it brings. We're also reverently grateful for all the benefits that we can't even imagine as these new masters join us and shine a new light in our world.

Uriel Light is an Ordained Minister, Naturopath, Homeopath, Emotional Life Coach and currently involved in construction of the New Jerusalem/Garden of Eden in Quito, Ecuador. **www.galacticspiritualcenter.com**

The Little Masters; An Interview with Spirit Guide Hector

Channeled by Stacie T. Lau
Written by Nancy Lea Speer

The Skype-line goes quiet as Stacie lapses into a trance.

I hear her soft breath and follow its rhythm until the energy shifts.

Hector's rhythmic voice distorts hers, vibrating through the ear piece: *"Hello, dear friend, how are you today?"*

"Hector, how are you?"

"I would say, I am most-assuredly, light." Then we get down to business as Hector asks, *"...very well, my friend, we have much to discuss today. So, what questions do you bring to the table?"*

"Hector, I want to talk with you about the children coming to Earth who are already arriving. Who are these children - and who are the children of the future going to be?"

Hector is delighted by my question, beginning by saying the children who are already here are the ***Indigo, Crystal*** and ***Rainbow Children***.

Then he says, *these children "... all are (how do I say this?) Beings of Light, or perhaps aspects of Beings of Light -**aspects of the Masters themselves**."*

Awe washes over me. *"... Each hold, besides the Creator particle, an aspect or partial aspect of the soul of the Masters in the 6th Dimensional Realm, ...* ' You see, *"... a Master can have many, many aspects of himself on this Earth plane."*

As I suspected from childhood I know each of us carries in our heart, a spark of God, the Creator, or Source of all that is. We also have our own souls and higher selves.

Young souls incarnate using a large percentage of their soul. Older more evolved souls incarnate using a much smaller percentage of their soul.

Saying a many of the children on the earth plane are bringing with them *"...a partial aspect of the Masters of the 6th Dimensional Realm..."* Hector throws something new at me.

185

My mind is racing: "Imagine the effect this will have on the consciousness of these children!"

Hector interrupts my musings, saying, if they will it so, "... *with this soul aspect ... they will be able to ... go forward... with the messages that the Masters want the rest of the human race to learn...*"

I wonder, "What is that Biblical saying about the Children?"

"The wolf will live with the lamb...; and a little child will lead them." [Isaiah 11:16] It feels like Hector is reading my mind when he answers my thought.

"... *the children shall step forth and begin teaching the adults. Perhaps I should not say, teaching... perhaps I should say...awakening the Light in the adults.*" Just as the *Bible* says, Hector confirms: "...*the little children are going to lead...*" the adults ....

Many adults today are looking to the stars and the heavens, some for the first time, proclaiming, as Hector echoed to me, "There is more to life than just this physical body.

There is more to life than just making that proverbial dollar bill."

He says **many children are already stepping forth and activating the Light within their parents and others.**"*Thus will the human race, in a matter of time, so to speak ... be awakened and ready for the* **Grand Shift in Consciousness**."

Then he shows me what it is like to be in close proximity to one of these children who carries a speck of the Light essence of the Masters: "... *he or she would be vibrating at that energy of ...*" the Master-essence. While most of us will be unable to see or feel it, when in their presence our cells will delight within us and spontaneously match the child's vibration.

"*As that child grows to begin to speak, to begin to draw, [to be] the artist, to begin to sing...more, and more, and more of the teachings of that Master...*" can be brought through. It depends on the will of the child...

Being taken aback, I want to know how many Masters are participating in this when Hector's voice jars me, asking, "*How many people are on this planet, my friend?*

"Billions."

He then asks me how many people on Earth are holding the Light of the Creator in their hearts?

"All of us." I mumble.

And Hector says, "… *we could list a line of many, many, many Masters, could we not? It could possibly go on, and on, and on. If it were to fill the pages of a book, I would say the book would have no end.*"

I ask if this has been happening already and he answers, "*I would say, most assuredly, yes,*" announcing that if we were to look back over the years, far fewer children held this energetic Light in the past: "*…now that the floodgates are open, perhaps you can say, it is an 'All Go,' my friend, the Shift is on.*" Many of our children "*… indeed are carrying that Light.*"

"OK… so the **Indigo, Crystal and Rainbow** children are carrying the Light?"

"*Indeed. And each one carries…, in their subconscious mind, their mission… what they are to complete on this Earth plane.*"

He stresses the children's mission is not an individual mission: "*Not so... These children …will show signs of telepathy, …. They will know how to work consciously as a whole in numbers [as a group]. So the mission of one indeed is the mission of many.*" And Hector adds: "*…*

I am saying that you will be, and the Earth is, in good hands."

My son, now a twenty-two year old man, was diagnosed at twelve with a form of what our culture calls, *autism*. When I was a child, one in ten thousand children were born with some form of *autism*. Today it is epidemic: one in one hundred-ten children manifests symptoms of *autism*.

I have to ask, and shift the subject, "**Hector, are the children with what our culture calls, 'autism,' here to teach us something?**"

"*I would say, my friend, if we were to use the word 'autism,' …. These children,… have a defined, specific talent, …. There may be one who knows how to calculate the numbers further and beyond….*" Hector suggests that such a child could be the smartest human being on the planet.

Then he indicates the way another child looks at the world may render that child able to beautifully express through artwork, a masterpiece that would rival that of Van Gogh.

And I know one of these children. His name is Kevin Hosseini. http://kevingallery.com/

"...*Yes, indeed,*" says Hector, answering my question, affirming that these children with what we call *autism* are here to teach us!

He says they were initially **scouts**, sent here to "...*take it all on, to say. ...'Hey, I am different, I have different talents. Please do not judge me for who I am because I can be brilliant in a specific way -if you let me. You must accept me. Open your arms and I will open my arms back to you.'*"

As the mom of a child with autism, this comes as no surprise to me.

I politely ask to return to discussing the **Indigo, Crystal and Rainbow** children, "**Is there guidance you can offer these children and their parents?**"

Hector is again excited to answer and says, "*Ah, to the parents I say, dear ones, you indeed have the majestic honor of raising* **The Little Masters**..." clarifying later that these children include the "normal" [I hate to use that word] and many children with different neurological ordering. His advice is the same for all Little Masters:

"**Be patient with them**, *for they will be at times ... a little different or ... a little frustrated with life... they do not, how do I say this? "...they do not feel comfortable within a little body...*

"**Allow them not to hurt themselves**.

"*Allow them to* **adjust to the Earth plane**.

"*Just as they are teaching you, you need to be firm and teach them.*

"*Yet,* **allow them their own creativity** *for they will paint [and] sing the colors of the rainbow that have been lost on this planet for so long.*

"*They will show you beauty beyond beauty and indeed they will love you ten thousand times more than you love them.*"

Then Hector proclaims, "*My friends, when the* **Grand Shift in Consciousness** *indeed hits its peak and we wake up on the other side in that planet of Light, you will all look to each other in recognition ... see, indeed, your children were not your* *children here in this three dimensional Earth, but … they were there standing next to you, choosing you as part of their family.*

"They indeed are your best friends."

This is beautiful to me.

I ask how parents and adults can communicate with these children and Hector answers, "*… here is a small exercise.* His voice is soft with compassion as he points out that, in raising one of these children, it is crucial to pinpoint a talent or passion within each child.

Behind my thoughts I hear Hector saying that one child may exhibit a facility for music, another, a talent in dancing, yet another, a gift for art….

"How can you best communicate with them? Well, they indeed will show you where their specific field or expertise will be." Once they have done this, Hector says it is up to the parent.

Considering the child who is intrigued by music, and stimulating the child's mind at all times, choosing music that will express what you wish to express to that child.

If you are looking at the child who has a gift for art, "… *perhaps you pick up the crayon and draw next to them.*" Expressing what you wish to express through your art. "*… the message in your drawing need not be perfect…the child shall understand the vibration of the essence of the message that you are trying to give them through that form of communication.*

"*Does that make any sense, dear one?*"

Yes, Hector, it makes perfect sense to me.

"Will these children have greater access to past life memories?

"*I would say, most assuredly yes, my friend.*" Hector did, however, clarify one thing"… *I believe for them, the past is indeed something that…*" exists, but it is different for these children.

While we have to seek a past life, for children coming into our world, past lives are "*… integrated within them. They will remember a past life or an experience, as if it were in **this** physical body…say you were the age of forty-two and you had a memory of a … pet… when you were a … seven old;*" this is simply a memory for you. You need not go into a meditation or seek the Akashic Records to recall that pet when you were seven.

"...*with these next children, the next wave of the light, their memories of their past lives will be...*" like that, as if the past life memory were in this life body.

"Hmmm... are there other ways these children will be different?

"*Ok then, I would say this,* **they ... perhaps will begin talking to something that...**" **to you, seems to not be there.**

"**Yet, it is**, *for they are able to see... people in other dimensions... the particle they hold within them...*" vibrates higher than most people on Earth vibrate. These children will therefore see things many others cannot see.

Awed and concerned, fear teases my consciousness and I ask, "If they are hearing voices, how do we protect them? Will we need to protect them as much in ten years as we would need to protect them today? How do we safeguard these children from being misjudged and misunderstood? Will others think they are schizophrenic?

"*Ah, I believe with more, and more, and more of these children exhibiting their grand talents, it will be looked upon as less, oh, how do I say this, uhhh, undesirable...*"

Then Hector expresses another truth I have also discovered in parenting my "different" son: "**The adults are the ones who are going to need to adjust to them**."Hector goes on to say that as incarnations of these young-old souls of Light grow in number, "*... the less and less 'abnormal,' (I hate to use that word)...*" they will seem.

Hector urges us to nurture these children in all the ways we have learned: using Light energies, using sound waves. He laments that he "*...could go on, and on, and on,*" saying that as we spiritually nourish and teach these children and they go to school, "*... being indeed much more secure in this world. The other parents will begin to notice ...*" and ask what we are doing differently?

"They *ask the questions and then it becomes a time for sharing the knowledge, my friend. The barriers are already breaking down. People are willing to listen ....*"

I am again reminded of my son, who had tantrums, when Hector shares that another way in which these children will be different is "...*they will indeed ...throw tantrums...*" He says this is because "...*they remember that indeed they could fly in the blink of an eye.*" Being here in a human body "... *will frustrate them a lot...* . Because of the tantrums, "... *in the beginning, the early years, ... you may think ... something may be wrong with your child...*"

"*Fear not. They just need to know to adjust to this realm and you have ...'time on your side.'...*

"*Each step forward in the awakening of humanity, ... brings humanity itself to a higher level of existence, a higher vibration, ... and that vibration is the vibration that the Children of the Earth currently are used to living in..If you were to be put in a much denser place physically than you were accustomed to, would you not feel a bit upset also?*"

Looking back at Hector's message I ask Hector for clarification and he mirrors my question back to me, asking me to consider "... *how many children have different labels put forth on them in this current time, autism, downs' syndrome, ADD, to name a few....?*"

"*We could say each 'label' is carrying a different Master Light essence that is engrained in...*" each of the affected children, whether they are **Indigo, Crystal** or **Rainbow**.

"*Now why would a Little Master take on such a hard life -to be labeled and called 'different?'*" In the case of children with different neurological wiring, their ways of being different are even greater. Why would a soul take on so much? Hector answered his own question, saying that Humanity is constantly evolving and these young-old children are here on the Earth Plane to stretch the way we humans think, to open Humanity's mind to accept that change IS here, the Shift is on, and wondrous souls come to us in different and amazing packages!

Pay close attention to the children among us who are considered "different." They just may be harbingers of change.

Be they Little Masters, or just different, all children come to Earth with the same loving message, "*Open your arms and I will open my arms back to you...*"

Please hear their messages and be awakened.
It is time!

SPECIAL NOTE: A pretty good description of **Indigo and Crystal Children** can be found at:
http://www.starchild.co.za/what.html and
http://en.wikipedia.org/wiki/Indigo_Children;
A pretty good description of **Rainbow Children** can be found at:
http://www.starchildren.info/rainbow.html **and**
htttp://en.wikipedia.org/wiki/The_Rainbow_Children.

The transcript of this interview is available at www. SpiritualReader.net

Medium/Channeler
Stacie T. Lau is a Medium and Signature Cell Healing Practitioner. She offers private sessions with Hector, healings and classes. Visit **www.spiritualreader.net/** for more information.
Arc-Guide from the other side
Hestectoramus, "Hector" is an ancient energy force from the Sixth Dimensional Plane -the plane of guides and Ascended Masters. A former guide to the powerful Egyptian potentate Imhotep, Hector has returned to serve Humanity during these uncertain and turbulent times. Hector is here on Earth to share in her Great Planetary Shift, assisting those participating in this unprecedented evolutionary leap in human consciousness.

Interviewer-Writer/Editor
Nancy Lea Speer, J.D., is the co-author of the soon-to-be released book titled, **Wondering into Wisdom**. She was a founding board member of the Santa Barbara Chapter of **Autism Society of America**, later also a founding member of Santa Barbara **TACA**.

Soul Groups: "All" in the Family

by Michelle A. Payton, Ph.D., D.C.H.

The door whooshed open and shoes thudded on the floor by the front door as my eighteen year old son entered with his previous night's attire on. Not sure what mood darkened the door I chirped, "Well Hello!" and left it at that. "Hey Mom," he greeted and padded heavily through the hall then took the steps two at a time to his bedroom. Within minutes, music blared as he yelled from upstairs, "Mom why is this internet so slow... I swear I'm gonna shove my foot through this computer screen... I need to download some music!" Clearly this was my fault, but somehow he completed his task, made it back down to the ground floor with a clean outfit, wet hair and CD's in his hand announcing "These are the best mixes I have ever done! And, oh, by the way, Carol's (15 years old) brother's kidneys are failing and he only has about five days to live... He isn't in any pain... We're all over at the hospital supporting them." And he vanished.

If a picture manifested that moment it would have shown a forty-something, dumbfounded woman with a text cloud overhead reading "What am I supposed to do with that?" After I took a few deep breaths my consciousness floated to a solution that expanded my idea of synchronicity --that every situation I came in contact with is a 100% reflection in me in some way. So I looked in the proverbial mirror and wondered what I would do if my child was lying in bed and waiting to die---no pain, coherent, and had only five days. Initially my logical mind looked for a process-- on day one I would... then... then... Lackluster energy dripped from every linear thought until inspiration seeped through my left brain clutter and the answer emerged, "How did we live? Celebrate that!"

Life has become even richer as I've considered how far family extends. Family can be loosely defined as a group of people connected through love and affection. But what if we simplified this and proclaimed family is a group of connected entities (people, animals, spiritual guides...)? If I combined the idea that every situation I come in contact with is a 100% reflection in me then each time I brush up against a reality (even if I accidentally hear a conversation not meant for me... Or was it?), then I connected to a family labeled soul group.

For instance, it was "Meet the Teacher" day for my daughter in intermediate school (fifth grade in our area). Halls hummed with the combined sounds of teachers, administrators, parents, and students completing missions-- finding classrooms, finalizing paperwork, some children celebrating classroom soul groups and others mourning, and parents sharing phone numbers for emergency contacts. It was a chaotic, mainstream, hot bed.

Being a mainstream metaphysical mom--observant to energy around me--I've learned to flip a switch in these types of situations and own the idea that I am connected to a soul group for a duration of time. That translates to a form of "all are one" and we create a type of dance. We may demonstrate similar needs, but it doesn't mean we are completely like-minded. It does mean we have roles to play to create harmony, goodwill, and community--to feel helpful and feel helped, to accept and feel accepted, and to be interesting and interested. Being of service to one another can be a simple nod and non-verbal communication that fits the moment to more complex engagements.

I'll admit that there are days when I don't always feel comfortable in random soul groups. To experience soul groups that I have less obvious connections to, my physical body has to be rested, be at average blood sugar levels, and ample time has to be budgeted to manifest patience on my part. And when I can accept my roles, the experiences are enhanced and I appreciate being united with a soul group for that specific time frame--from the most platonic to the most intimate contact.

Soul groups change regularly in a 24-hour period--perceptions could be that they are random or (the opposite) fated depending on philosophies. There could be a grocery store soul group, work place soul group, meetings in the work place soul group, yoga class soul group, highway traffic soul group, meal at a restaurant soul group all playing out parts in each family. If we grew accustomed to this and taught it to our children by example then what might happen? Would insensitive bullies, thoughtless discrimination, and painful exclusion disappear? If all adopted these patterns as adults how would peacekeeping measures, safety, and inclusion be expressed?

When the body isn't well--lethargic, nutritional shortages, immune system deficiencies--interest in interacting with soul groups drops. Rapidly. The low energy body either sees groups coming and turns the other way or forms various types of attacks like animals backed into corners. Being reclusive or aggressive gives an artificial sense of working for only so long. Waking up and becoming seekers, there are wholistic integrative tools that can successfully create a more conscious, connected life. Notions that get emotional duress to zero (one way to process tension is to benchmark levels from ten--the highest--to zero-- no stress) --like Emotional Freedom Technique, Ho'oponopono, self-hypnosis, and ritual sayings-- have served as effective pattern interrupts for many years (we'll get into process details a bit later).

As parents and overseers we've used pattern-interrupts intuitively. If children have metal objects and are about to insert them into electrical outlets we want to pull their attention away from that destructive decision. Shouting proper names--Johnny and Cindy--may or may not work effectively, but sharing more attractive options ("Do you want to play with this toy?" or "Would you like a snack?") encourages the children to turn around and reach for something else. And that is the gist of the concept; we're reaching for things more productive.

There are few incidences less productive than sports rage. We see it in local, national and even international news, but why do we see it in youth leagues? Media cameras capture what would seem to be terrorist attacks--over-turned, burning vehicles, blood running down an onlookers face, and others fleeing in fear--until the headline reads "Ohio State Michigan Game Ends with Appetite for Destruction." These students become adults and reports emerge: a "Hockey Dad" is found guilty of murdering his 12-year-old son's coach, a parent body-slammed a referee, a father knocked down and kicked a baseball coach when his son was not chosen for a team. Connecting to soul groups of parents watching their kids play sports can be energetically draining, and now even deadly. Competition runs high – cheering for the team and individuals, coaches pulling kids in and out of matches, parents critiquing the coaches and referees, mobs remarks in the stands--and it quickly becomes cold, cruel, envious, judgmental, angry, and violent in a flash.

Sports are a big piece of the rearing mix in American children's lives. Statistics quoted from a NY Child Study Center article revealed that up to 45 million youths from 6 to 18 years old participate in at least one community-based athletic program. And while these types of activities can create socialization, leadership and teamwork skills, enhance self-esteem and overall well-being, there's a dark side in spectators' sections. Maybe it's connected to measurement sticks put on success, and the messages that accompany being winners and losers. This seems to be one of the spaces where the switch is flipped and connections are broken.

I've taught my children that we really know who people are when the chips are down--when they perceive loss. Disconnected enthusiasts can, not only, sneer at opposing teams but also create friction in the name of winning even when their own coaches make decisions. These are the moments that people become less concerned about others. Self-control is non-existent. Taking personal responsibility for actions afterward has no impact because the connection to the group and combined consciousness is lost while exhibiting overly vain, self-serving behavior in the name of conquering at all costs.

What is the 100% reflection in me? I have been that mother tensed up as my youngest daughter ran to the soccer goal and made or missed scoring screaming "Go, Go, Go! Kick it in! Kick it in! Kick it in!" I have been that spectator bellowing from the stands "Be Ready! Spike It!" when my oldest daughter played varsity volleyball. I have also been that parent that has been projected onto when my coed replaced players and felt the burrowing eyes of parents who felt their children were somehow cheated. Entitlement prevails and trickles down to youths and history repeats itself.

One day (as mainstream metaphysical soccer mom) when I was cheering my daughter on, she yelled from the field "Mom! Calm down!" Other rowdy parents didn't notice, but those connected to the soul group off the field did and I desisted. But what if I wasn't a parent that could hear, feel or see the messages? What if she adopted my behavior over time? Reaching for something more productive, we can redirect and suggest new choices of perceptions.

If we foresee energetic exhaustion and don't want to participate, follow that intuition. Exiting, in essence, may be our character roles in certain soul groups. However, being mainstream metaphysical parents there are times that mingling is required--school functions, athletic games, play dates. Getting to emotional zero with Emotional Freedom Technique, Ho'oponopono, self-hypnosis, and ritual sayings can interrupt patterns and reshape experiences in the moment and future. Let's start with the Emotional Freedom Technique or EFT.

EFT is a process that utilizes the body's meridian system (specific nerve endings). It involves tapping--with fingers, on a series of acupressure points on our faces, body and hands while focusing on a thought to reframe. Reframe is a common term used in hypnotherapy and neuro-linguistic programming with the purpose of changing the meaning of the experience--changing the memory of the experience to something more neutral or positive. Inevitably, the process allows us to remember the thoughts, but in a more productive fashion.

Here are some easy steps when using EFT with children (with a pinch of hypnosis suggestion):

1. The parent, teacher, or coach should use an anchor statement (meaning expectation) to prepare for the EFT exercise. For example: "Johnny, can you help me? Children, can you help me?" The child(ren) must be aware that this statement is an anchor to stop, look and listen to the parent or teacher, and begin tapping (it's even more effective if both adult and children tap simultaneously to create energy exchanges).

2. Children seem to be most comfortable with the karate chop area (the pinky side of the hand)--it's easy to remember, and the term karate chop area makes sense to them. Another literal verbal anchor could be "Johnny can you tap on your karate chop area, and listen and look in my direction?" Then voice the expectation.

3. The parent, teacher or coach then requests a new action. For example, (as tapping) "Could you think of your favorite place to be calm and quiet?" (This is a self-hypnosis visualization that can be accompanied with "What colors do you see? How is the weather? Do you hear any sounds? Are there any aromas?" can increase the sense of calm and quiet.) (If Resistant) "Johnny I know you would rather talk with classmates (or teammates)" (the problem), "but can you tap your karate chop area, and remember how calm and quiet you feel in your favorite place (neuro-linguistic programming anchor) through the rest of the reading period?" (the solution). Repeat until the desired result is reached.

4. Experiencing certain issues consistently? Write the problem and the solution on a slip of paper and hand it to the child to work independently (handing the paper to the child would serve as an anchor as well).

If parents, teachers or coaches expectations are less than optimistic then take time to tap prior to approaching the problem and reframe or change the negative perception. Say out loud or in our minds that "This has been a bad situation for so long how could it change? I'm ready to be a part of a new and positive situation." Or "This is a frustrating situation. I'm ready to create a positive situation." Clear out the residue as a result of the negative experience (the problem), and EFT/NLP reframe (the solution). Another option is to decide not to solve problems in moments of duress (exception is if safety is being threatened), but open ourselves up to possibilities we may not be aware of until after clearing our minds. To achieve this we would change the statement from something like "This is a frustrating situation (the problem). I'm ready to create a positive situation (the solution)." to "This is a frustrating situation (the problem). I'm sorry, please forgive me, I love you, thank you" (not concerning ourselves with negative or positive labels, but simply getting ourselves to zero and relaxing). This creates a mental environment of being open to inner compromise, and positive inner dialogue

(Examples: "This situation is better than I initially thought." "Now that I've distanced myself from the situation I can return and address this more calmly."). These phrases are part of a practice called Ho'oponopono and is considered mental cleansing in the Hawaiian culture. Ho'oponopono means "to" "correct, revise, adjust, amend, rectify." The expressions associated with this practice are "I'm sorry, please forgive me, I love you, thank you."

In the earlier example with children, we didn't rank the emotional duress from zero to 10. With adults we can more easily narrow duress from 10 to zero and tap until the numbers get as low as possible (zero being the goal). Some say phrases from Ho'oponopono only. Others use EFT only. Still others use a combination and add their own little twists—maybe cite ritualistic chants, prayers, and poems used regularly for pattern interrupts depending on philosophies. But whatever the process, repeat the steps until interrupting negative thoughts are successful.

What would happen if we considered all interactions reflections in us? How differently would it feel if we considered our interactive experiences as families or soul groups in the moment? Our lives are, many times, plagued by the small stuff; yes, I know that we're told not to sweat those, but why not nip those in the buds before they grow? Beware of the sneaky "And, oh, by the way" comments. Turn "What am I supposed to do with that?" into synchronicity gifts and celebrate those!

Michelle Payton has written numerous books on mainstream metaphysical living, has a Doctorate in Clinical Hypnotherapy, Mastery in Neuro-linguistic programming and Emotional Freedom Technique, plays, lives with her husband/partner and three children, and has a private practice (Mind Over Matter) in Asheville, North Carolina. See more at **www.MichellePayton.com**.

Empowering the New Children

by Diana Cooper

At last people are starting to recognize that the greatest spiritual responsibility anyone can undertake in their lifetime is to bring up a child and develop its unique gifts.

The children being born now are very high frequency, high energy, psychic, intuitive and gifted. They also have a need for freedom and creative expression.

If the parents of the new children are fifth dimensional then the possibilities for those children are limitless. If they are not, the potential they incarnate with will be squashed. So the greatest gift we can give to our children is to raise our frequency to the fifth dimension. This means we can cherish our offspring and make their welfare and happiness high priority.

Who are the new children?

All babies born after 2012 will have a contract to serve in some capacity. Already waves of special children are incarnating from all the Universes to prepare us for the transition to the new Golden Age. These children include:

Wise old souls
Many of the Wise Ones of former times have returned already or will be born in the next few years to assist the planet. They are encoded with their former gifts, prepared to teach, heal or hold the light. The information they hold is fifth dimensional and does not work at a third dimensional level for example allopathic medicine is third dimensional while light healing is fifth.

Star Children
Star children do not originate from Earth but their souls come from other planets or universes. They include:

Indigo, rainbow and crystal children
These children originate from Orion, the planet of wisdom

and enlightenment. They have never incarnated on Earth before, so this material plane is very difficult for them to comprehend. Not only are they very high-frequency but they are extremely psychic, often enlightened and many have gifts of healing, telepathy and clairvoyance. Some have advanced powers which need to be carefully nurtured and trained. Occasionally these children withdraw into autism and shut down their gifts because their vibration is so pure that they cannot cope with the energy around them.

IVF children
In the thirty years since the first IVF baby arrived a wave of them has followed. They come from other Universes and have never incarnated here before. IVF souls are not conceived in a moment of emotion so are not clouded by this; rather they witness the conception. With the ability to stand back and examine things from a different perspective, they observe situations, often bringing fresh and different ideas, viewpoints and solutions.

They are very special because they are so wanted. Also their purity means they can tune into their parents and heal them.

High frequency souls
They are bringing in new and exciting information, for example those entering from Sirius are programmed with spiritual technology. Having expanded their higher minds they are developing new advanced concepts to take us into the Golden Age. They will 'invent' methods of travel, power, communication and weather control that are currently beyond our comprehension. The capturing of angelic vibrations as Orbs on digital cameras is a recent example of spiritual technology.

How can we help to empower the children?

1. Keep yourself and your home at a high frequency.
To do this watch your thoughts, play harmonious music and fill your home with beauty and light. Do things that make you happy and feel fulfilled.

2. Listen and validate their experiences.

The psychic children can see or sense into other dimensions and may experience spirits, angels and elementals. If they say they saw their dead Granny, talked to an angel or remembered another life, don't tell them they imagined it. Be prepared to listen with open minds and hearts.

3.Tell the truth

Children intuit all that is going on around them. If you tell your child that everything is fine when the reality is that your relationship is breaking down, they feel unsafe and disempowered. It means either that you are lying which is scary because they can't trust you or their intuition is wrong which is also scary because they can't trust themselves.

Truth, however uncomfortable, has a pure, clear vibration and they respond to this. We are moving into an Age of Transparency.

4. Ground them and attune them to their Higher Selves

Many high frequency children find it hard to ground into the low vibration of the planet so their crown chakra doesn't link directly to their Higher Self.

My granddaughter was one of these and my guide asked me to put her photograph onto Orbs of Archangels Sandalphon to ground her and Jophiel to attune her crown chakra to her Higher Self, for pictures of Orbs continue to radiate the energy of the angelic being and this will enfold you or your child. I did this and the change was remarkable. She has never looked back.

If a child is withdrawn place their name or photograph on a unicorn Orb.

If your child needs protection put the name on an Orb of Archangel Michael.

If they need confidence place them on an Orb of Archangel Uriel.

Then watch the changes.

5. Ask the angels and unicorns to help them

Unicorns and angels love to connect with children and will

assist them if asked! To facilitate this, talk about and read stories about the other realms. Teach children to ask for help.

6.Education

Children are unique souls whose individual talents need to be nurtured. The new ones are born with exceptional knowledge and wisdom and we must find ways of drawing this out rather than teaching them someone else's ideas. As we cultivate and honour their innate gifts they will feel happier, socially belonging and responsible.

Education needs to be right and left-brain-balanced, with more emphasis on social skills, creative expression, honest communication and living in harmony with nature and other cultures.

Help them have a growth mind set so they can fulfil their potential. For example when a child passes an exam we may say, 'Aren't you clever,' and this starts to become their internal label. The next time they are presented with a harder test they may feel they will fail if they do not pass, so they find an excuse not to accept the challenge. However if you focus on the process by saying, 'You studied hard and did your best. How wonderful that you passed,' the next time there is a test, the child can study and try and is more prone to accepting an opportunity for growth.

When smaller community schools with smaller classes replace the current ones, children will flower as they feel noticed and important. These local schools will allow contented, balanced and evolved children to emerge, ready for the future.

7.Space for games and sport

These high energy children need plenty of space to let off steam and play sports so we need to encourage sports and physical activities.

8.Connecting with nature

Nature helps to ground people and keep them in the fifth dimension. It is important that children learn about and are connected to the elementals, for without them our planet could not flourish.

9.Food

Good food and pure water is essential for these children to maintain their frequency.

Children's books

I feel very passionate about the importance of helping the children, so I kept asking my guides and angels to show me a way. One day a story about a little girl who finds relationships, school and life difficult came into my head. She is confused and anxious until she is given a little grey kitten who can talk to her. He becomes her guide and empowers her to find friends, deal with situations and feel confident. Through him she meets elementals, her guardian angel, other angels and unicorns and together they help others and the world. Now I have written a series of books and CD's about Tara and her Talking Kitten, which enchant and illuminate children and their parents.

Diana Cooper is author of 24 books and is Founder of the Diana Cooper School **www.dianacooper.com**

Occupy Earth...

by Nina Meyerhof

It is time we consider that we, as EARTH's occupants, must live in harmony and balance with equity for all. The movement of Occupy Wall Street, Arab Spring, and all the others uprisings are now the call for humanity to go beyond what systems exist and topple the old institutions and have them follow human's needs. These needs once seen as an aspect of dominance now are a call to realign and circle the earth as one world family in service to all of life.

Children of the Earth is a youth spirit/peace organization acting around the world as the "Hope Generation" to create positive social action through local projects as well as organizing other youth.... thus translating our mission into a movement -- the worldwide OCCUPY EARTH movement.

Youth with proper skills and inner realizations will initiate a relevant transformation of society. We believe in peaceful changes that include skills in dialoguing with the "oppositional party" to create a holistic understanding and conversation. If you look at Mandela, King, or Gandhi, they each had methods that truly impacted not only their own country but also the world at large. We believe that embedded in all religions is a heritage of peace. So it would be our purpose to uncover this and bring forward these memories. With these memories, a youth movement that does not instill fear, but rather, love and compassion could stand out as a poignant and powerful movement. We are training young adults as well as leaders to learn these skills and then develop goals for social change, and go into peaceful warrior action.

Youth empowered will occupy Earth in right relationships. As the next generation discovers their inner authentic call, understanding the interconnection of life, they are organizing themselves in connecting to deal with civil unrest as it is occurring in the world with goals and action plans.

The future must move from problem focused to integration of holistic understanding, so that all peoples of the world may live a life of peace. Civil unrest is only a symptom of a deeper cause. Now all are organizing, but have not yet understood that this is the prophesied 2012 reorganization or shift. It is the time of the birth of change and our great opportunity to move into a family of one humanity, caring for ourselves and each other.

This is the time of re-evolution and youth are ready to move into world action. The commitment is to build positive and lasting change, and to help launch and nurture a millennium of peace.

Dr. Nina Meyerhof is the executive director of Children of the Earth, an international organization that inspires and unites young people, through personal and social transformation, to create a peaceful and sustainable world. One Earth....with all her Children smiling! **www.coeworld.org**

A New Breed of Activist

by Oran Cohen

Imagine, if you will, a wave, a movement of youth who walk this planet and feel a deep urge to change it. This wave of consciousness is made up of individuals from every corner and every faith of Mother Earth. They live with a certain sense of reverence, respect, and love for all sentient beings that transcends the boundaries of countries, cultures and traditions. They feel, somehow, that they have a responsibility to humanity and to themselves to impact their world.

They believe that action alone will not save humanity from it's present trajectory. They also know deep within their hearts that sitting in a candle-dimmed meditation room or place of worship and praying for world peace is great, but still, not the whole picture. These individuals believe that to truly transform this world for the better, a future of unity and collective conscious evolution, the way forward is for those who are spiritual to dare to become active, and those who are active to dare to become spiritual.

They're starting NGO's (non-governmental organizations), occupying the streets, and they are self-organizing, balancing spirituality with potent and deliberate acts. Learning to walk in both worlds. They are strategists, mediators, pioneers, system breakers and system makers who can sense that the status quo is ready to be challenged! Oh, and a large majority of them also happen be under the age of 35.

Welcome to the new breed of activists. This is the new paradigm of thought. More and more individuals understand that to fundamentally transform the culture of war, physical measures will never be enough. If they truly wish to shift this planet, they need to shift their inner warring nature as well --on behalf, and as part of, humanity. They know without a shadow of a doubt that their world mirrors their beliefs, judgments, values and perceptions. No one knows this better than these new activists. In fact, more and more people are awakening to this realization everyday!

They are learning that waving peace signs and marching

won't change the world, but spiritual and conscious action taken with discernment and long-term planning just might. These individuals realize the need to deepen their spirituality and then transform that beingness into action.

They feel that the more we, as humanity, look at ourselves as the cause of our external experiences, the more we can stand accountable and learn to change our world. They know that by changing themselves, they can re-write their social script, and they use their writing tools with passion and determination -- compelled and inspired by something deeper, by an internal call from the genius inside themselves. They are aware that every thought, emotion and belief takes them closer or farther away from unity with themselves, their community and their world.

We are in critical times, and the movement is at a critical stage. On the surface, you might call one face of this movement Arab Spring or Occupy Earth. However, something deeper is stirring underneath the contempt and the call for change. A movement that takes us closer to our divinity is under way, and our most prized possession during this shift is bringing our individuality AND our indivisibility into play.

For humanity to thrive in the transformation that awaits it, we have to realize the truth about our nature on an individual, communal, and global level. We need to bite the bullet, and own up to the fact that humanity is an organism. It's a system in a sea of systems, a player in the grand orchestra of life. We are now being called to learn to see our world as systems rather than live under the illusion of separateness. And the destiny of a thriving system is fueled by the mechanisms of collaboration, decentralization and constant innervation. The new activist knows this intuitively.

Our role is to listen to what emerges, see what is needed, and act as facilitators rather than dictators --as collaborators and students of the future. Our part is learning to create conditions conducive to life! These "New Activists" are the Mapmakers of the future. They carry the pin-code for the change humanity is destined to undergo. They represent the new order of freedom that is emerging! This "movement" has no borders, no criteria, no categories and no dogmas. So, all are called to join this growing force! It is about the freedom to love and the love of freedom. It is about awakening to our highest truth, whatever that may be, and uniting as humanity to fundamentally transform ourselves and our world. It is about living our highest values of love, truth, unity and peace.

Our only undoing is our inability to see the trends and signs that lead to the new positive, supportive ways of being in the world. There is a call now to re-imagine the way we relate to ourselves, to one another, to our world, and to the mechanisms to which we choose to engage. We are being asked in no uncertain terms to rethink our thinking and use tools that relate to the monumental times of exponential shifts that we find ourselves in.

Our most valued tool is our hearts and our ability to listen. Our gift is our uniqueness, our individuality --our personal genius. We can only do this by listening with intensity and humility. And we can only change things by acting with intelligence, discernment, passion and reverence. This is the path of the spiritual activist.

This, I suspect, is our mandate. It is not an option, but the very foundation of the future we constantly say we desire to experience. The 'new breed' knows this and walks that path as a daily discipline.

If these words move you, then, my friend, you are one of those activists.

Your work is to learn this new way of being while simultaneously conjuring up new systems, paths and visions, to expedite your desires and ideas, many of which are still waiting to be born. Our work is to create places of refuge where magnificent souls, just like yourself, can safely explore mew models for the future --dreaming, loving and daring to-get there, romancing ideas out of the collective wisdom and finding the clarity to act on these treasures. The more outrageous and courageous, the better!

Within each individual is the indivisible. Your mission, if you choose to accept it young grasshopper, is to unearth the song that rumbles in your heart, to uncover and discover your genius, and to courageously bring it to the world with audacity, imagination, passion and grace! Know that through doing this, you'll inspire others to do the same. That's how a movement is made. One crazy and inspired soul at a time. Thank goodness you exist!

Oran Cohen is a passionate facilitator, scriptwriter, Singer-Songwriter, designer, social entrepreneur and Change Artist. Oran has traveled the world facilitating peace and aiding in conflict resolution with the focus on the development of young leaders to fulfill a vision for the future. During his time in the Middle-East, he worked with Palestinian and Israeli youth in inter-faith dialogue. and is now on the CHILDREN of the EARTH BOARD that fosters, inspires and activates spirituality within youth."

Death hangs over thee. While thou still live, while thou may, do good! - Marcus Aurelius
Antonious

Picasso

The Code
For the 21st Century Knight

I swear loyalty and all the power of protection at my disposal to my family, loved ones and any other worthy soul. I promise to do everything possible to help the helpless and rescue those I can. I further swear to hold tightly onto love and faith when challenged by the despair of human failings – my own or others.

I seek excellence in all endeavors, the strength to complete all worthy causes, and the divine help to right all wrongs. I value the contributions of others above my own and don't boast about my accomplishments.

As knights of Don Q's court, I have the wisdom to know that craziness and courage are cousins. I do not confine my hopes to the small world in front of me, but do all things, however small, with the impossible dream of infinite love and blessings for all in mind.

I recognize that the sword of justice needs to remain sheathed so mercy can work its magic. I further recognize my enemies as potential loved ones, and seek to incorporate nobility, bravery and love into every aspect of my life, never seeking rewards but always knowing they are at hand.

Harmony Through Chivalry

by Hunt Henion

"**C**hivalry (derived through the French *cheval* from the Latin *caballus*) as an institution is to be considered from three points of view: the military, the social, and the religious." – The Catholic Encyclopedia

It was a knight's sacred (religious) duty to protect (militarily serve) society. The rules of conduct on the battlefield and in society were quite elaborate. His word was literally his bond, even with his enemies. A knight was completely committed, heart, mind, body and soul, to this code of honor in everything he did.

There was opposition to be sure. After all, chivalry was born in the selfish, lawlessness of the dark ages. Still, there was comfort and inner harmony in the selfless code of ethics that has become known as chivalry.

The castles of the knights crumbled with the advent of cannons, and the medieval knights have faded into history. Still, you just can't kill the hope and harmony that the code of chivalry inspires. Even today, the U.S. ***Army's Laws of Land Warfare (FM 27-10)*** states that soldiers must always conduct themselves "*with regard for the principles of chivalry and humanity.*"

Today, business professionals, athletes, politicians and students are all wondering, "Why should I play fair when everyone else is getting ahead by cheating, and sneaking around and not being honest? Well, knights don't sneak! A warrior must act justly and honorably, even when competing against someone who "does not deserve it." When people in any field demonstrate to their friends and associates that ethics and ideals are just as important as their objectives, they elevate the whole playing field, and inspire others (including girls and women) to be the best they can be too.

Men don't have a monopoly on chivalry any more than women have a monopoly on poise. The counterpart of the male "*knight in shining armor*" is what has been called a the "shieldmaiden." This is the perfect balance between the nurturing female and a woman warrior.

213

She's the one who keeps the home fires burning. She provides a safe nurturing environment for her family. She is the teacher of her children and lady for her lord. The shieldmaiden has the courage and fortitude to do the thankless daily jobs with grace. She is an example of service and poise to her family and the keeper of the peace. She keeps her word no matter how hard to fulfill, and she stands by her beliefs, serving selflessly.

Many more knights have fought for the sake of their chivalrous shieldmaidens than for all the princesses or damsels in distress that ever existed! In today's world,where roles aren't so clear-cut, frustration about what is expected and what is right is natural. Unfortunately, this conflict in understanding and the resulting frustration has separated many a knight from his shieldmaden.

There are many shieldmaidens who work tirelessly without the benefit and comfort of a knight, and there are probably just as many knights who long for the nurturing feminine inspiration to continue their battles. Still, the chivalrous attitude is to selflessly do our duty to the best of our ability, never compromising our honor, "never seeking rewards but always knowing they're at hand." When our chivalrous path is clear, harmony sets in, frustration disappears, and the laws of attraction begin to work in our favor.

We were reminded of the ancient tradition of the shieldmaidens in "The Lord Of the Rings," by the character Eowyn, who was a shieldmaiden of Rohan. Her journey also took her from being cold and distant to finding the strength to be vulnerable -- opening herself to love and loyalty, which is at the core of chivalry. In the end, she fought along side her knight. She accomplished what no man could. Because it was the love and obvious devotion between her and her knight that inspired hope in her people and peace in her enemies.

Today's youth are getting a lot of mixed messages, and I just wanted to add the notion of chivalry to that mix. When The Code is kept in mind, anger can be directed. Courage falls into perfect harmony with justice, mercy, generosity, faith, hope and nobility.

There's no reason to live with inner conflict, when taking on the the code of chivalry can bring so much harmony into our personal lives at school or at work. It can elevate our relationships, and heal community issues --which are brought on by the opposite of chivalry.

It's a matter of personal application, but the code is clear and the path is as simple as doing your best to adhere to the seven virtues. The Children of the Earth organization expresses their code of ethics in this way:

LOVE.....for the form, voice, thoughts and spirit of each person

RESPECT....for differences

HONESTY....of our feelings, thoughts and behaviors to be transparent

TRUTH ....in feelings and thoughts

COURAGE.....to take a stand

HUMILITY......to reflect inner peace

WISDOM...... to be a seeker

Or, the knightly code of ethics I've seen is expressed like this:

Harmony: Happiness is when what you think, what you say, and what you do are in harmony ~ Mahatma Gandhi

Justice: If we do not maintain justice, justice will not maintain us. ~ Sir Francis Bacon

Mercy: I have always found that mercy bears richer fruits than strict justice. ~ Abraham Lincoln

Generosity: Generosity is not giving me that which I need more than you do, but it is giving me that which you need more than I do.~ Kahlil Gibran

Faith: The moment we break faith with one another, the sea engulfs us and the light goes out. ~ James Baldwin

Hope: Without hope I would sit motionless, rusting like unused armor. ~ John Steinbeck

Nobility: To be humble to superiors is duty, to equals courtesy, to inferiors nobility. ~ Benjamin Franklin

There is nothing noble about being surperior to some other person. True nobility is being surprior to your former self. -Hindu Proverb

Nobility and chivalry aren't in the public consciousness nearly as much as they were back in the middle ages. In fact, those concepts faded quickly after the last knight took off his armor for the last time. Some say that chivalry died then. Still, every once in a while someone comes along who tries to resurrect it.

One such man was written about in Cervantes's book Don Quixote. Cervantes tells about how this man read about chivalry all night long "until finally, from so little sleeping and so much reading, his brain dried up, and he went completely out of his mind." - from *Don Quixote* by Miguel De Cervantes

Still, the inspirational spirit of working toward an "Impossible dream" is still epitomized today by that crazy Quixote, who definitely had his faults. Still, "...his approach to life uses human failings as a tool for motivation and blindness an an instrument of focus. With the right blindness/focus, our failings actually feed our Don Q point of view. So, this really is a game anyone can play!

"Those who try on this point of view find that their passions grow and their fears dissipate. They can take a stand against injustice and tyranny, while they understand the human failings of their enchanted tyrants... Their creed of chivalry may seem crazy, but it's a craziness that comes with the rewards of a calm heart, a steady hand, and an entire world of blessings that others will never know." --

From **The Don Q Point of View**, *the true story of Don Quixote.*

Blessed are the meek and quixoitic, for they shall inherit the Earth!

Hunt Henion is the author of four books, including the cult classic *The Don Q Point of View.* **www.shiftawareness.com**

Inheriting the Earth

Blessed are the meek, for they shall inherit the earth.
Matthew 5:5

Who's In Charge of Who's In Charge? Why Changing the Political Game is the Only Game in Town

by Steve Bhaerman

Reprinted with permission from his blog Posted on May 19, 2011

"Of course there is a difference between the two political parties. The Republicans bend over backwards for the banksters and special interests. The Democrats are exactly the opposite. They bend over forward."
– Swami Beyondananda

No matter which issue is closest to your heart (or, if it is particularly infuriating, your liver or spleen), EVERY political issue boils down to just one:

Who's in charge of who's in charge?

The founders of the United States of America addressed this issue directly in the Declaration of Independence, putting forth the profoundly radical notion that the legitimacy of government rests on the consent of the governed. Furthermore, they declared that every free individual is sovereign (i.e., has the same rights as a king) with the same natural right to thrive as the grass has to grow.

In creating the Bill of Rights and the Constitution a dozen years later, our country's founders designed a republic (from the Latin *res publica* meaning "thing of the people") as the structure that would serve as an alternative to rule by monarchy and oligarchy. However, the forces the American patriots fought in the Revolutionary War have retrenched and re-grouped. Instead of one multinational corporation (The British East India Company) backed by the power of the military, there are now many. And because these entities have access to so much wealth and resources, they have been able to overrule the rule of law. In some cases, they simply factor in any financial penalty as "the cost of doing business," and go on perpetrating their sociopathic behavior. More often, they do the easier thing. They "invest" in government, and by paying legislators directly (why pay taxes when you can avoid the middle man and go direct?) they can simply buy new laws, or negate old ones. Oh, and when they need to, they can – thanks to the military-industrial complex that really rules America — employ the U.S. military as well.

Now while some might see this as a cynical assessment, I see it as just the opposite. Cynicism is a rationalization of powerlessness, an excuse for apathy, a reason to go back to sleep. I view the stark assessment above as the first truth-telling step on the road to recovery. Despite our nation's unique legacy, we the people have become addicted to powerlessness and dependence on a ruling elite whom we hope will trickle some wealth down onto us "pee-ons." But, as the Swami says, "The ruling class has flunked ruling class. They get an F."

Whether that "F" stands for freedom or fascism is up to us and no one else.

We Have A Deeply-United Body Politic

No, that's not a misprint. While the mainstream media would have us focus on our differences, here is a very important point. Ready? Awakening individuals on all sides of the political divide – from Coffee Party progressives to Tea Party conservatives – overwhelmingly agree that our country is being turned into a third world nation by the unchecked power of money. I am not just speculating here. The work that my friend and associate Joseph McCormick has been doing in large cities and small towns has proved this again and again.

The dysfunctional function of the media has been to prevent civil discourse between the red and blue tribes. Think about it. Where, on mainstream radio or TV, can we find a real forum? All we have are "againstums." Those who are turned off by "massdebating" and "detestimonials," turn off their TV, and then what? They fall back into cynicism and apathy, which further entrenches the powers in power. Or, they redouble their activist efforts on behalf of the thousands of worthy issues related to peace, personal freedom, economic justice, ecological sanity, etc., etc., etc. Each of these worthy organizations and causes are like single cell organisms competing with one another for a dwindling "food" (i.e., cash) supply.

Because this well-intentioned activism is going off in all directions at once, it is actually dissipating our energy. Go ahead. Pick the concern that is most important to you:

• Uncontrolled power of the military industrial complex, and the mind-boggling (and secret) budget for war and weaponry

• Loss of civil liberties

• Power of lobbyists to buy and own legislators

• Choices limited to two pre-selected candidates, and very limited parameters of debate and discussion

• Growing gap between rich and poor, with the middle class becoming a vanishing species

• "Health care" where individuals are forced to purchase insurance from a "company store" monopoly

• Mind-boggling regulations that can be defied by huge corporations but are costly to smaller entrepreneurs

• Clean water, clean air, clean food compromised by those who benefit from not having to clean up after themselves

• GMO foods and the monopolies like Monsanto (who want to control the world's food supply)

• Big Pharma making selling herbs illegal in the European Union in preparation for doing the same in the USA

• Chemtrails, HAARP and other dark conspiracies that one finds going deeper down the rabbit hole

• Etc., etc., etc. Every one of these issues – every one –

boils down to just one issue: Who's in charge of who's in charge? Is it we, the people? Or they, the very, very few people? It's as simple as the old maxim, "When few rule, few benefit."

It's Time For We the People To Gather Under One Big Intention

What is now required is a "movement of movements" or, as Swami Beyondananda would put it, "gathering all the tribes under one big intent." Only by unity of purpose – around the core virtues and values 80% to 90% of us share in common – can we "overgrow" the current deadly, dysfunctional system. We cannot do it while separated into progressive and conservative tribes. However, by integrating the healthiest and most functional aspects of the natural impulses of growth (progressive) and protection (conservative) we can create the whole-brained, whole-hearted politics needed for massive evolutionary change.

Sound too idealistic?

Well, consider the alternative: More of the same, only worse.

For the past ten years since the oxymoronically-titled "Patriot Act" was passed, we've been seeing "soft fascism," the kind that quietly installs the machinery of the police state just in case our collective awareness breaks through the carefully-crafted illusion of freedom. It is a disease process that has been robbing us of our heart, our soul, and our spirit – until now. Because as the Swami says, the truth shall upset you free. As with any disease process, there comes a time when the symptoms can no longer be ignored. And the usual "treatments" – petitioning our "leaders" with demands or waiting for the next tweedle-dweeb / tweedle-dumb election – won't do the trick.

It's time for us to stop banging our heads against police batons and being drawn into the culture wars, and emerge to a new level of power.

It's time to use the ace-in-the-hole … the dormant yet powerful moral authority of the 99%. It's time for the 99% to "occupy" the Occupy our political system.

OK. But how?

By first of all, convening conversations across America, and inviting anyone who identifies with the 99% to participate. A Fox News poll http://www.bradblog.com/?p=8837in early 2012 indicates that 67% consider themselves part of the 99%, and that's not a bad start. In fact, let's invite the other 33% as well, and even the 1% -- provided they speak as individual citizens rather than controllers of the conversation.

Imagine what it would be like to really find out what the 99% of us feel, think – and have in common. What if 80% or even 90% of us supported just one idea, just one rule of governance? What if – for the first time – a unified voice of We The People said, "We the People of America stand for THIS" (however "this" is articulated) and that voice spoke with such collective authority that our legislators had to legislate it – or face certain defeat in 2012?

The same with the President.

Think we can't do it? Thanks to the Internet, we can gather millions in a matter of days, if not hours. The question is, of course, gather around what?

As a first small step, how about gathering in a massive national conversation to decide what unifying theme to gather around. Imagine ... moving the conversation from the Internet to the "outernet" and using the Freedom of Assembly to ... assemble – not just to protest but to pro-actively envision what we would like instead. There are numerous models for gleaning the wisdom of a group in the context of respectful communication, including Jim Rough's Wisdom Council concept http://www.wisedemocracy.org/page11/page18/page18.html, the pioneering work of Tom Atlee's Co-Intelligence Institute http://www.co-intelligence.org/index.html and the Transpartisan Toolkit articulated in my e-book with Joseph McCormick, Reuniting America. http://reunitingamerica.org/

While conversations can certainly happen informally, for these to have greatest impact – and like Occupy Wall Street, become mainstream news -- there would have to be a "neutral convener" outside the current political order and beyond the influence of special interests. Who might be capable of that? How do we call forth the leaders in our spiritual communities, our business communities, in the domains of academia, the arts and sciences who recognize that politics is too important to be left to the politicians? And who or what does the "calling?"

Not since this country was founded have we faced a greater crisis or stood on the threshold of a greater opportunity. We don't need a revolution in this country. We already had one, thank you. Some 235 years ago, a band of courageous and forward-seeing individuals risked life and fortune to stand up to the tyranny of a previous-incarnation of the corporate state: The multinational British East India Company, and the British army and navy.

That was then. This time, what is required is an evolution, where we the people declare ourselves worthy of self-governance and become the sovereign "king" America's founders intended. Can we do it? The only way to find out is to go for it.

Interested in creating a Department of Heartland Security to bring red tribe and blue tribe together in sacred circle to talk until they are purple in the face? Contact us at swamib1@gmail.com

Steve Bhaerman is an internationally-known author, comedian and political visionary, who has spent 25 years writing and performing as Swami Beyondananda, the "cosmic comic." He is the co-author of Spontaneous Evolution: Our Positive Future and a Way to Get There from Here, and 2012, Creating Your Own Shift. He can be found online at **www.wakeuplaughing.com**

We Can Have It All: The Beauty of Value Capture

by Edward Miller

Reprinted with permission. Posted on October 25, 2011 at *Discources on Liberty*

As anyone familiar with classical political economy knows, true property rights are rooted in self-ownership. You own yourself, and by extension you own what you make through labor or voluntary transactions thereof. Land, however, is not a fruit of labor.

One might reasonably suppose that land, being unlike other things that are called "property," would have special economic characteristics. Classical economists recognized this to be the case, and spoke at length about the implications of it. Neoclassicals and their Austrian copycats insisted on lumping everything together under the solitary label of "property," which served to obscure these implications. They simply bicker about how best to achieve equilibrium and Pareto efficiency, given value-free analysis of the system that exists. Some might call that dispassionate analysis; others might call that bean-counting for elites.

Unlike the priesthood of the status quo, I am interested in making moral judgments about the system we live under. I am not talking about a revenue model. I'm talking about a revolution: a revolution of liberty, of prosperity, of human relationships, of ecological relationships.

We can eliminate taxes and debt, poverty and special privilege. Contrary to the dour pronouncements from the curators of the dismal science, we can have it all.

The Basic Properties of Land

In terms of political economy, "land" refers to access rights over everything that was here before us humans. When you buy land, what you are really buying is a bundle of rights, be they air rights, mineral rights, drilling rights, surface rights, spectrum rights, right of way, you name it. Such rights are necessary for all production, and even life itself.

Supposing the entire habitable globe to be so enclosed, it follows that if the landowners have a valid right to its surface, all who are not landowners, have no right at all to its surface. Hence, such can exist on the earth by sufferance only.

They are all trespassers. - Herbert Spencer, *Social Statics*

That is a simple illustration of the absurdity of the current system, when taken to its logical conclusion. Indeed, we aren't far from that.

When land is made into a commodity, the progress of society, be it in terms of productivity, philanthropy, or the rule of law, tends to be encapsulated in land values.

> ...every improvement in the circumstances of the society tends either directly or indirectly to raise the real rent of land, to increase the real wealth of the landlord, his power of purchasing the labour, or the produce of the labour of other people. -Adam Smith, *Wealth of Nations*

So the community as a whole is what generates all this value, and yet the windfall gains accrue only to the holders of these access rights. In fact, under feudalism land titles these were the root of noble privilege, and although we have left behind the aesthetic trappings of feudalism, we have yet to be rid of the core component.

That means in practice the payments which can be demanded for these access rights are not like other sorts of payments.

> Moreover, wages and interest, when there is no rent, are regulated strictly by free competition; but rent is a monopoly-charge, and hence is always "all the traffic will bear." -Albert Jay Nock, Henry George: Unorthodox American

Essentially, when private individuals get to levy a charge on others for the mere privilege of existing on the planet, this creates an endemic state of poverty for large masses of people. Just as land titles are the essence of noble privilege, so is landlessness the essence of serfdom.

It is through this logic that David Ricardo debunked Thomas Malthus's "Iron Law of Wages." He developed his own "Law of Rent" to show that when the produce obtainable on the best available rent-free land (the margin of production) is high, wages will also be high since everyone's next best alternative to wage labor is improved.

When Malthus and Ricardo were debating, the Old World was all built up and many people were living in Dickensian squalor. Yet, the New World of America had lots of free land, and it witnessed growth rates comparable to those of China today. Unemployment wasn't even part of our vocabulary. True, many homesteaders did not have an easy life, but everyone who was willing and able to work could simply go work. Why is that no longer possible?

The Remedy

The commodification of land itself is not the issue. The issue is who gets the benefits of the access rights. Anything less than an equal share is a violation of the Law of Equal Liberty, for any exclusive claim over natural opportunities necessarily reduces the opportunities available for everyone else. There is only one way to ensure equality of opportunity: for the community to recapture the value of land.

It is for these reasons that virtually all the notable classical liberal political economists supported the idea of the community recapturing the land values, using the discourse of taxation.

A tax upon ground-rents would not raise the rents of houses. It would fall altogether upon the owner of the ground-rent, who acts always as a monopolist, and exacts the greatest rent which can be got for the use of his ground. - Adam Smith, *Wealth of Nations*

A tax on rent would affect rent only; it would fall wholly on landlords, and could not be shifted to any class of consumers. The landlord could not raise his rent, because he would leave unaltered the difference between the produce obtained from the least productive land in cultivation, and that obtained from land of every quality. - David Ricardo, On the Principles of Political Economy and Taxation

When you impose costs on man-made objects, you see a reduction in supply. The supply of land, on the other hand, is fixed.

Income taxes discourage production, sales taxes discourage consumption (which drives production), tariffs discourage trade (which is really a form of production), but value capture only discourages the unproductive holding of land.

Instead of hampering production, it would boost it. Think of every vacant lot or surface level parking lot in a city, every abandoned building, every single-story fast food franchise amidst skyscrapers. Those are all examples of the waste and underdevelopment of the current system. These things occur simply because it is cheaper to sit on the land and hope others put in the work necessary to make it valuable, compared to the expense of undertaking a risky entrepreneurial venture.

Taxes? What Taxes? We Don't Need No Stinking Taxes!

Landholding ought not be seen as a no-strings-attached sovereignty. A true libertarian position recognizes that landholding comes with obligations: obligations to internalize negative externalities, and obligations to respect the Law of Equal Liberty. Sure both of those things may be difficult to do, and may not be accomplished perfectly, yet we must try to achieve them one way or another.

My goal is not to say exactly how the land value should be recaptured. Whether this is done by a municipality, a nation-state, or a Charter City is not the topic of this paper. I only aim to spread a general recognition that it is an essential prerequisite for a just and sustainable socioeconomic order.

Value Capture is most commonly advocated as "Land Value Taxation." However, it is a tax only in the sense that Pigovian "Taxes" are. It is not a tax on production, and thus there is nothing objectionable about it from the perspective of classical liberalism. Indeed, I'd argue that without it, classical liberalism is a cruel joke. Value capture is simply a reconceptualization of who owns the value of the access rights over the Earth.

> Rent is not a tax. It is payment for the use of a location, determined by the higgling and haggling of the market, and it makes no difference to the land user whether he pays rent to the city fathers or to a private owner. -Frank Chodorov, *Out of Step*

Under the current system, rent is like an extractive force upon laborers and capitalists, and that can only be fixed by preventing the private appropriation of land rent. I care not whether the person pocketing the rent is an ideal Lockean homesteader or Donald Trump, it is unjust either way, just as it would be unjust for either of them to unaccountably create negative externalities.

The land value must be recaptured to the fullest extent possible, not simply as a means for funding essential services. If the government is limited enough and well-managed enough to not require all of the land rent, it should still recapture all of it and distribute the surplus as a flat Citizen's Dividend, since that value truly does belong equally to all. This dividend would not only be essential for justice, but would provide a strong incentive for all parties to keep public services lean and efficient.

That which makes public services more efficient would be of direct interest to citizens. That which makes land values higher, would be of direct interest to bureaucrats, which means their incentive would be to create value for the community, rather than to take from productive activity. The incentives between individuals and their community are aligned.

Steady Growth

The ideal of steady growth is completely feasible. Monetary policy is not the root cause of the **business cycle**. Borrowing fuels speculation, but it isn't the ability to borrow which creates the business cycle. That merely amplifies it. You have to ask why they are borrowing. If the borrowing were for normal productive purposes, the borrowing wouldn't be inflationary.

No, the root cause of the cycles isn't borrowing, it's when we leave for the taking a giant pile of community-generated wealth. We shouldn't find it unusual that people should want to pocket unearned wealth. Or even that they should want to undertake bouts of debt-fueled speculation. "Safe" unearned income sure beats working. Who wouldn't want that? It is the system which is corrupt.

Land shouldn't be seen as this "safe" investment, which grows over time with the progress of civilization. No other asset works like that. It ought not even be seen as an investment; if anything, it should be seen as a liability. That we have obligations when we take on the duty of landholding might come as a shock to some, but it is the only position consistent with liberty, and key to our success.

Though it isn't calculated in official statistics like the CPI, rent is what drives much of the increase in living expenses, and why the working classes often never see a piece of their increased productivity during booms. What good is it that the GDP has risen if the general level of wages do not rise as well? That is not the sort of steady growth I'm interested in.

Unemployment during busts is a result of the market correcting for the inflated cost of production resulting from land speculation and other rent-taking. Remember, land is necessary for all production, and life itself. I don't care if your business is all Internet-based, you and your employees still require access rights to the Earth, as do all the producers of the capital goods you consume. Conversely, if people have access to land, there can be no unemployment.

Really Smart Growth

Another cruel joke of the current system is the notion of Smart Growth. We cannot possibly curb sprawl as long as land speculation occurs. Let's say a really nice community is developing. Businesses are sprouting up. This increases the land values. Before you know it, the land values exceed the ability for many people to pay. Even though the transportation infrastructure isn't anywhere near capacity, and density living is far more ecologically efficient, people begin to go elsewhere in search of a place to live. It is simply too expensive in town.

They buy up land outside of town. Yet, before you know it, the new settlement is getting built up, the community is generating lots of value, and they begin construction on new infrastructure, and again before you know it the land values exceed the ability for people to pay. How could anyone believe that people would make different decisions simply because a few do-gooders built pedestrian friendly development? It is absurd to believe this process of sprawl can be halted through zoning, light rail projects, philanthropy, or any sort of central planning. It can only be halted through systemic change.

Land is artificially scarce under the current system of

land tenure. We've already discussed the issue of vacant lots, abandoned buildings, and underdevelopment. Those are just the most visible signs. What about the things we don't see?

For instance, think about our industrialized agriculture system. It is probably the most land-intensive production there is. Wasteful production practices are essentially subsidized by this system. Why aren't we moving towards more high-tech and efficient forms of production? You may have heard about the concept of vertical farming. People often ask why it isn't common practice, and the answer given is that it is "not economically viable." A primary reason why it isn't viable is that holding lots of land is under our system is very cheap, and even profitable.

This insanity isn't just contained domestically either. All the waste of the current system creates this compulsion to expand abroad, to continue fueling the land speculation Ponzi schemes. This creates international resource conflicts, and may even trigger war. It is no wonder that the Old World, where all the land was parceled out and the Commons long-enclosed, became the aggressors in the Scramble for Africa. Of course, eventually they gobbled up all of Africa, and finally turned inward on themselves in the form of the First World War.

What does this mean in practical terms?

You don't have to be a political economist to see the common sense truth of the matter. Some people just care about practical or personal concerns, and value capture is just as relevant from this perspective. Through it we can replace income taxation with a straightforward, efficient, and non-invasive revenue source.

It doesn't require teams of IRS auditors to snoop into every transaction you've ever made. You can't hide your land in a Costa Rican bank account. The current "property tax" system isn't even that different from a methodological perspective; it would only need to change in two ways. It would need to stop including improvements as part of the taxable value of real estate, and it must raise the rates up to near the full annual rental value of the location.

The one thing basically all economists agree on is that "incentives matter." The shift in incentives under value capture would cause dramatic and positive changes in the relationship between citizens and their community.

> Well, then, since natural+55 resource values are purely
> social in their origin, created by the community, should
> not rent go to the community rather than to the Individual?
> Why tax industry and enterprise at all--why not just
> charge rent –Albert Jay Nock, *Henry George: Unorthodox
> American*

Our current system has very perverse incentives. Want to go build a restaurant? Pay up. Want to buy up a prime location and hold it out of production? Under laws like the State of California's Prop 13 we've made sure you get to keep nearly the full value of your precious title. Want to build a community center to help the poor? Congratulations, you've just raised the rents for all the landless people in the area, and may have just "helped" them right out of a home. As a landless person you have essentially no stake in your community. I walked through a poor neighborhood once and was shocked to find a big pile of garbage sitting out in the open in a vacant lot. I then saw one of the local residents walk by and chuck yet more garbage into it. I was puzzled by why anyone would do such a thing, but it makes perfect sense now. Even caring for the cleanliness of one's community is of little benefit to the landless. Cleanliness raises rents, and littering lowers them. You can see the same thing with the contentious issue of gentrification. Have you ever wondered why gentrification is so despised? Why should people hate that their community is improving? They should be rejoicing! Right? Well, they would be under any sensible economic arrangement, but now it merely causes displacement and hardship. Wouldn't it be great if improving the community actually... you know... improved the community. What a thought!

Inequality

> I do not claim that George's remedy is a panacea that
> will cure by itself all our ailments. But I do claim that
> we cannot get rid of our basic troubles without it." John
> Dewey, *Steps to Economic Recovery*

Given the fundamental nature of land, and access rights

over it, unless the land question is taken into account, one of the primary consequences of any otherwise-positive economic reform, including the repeal of other special privileges, will be an increase in rent to landlords.

> What has destroyed every previous civilization has been the tendency to the unequal distribution of wealth and power. -Henry George, *Progress and Poverty*

Inequality is dangerous to liberty, and can enable vicious feedback loops of rent-seeking, which sets the stage for corporatism on one hand and state socialist counter-reactions on the other. Vast fortunes should not be worshipped by those who love liberty. They should be looked at skeptically, and seen as a red flag that something is amiss. Most great fortunes are not the result of voluntary interactions in the market, but by direct or indirect state intervention on behalf of the powerful. The mother of all those privileges is land speculation.

It's time we heed the actual words of the classical liberals, so that we may create a system that works for everyone. No more compromises between prosperity and equality, freedom and justice. We can have it all.

To read more of this type of article as well as more of Mr. Miller's thoughts go to
http://www.discoursesonliberty.blogspot.com/

The economy is SO bad that...

Now they're sending out pre-declined credit card aps in the mail.
CEO's are now playing **miniature** golf.
Exxon-Mobil had to lay off 25 Congressmen!
Angelina Jolie adopted a child from America.
Motel Six won't leave the light on anymore.
A picture is now only worth 200 words.
They renamed Wall Street " Wal-Mart Street".
And finally, when I called the Suicide Hotline, I got a call center in Pakistan.
When I told them I was suicidal, they got all excited, and asked if I could drive a truck.

Open Discussion

by Hunt Henion

In the chapter titled *The Golden Thread*, I pointed out how all religions have the same sacred sense at the core of what they believe. Just as the followers of those religions all pray to the same God, each in their own way, all people also have the same concerns about their place in the world and their ability to provide for their families and loved ones.

People break up into different religious perspectives, and they break up into various political and economic perspectives. However, when we can sit down and discuss the core issues calmly, we discover that we all want the same things, and there are some simple answers that we can all agree with if we are open to that discussion.

For instance, ever since Rome swept across Europe privatizing all the land, the powers-that-be have done everything within their power to enforce this notion that land must be held privately. There are some very good reasons spelled out in this section as to why this arrangement is generally not in our best interest. There are also many examples of how natural assets can be most successfully held in common. And finally, there is the Henry George strategy of leaving ownership alone and simply taxing natural assets and returning the value to the people.

This final strategy has been seen by prominent thinkers from Tolstoy to Thomas Paine and John Locke as THE answer that our world could put into effect right now, without rocking the ownership boat. The powerful elite have fought this common sense solution with inflammatory accusations of "communism" and the vague threat that the common man would lose their homes or maybe the property under their homes.

Still, when we dismiss the illusive threats and sit down to discuss the real issues and proposals, as we do in this section of this most amazing anthology, we see that there isn't any fire to fear behind all their smoke. In fact, intelligent people from all political backgrounds can agree on some simple humanitarian measures that would renew the common man's fighting chance for a respectable life.

We asked Edward Miller about the all too common initial reaction when people first hear about the theories of Henry George. The common knee-jerk reaction in capitalistic countries (which is almost all of the civilized world now) is that those ideas sound communistic. We asked his advice on how to approach that objection. This was his reply:

"With these sort of people, I like to turn their attention squarely on the fact that no principle of liberty can justify eternal monopolization of locations, regardless of whether one is using the locations or not. I like to point to all the many conservative folks who have enthusiastically supported the Land Value Tax.

"For conservatives, I like to point to Winston Churchill and William F Buckley.

"For libertarians, I like to point to Thomas Paine, Thomas Jefferson, Frank Chodorov, Albert Jay Nock, Herbert Spencer, and also various quotes by Adam Smith and John Locke.
https://www.facebook.com/note.php?note_ id=10150285736249720

"The earth is given as a common stock for men to labor and to live on... Wherever in any country there are idle lands and unemployed poor, it is clear that the laws of property have been so far extended as to violate natural right." -Thomas Jefferson

"...every improvement in the circumstances of the society tends either directly or indirectly to raise the real rent of land, to increase the real wealth of the landlord, his power of purchasing the labour, or the produce of the labour of other people." - Adam Smith (Wealth of Nations, Book 1)

"Men did not make the earth... it is the value of the improvement only, and not the earth itself, that is individual property. Every proprietor owes to the community a ground rent for the land which he holds." - Thomas Paine (Agrarian Justice)

"When the 'sacredness' of property is talked of, it should be remembered that any such sacredness does not belong in the same degree to landed property." - John Locke

"The land is the original inheritance of mankind. The usual, and by far the best argument for its appropriation by individuals is that private ownership gives the strongest motive for making the so loyal yield the greatest possible produce. But this argument is only valid for leaving to the owner the full enjoyment of whatever value he adds to the land by his own exertions and expenditure." -John Stuart Mill

"As soon as the land of any country has all become private property, the landlords, like all other men, love to reap where they never sowed, and demand a rent even for its natural produce." Adam Smith (Wealth of Nations, Book 1)

"Landlords grow richer in their sleep without working, risking or economizing. The increase in the value of land, arising as it does from the efforts of an entire community, should belong to the community and not to the individual who might hold title."--John Stuart Mill

For anarcho-capitalists, I like to point to Fred Foldvary http://www.anti-state.com/geo/foldvary1.html

Here's an excerpt from that site:

...if we look at markets today, we see instead contractual communities. We see condominiums, homeowner associations, cooperatives, and neighborhood associations. For temporary lodging, folks stay in hotels, and stores get lumped into shopping

centers. Historically, human beings have preferred to live and work in communities. ...Henry George recognized that site rents are the most efficient way to finance community goods, because it is a fee paid for benefits, paying back that value added by those benefits. Private communities today such as hotels and condominiums use geoist financing. Unfortunately, governments do not.

Fear and prejudice are the weapons that have been used against us for time immemorial. Without them, we have no enemies!

The answers that our society so desperately needs are literally at hand! Open minds and open discussions are the key. So, give the brilliant authors of this section a chance.

Come back to this chapter and look over the quotes above whenever you start to feel a reaction to the material presented in this section. Work to break down those hidden prejudices that have been programed into our minds all our lives. Think it all over carefully. Discuss it with anyone you can. Let's give peace and prosperity a chance!

Hunt Henion holds a PhD in Religious Studies and is the author of four books.
www.shiftawareness.com

The Land Ethic: How to Address Inequality and Financial Instability

by Alanna Hartzok

The global financial crisis has demonstrated a deep systemic failure of the prevailing economic paradigm. So far, efforts to remedy the situation have failed to address the root causes of the meltdown and are digging the American people deeper into the hole of public debt.

In an op-Ed titled "Obama's Ersatz Capitalism" earlier this year, Joseph Stiglitz wrote that the bailout of banks by taxpayers is a "partnership in which one partner robs the other." Considering that in 2004 the top 1 percent of the population of the United States owned more than $2.5 trillion more wealth than the bottom 90 percent, and that even in 1996 about 350 billionaires held more wealth than nearly half of humanity, we have surely arrived at the end of the capitalist monopoly game.

Rent-Seeking and Economic Restructuring

Alternative economic analysts have traced the severe wealth gap problem to the ability of the so-called FIRE sector—finance, insurance, and real estate—to concentrate large amounts of money, resources, and power into ever fewer hands via a variety of rent-seeking behaviors. "Rent" connotes unearned income. Alternative analysis considers economic rent to be a socially generated surplus that is being privately captured.

As an economy generates wealth, the price of land and other natural resources increases. Because the gifts of nature cannot be produced by human effort and supply cannot be increased to meet demand, holders of land and natural resources are in a position to capture the surplus—economic rent—generated by labor and capital.

While economic rent is essentially a measure of the social surplus it is not regarded as such under neo-liberal economics, which treats this value as a market commodity for private profiteering. This fundamental flaw in market economics has created a highly inequitable global economic system. Lack of knowledge as to how to correct this flaw, and retain the benefits, efficiencies, and individual freedoms of the market, was the impetus for the emergence of centrally managed and controlled state socialism. An economic restructuring based on a full understanding of the role of economic rent is needed for a new economic framework beyond both the old right and the old left.

Real Estate and the Land Problem

While many subprime mortgage lenders are guilty of immoral activities, their business was perfectly legal in the game of real estate "investment." To generate more profits under the guise of fulfilling the American dream of home ownership for more of America's workers at a time when capacity to purchase a house from wages had been decreasing, new financial instruments made it easier for poorer people to acquire mortgages.

During the expansion stage of the economic cycle, when land values were rising, banks and others invested in real estate. Banks loaned money to people to play the real estate speculation game. This behavior further drove up land values. We know that 20 percent of all homes bought in this last up-cycle were on the expectation that land prices would increase.

This Ponzi scheme brought the cycle to a frenzied peak and then a total crash, derivatives and all. Land-rent economists understood and predicted the entire scenario, based on detailed analysis of 18-year real estate cycles traced back as far as the 1840s.

The point is this: Underneath the money and banking problem is the land problem —treatment of the gifts of nature and of socially generated land rent as commodities for speculation and profiteering. The land problem is the ultimate genesis of the global financial crisis.

Property Tax and Wage Tax

A solution is to publicly capture the full value of socially generated rents to curb land speculation and stabilize land and housing prices. This can be done by a land-value-only type of property tax. Socially generated land rent is an enormous sum, estimated to be as much as one-third of GDP in developed countries. This is more than sufficient to pay for true social needs including education and health care for all.

With full land-rent capture by the public and for the common good, there would be no surplus rent from land to pledge to banks as interest. There would be no more land-backed borrowing. Financial capital would find no profit in land and natural resource rent-seeking. Substantially more funding would thus be available to invest in productive goods and services.

A necessary policy corollary entails the elimination of taxes on wages in order to secure the full return to labor. Un-taxing wages will of course immediately increase the purchasing capacity of all who work for a living. The highest incomes are generated not from wages but primarily from economic rent (unearned income). Maintaining a tax on people at this level would be another important way that the social surplus can be captured back to society as a whole.

Public Finance: Money as a Social Technology

Another part of the solution concerns the treatment of money as a mechanism of wealth exchange. Money needs to be viewed as a social technology, issued into circulation directly by government as direct spending on public goods rather than as government and private debt. Seignorage reform would enable large-scale government projects, which would benefit large numbers of people. For example, public transportation infrastructure could be funded as a way of also issuing money into the economy. Since infrastructure improvements increase land values, capturing land rent would pay for the ongoing maintenance of public works. With seignorage reform, the money system can begin to function like a public trust.

The elimination of land hoarding and land speculation combined with the capacity of workers to keep all their earnings will enable more people to have affordable land access for housing and productive purposes. The trend would be to incentivize worker ownership of capital via the formation of small business enterprises and cooperatives. As this form of economy advances, more people will gain autonomy from monopoly capital. We can then more readily build movements to eliminate other forms of monopoly and rent-seeking.

This approach to public-finance policy enhances private sector economic activity and public sector goods and services. Taxes would function as user fees for common heritage resources. Economic-rent-based public funds can finance public education and health care for all; capitalization and maintenance of public infrastructure; and low-interest loan funds for housing construction and the development of small and cooperative business activities.

Global and Environmental Justice

Combining the land-rent-for-public-revenue policy with environmental taxation —"polluter pays"—yields an integrated approach to public finance. The resulting benefits would include a fairer distribution of wealth, environmental protection, and basic needs production.

The land ethic and public finance policies described in this article have roots in classical economic theory and the history of economic justice, such as the clean slate periods of antiquity. This is the kind of structural adjustment that the people of the world really need.

Taxes administered along the proposed lines would do much to level the economic playing field worldwide, both within and among nations. A coherent and integrated rent-based public finance system would fundamentally alter the status quo and give every person a stake in the planet as a birthright. With basic needs securely met for all, humankind would be freer to advance, physically, spiritually, and morally.

Alanna Hartzok is Co-Director of Earth Rights Institute and author of *The Earth Belongs to Everyone*, recipient of the 2008 Radical Middle Book Award. A United Nations NGO representative and former board member of United for a Fair Economy, she serves on the Advisory Counsel of the Prout Research Institute of Venezuela. Under contract with UN HABITAT's Global Land Tool Network, she developed an online course and program on *Land Rights and Land Value Capture*.

Toward a New Enlightened Economics

by Dale S. Ironson, Ph.D.

What will our legacy be to our children?
What might we do now to improve the future we can create for them?

We are clearly in times of economic crisis and uncertainty. While it is clear that there is a great need for workable solutions I believe there is a far greater and more profound need, for a deeper kind of discussion than the one that is currently going on in the media. This deeper discussion concerns the underlying foundation, or the context, in which we are viewing our current situation.

Our current economic debates are conducted in terms of conflicts between the rich and the poor, of the have and have-nots, the winners and the losers, the conservatives and the liberals, the Democrats and the Republicans, the strong and the weak, and many other such dichotomies and polarities.

As Albert Einstein once said, "we cannot solve our problems using the same kind of thinking we used when we created them." I believe that our brightest hope for a better future, and the practical solutions and cooperation needed to implement them, needs to come from a very different framework within which we hold our economic discussions.

In short, I feel that we need to move beyond our focus on conflict at the level of content and make a shift in our discussion at the level of context. What do I mean by this?

The Power of Frames / Context

Every discussion has three elements: content, process and context. The content of a discussion is what is discussed, for example taxing the rich, creating jobs, or controlling health care costs, etc. The process of a discussion is how we go about discussing it, i.e, public and political debates, town hall meetings, political advertisements, media coverage, internet forums, etc. The context of a discussion is the framework within which the discussion takes place. Context is the frame, our worldview, or the larger picture in which we are having the discussion. It is the frame of reference we are using within which we have the discussion.

The most common frames for most of our discussions, and for most of the current economic debates, is either – who's right?, or the frame of "government is the problem", or concern about some form of threat by "them". There is also the ever so popular "War on" series of frames – the "War on poverty", the "War on terrorism", the "War on drugs", etc.

The context, or frame, of a discussion contains an invisible set of assumptions which determine the range of our thinking about a subject. We all know how to fight a war – you find the enemy and you eliminate them. Such a frame has violence built in as part of the solution. Frames are powerful in that they are invisible and largely unconscious and they have profound effects on the way they shape the kinds of thinking we do and the kinds of solutions we can come up with. When they are used unconsciously they have power over us. However, when we use them consciously the context or framework we choose can be a powerful creative force in allowing us to see and come up with new kinds of solutions.

All of the frames cited above immediately suggest responses appropriate from within that frame of reference. For instance, when we have the discussion in the frame of a political debate of taking sides, the outcome is judged in terms of who wins? Or who is right? This creates winners and losers, those to be celebrated and those to be subordinated.

While common, to the point of being almost universally accepted as the only way to engage in discussions, this approach is not the only frame possible. In fact such a framing of issues can be seen as being less than ideal in getting us to where we need to go to create effective and workable solutions to our problems.

Why is this so? For one it creates winners and losers, it divides us into sides at war with one another. This is done by the very nature of how the discussion is set up in the first place – as a debate between sides. Such a divisive, polarized, competitive frame engenders competition where cooperation is what is most needed. While it is true that competition has its place in the world, it is also clearly the case that competition needs to be balanced with cooperation to enable organizations and society to function effectively. It is cooperation that will get us to where we need to go as a collective society – as groups of individuals working together cooperatively as an interdependent community.

Are there alternative frames for holding economic discussions that might be more effective and productive? I believe that there are.

New Frames for New Thinking and New Possibilities

One such possible frame for our economic discussions is the frame of "we are all in this together". This frame starts from the perspective that essentially we all share a common challenge and destiny. As Buckminster Fuller has said, we are all on the same spaceship earth, and we either all survive and thrive or die together. No one is here alone and we are all interdependently linked to each other. On this earth what affects one affects all. There is no place for us to escape our interconnectedness and our interdependence. We all breathe the same air and drink the same water. Holding our discussions from this context leads to a very different kind of thinking and makes very different possibilities and solutions possible.

Shifting at the level of context also provides us with new hope and new power in addressing the enormity of the issues that confront us. In a new context what was once seemingly impossible, such as instant access to the world's information, with the proper context and technology all of a sudden becomes real and accessible. Who in the 1950's, would have thought that such a thing as Google or the internet was even possible? In the economic sphere the "Asian miracle" of rapid economic growth and the rapid rise of China shows us what can be achieved with focus, alignment, collaboration, planning and commitment in today's technologically enabled world.

A New Context for Our Economic Thinking

Economics, in its essence, is about the flow of energies (money itself being but a symbol for stored creative energy to be exchanged) and life. The life force itself flows through us constantly in our breath, in the water we drink, in the many exchanges that take place within our bodies, in the blood flowing in our arteries and veins, in the air flowing into and out of our lungs, and in our societies where trade, exchange and communication represent the more physicalized forms of the flows of life's creative energies encapsulated into form. The Dead Sea is dead because it doesn't outflow. The same is true with money. Money that is not shared (circulated), doesn't flow and does not support life (resulting in death).

A few fundamental contextual shifts hold the potential for dramatic breakthroughs in the way we approach the challenge of reforming our economic system and evolving it into a system which more elegantly balances the needs and rights of the individual, and an equitable and sustainable distribution of economic flows that enhance the wealth and well being of both the individual and the community. Such breakthroughs would be based on our ability to find the higher spiritual common ground that comes from reconnecting with that essential part of our being that transcends the physical yet is the very embodiment of our physical life. **True spirituality is not escape from the earth but bringing the light of spirit into physical manifestation.**

Four Key Shifts of Context

Four shifts of context, which would be helpful in reframing our economic discussions, would include:

1. How can we all survive together on this precious space ship we call the earth?

As Bucky (Buckminster) Fuller has said there are no passengers on spaceship earth we are all crew."

2. What kind of legacy will we leave for our children?

This second meaningful shift of context can transform our relationships from one of conflict and attack to one of cooperation in creating practical solutions. We all have a responsibility to the future that our children will inherit from us, in terms of both the quality of life and opportunities for their personal and spiritual evolution as well. This legacy also applies to the needed social reforms, political climate and education that can either liberate us or cause future generations to suffer with political burdens of oppression and financial debts imposed by their unwise and irresponsible ancestors. This, of course, also includes the quality of the earth's environment and it's ability to support life as well.

3. A third needed shift lies in how we see ourselves: Do we see ourselves as separate individuals struggling for survival or as a community of spiritual beings evolving in a physical universe?

Or to put it another way, do we see ourselves, as animals struggling to survive in a dog eat dog world, as separate physical beings, or can we choose to see ourselves as a community of spiritual creative energetic beings who are inexorably linked together in a web of relationships spanning the globe? As such creative, interdependent spiritual beings we are all interconnected in terms of energy, consciousness, global communications and trade, and the shared environment upon which we all depend for our very physical survival and emotional well-being.

4. The fourth shift is about recognizing the inherent universal oneness of creation and the evolutionary nature of life.

This shift is about uplifting our vision of ourselves regarding the very purpose and meaning of life. Such a vision of Oneness incorporates the spiritual sense of the essential truth of our natures as evolving spiritual beings. Such a shift of framework, of coming from a universal sense of oneness and a focus on our spiritual evolution, might well be the most fundamental and transformationally important shift of all.

Key Challenges Moving Forward

In addition to these shifts, there are also some other critical challenges that we face as spiritual beings operating in human bodies which are important for us to consider in dealing with our economic situation at this time. Two of the most important of these challenges are:

1. The need to overcome allowing emotions like anger and frustration to lead to violence as a way of resolving conflicts. Instead we need to harness the power of our emotional energies through courage and commitment such as that seen in spiritual role models like Mahatma Gandhi, Martin Luther King Jr., Mother Teresa and Nelson Mandela have done. We should learn from them how it is possible to improve the lives of millions of people without the need to resort to violence as a means to create needed reforms.

2. The need to balance individual freedom, individual rights and personal initiative with the other equally essential need for the well-being of the whole community of mankind of which we are all a part. We need to more fully value and appreciate the importance of being part of the whole of the oneness of life itself. If our community, our society, or the earth doesn't survive neither will we.

The Art of Creating Societies and the Context of Oneness

The art of creating societies is to create institutions that balance the importance of freedom for the individual and the well-being of the whole community. The cost of not doing this can result in the kind of societal breakdowns we have seen so many times in the past such as the French and Russian Revolutions for example. We do not need to go down paths like these any longer. We can learn from history and avoid such tragic missteps which have caused humanity such great pain and suffering in our collective past.

It is within our power to create a new consciousness about life and economics by starting from a different place within ourselves. We can do this by operating from a new, inspired or enlightened context for our economic thinking, which can generate and implement effective solutions to the challenges that confront us. This new context can be summed up as a framework of oneness that is based on identifying with our spiritual natures and destinies as responsible creative beings operating cooperatively and synergistically with one another with good for all concerned.

Such a framework of oneness addresses how we relate to each other as creative spiritual beings, who are intimately connected with each other by virtue of sharing a common home, the earth.

In economic terms this translates into the immediate and practical priorities of focusing our efforts on creating and maintaining such things as the Commons[1]. The Commons are those shared resources that support, sustain and enhance life for all. The Commons includes natural resources such as land, forests, water, and air quality, as well as social creations that are shared by all such as culture, language, knowledge, the internet, and our biological design (genetics) etc. Such common resources, which are our natural inheritance, need to be maintained and managed for future generations (our children's world) in a responsible manner.

We also need to adopt a long-term perspective, much like the Japanese, thinking in terms of 100 or 200 years rather than 2, 4 or 6 year election cycles. In short. we need to develop a mechanism for long-term integrated planning and implementation at the local, national and global levels.

This all starts within our own hearts and minds. Can we give up the fear, the pain, the judgments, and the struggle and begin creating anew? Are we willing to start our discussions from a different set of assumptions and principles, beginning by the choices we make within ourselves about which frames to use in viewing our world and its situation? The frames we choose can then consciously inform the kind of thinking we do, and the kinds of decisions, institutions and lives we can create for our children and ourselves. Using these new frames can also help us to select the kinds of leaders that will help us move forward in creating a brighter future and serving the public trust which they are elected to represent.

The future doesn't just happen on it's own. We create our future. We need to plan for it. To abdicate responsibility for creating our future is to give up our power. It is up to us to choose and create wisely and well. If we can make the shift from taking sides to oneness, then perhaps we can create something new and marvelous that we and our children can be proud of and benefit from for centuries to come.

I believe that it is within our power to create a truly great new kind of civilization. I believe this is the possibility and potential of our time. We can do this. The question is will we? If we should choose, both individually and collectively, to make these shifts in context in our thinking and our consciousness then that would indeed be a fitting and most wonderful legacy to leave to both our children and ourselves.

Dale S. Ironson, Ph.D. is an organizational consultant who has worked with Fortune 500 companies and leaders in Silicon Valley California. He has written a monthly column on Enhancing Creativity for the Journal of the International Television Association. He is currently working on a book on Economics, Spirituality and Consciousness.

THE WORLD METHODIST COUNCIL SOCIAL AFFIRMATION

...We rejoice in every sign of God's kingdom:
in the upholding of human dignity and community;
in every expression of love, justice, and reconciliation; in each
act of self-giving on behalf of others;
in the abundance of God's gifts entrusted to us that
all may have enough; in all responsibleuse of the earth's
resources.

We confess our sin, individual and collective, by silence or
action:
through the violation of human dignity based on race, class,
age, sex, nation, or faith; through the exploitation of people
because of greed and indifference; through the misuse of
power in personal, communal, national, and international life;
through the search for security by those military and economic
forces that threaten human existence; through the abuse of
technology which endangers the earth and all life upon it.

We commit ourselves individually and as a community... to
seek abundant life for all humanity; to struggle for peace with
justice and freedom; to risk ourselves in faith, hope, and love,
praying that God's kingdom may come.

The Intricacies Of Taxes

by Rabbi Michael Laitman

Posted on August 10th, 2011

Question: Many economists suggest turning left toward socialism and raising taxes on capital in the entire world simultaneously. How realistic is this?

Answer: This will not help. Any action that does not facilitate unity among people will turn out to be disruptive. It will show you that you took the wrong course of action. The only action that can be beneficial is one leading to unity.

Today, in order to make any economic and government reform, you need to consider the laws of the integral system. You have to push and pull the world toward integrality, toward unity. This is the only way you can reach success. Otherwise, nothing will work out.

That is why it is not about taxes and laws, but about the approach. By taking money away from the rich and giving it to the poor, are you really strengthening unity? Let s say you distribute all capital equally and even the rich were left happy. However, the very next day, you will see that what you have achieved is complete failure. On the material level, your reform was large scale and effective, but its spiritual effect has remained zero. This zero will return to you in a negative sense.

Today, the world only needs unity. It must become similar to the Creator. Have you helped it on the path to unity? This is what the whole question is about.

In the worst case, if there is no other way out, people will be led toward unity by means of misfortunes and catastrophes. During a war, everyone unites. This is well known. If you don t want it the good way, you will be forced in the bad way.

This is the requirement of the forces of nature: Today, you have to be more united with others than yesterday. You haven t united? Well, then you will be pushed by the corresponding amount. This pressure may appear as poverty or, perhaps, in war, epidemics, and other disasters.

Daily development is defined by the growth in unity that we have reached. This is the only criterion. The actions themselves are not important. The action even may look negative, but if it leads toward unity, its result will bring benefit, at the end of which you will gain a greater correspondence to nature.

Nature nurtures us toward unity either by suffering or by the kind path if you want it. So, taxation on its own has no meaning. The key is to support the mutual guarantee and to build your calculations in the same way that it is done in a family. We need mutual care for the well-being of the home and the world. Then, everything will be in order.

This means that first of all, you need to come to a consensus in the entire nation of

those who are interested in the existence of the country including the rich and the poor. You can only move forward by way of education, without any pushing or forcing.

There is a place for everything: religion, beliefs, and the right and left points of view. Let everyone remain with his heritage. He must accept only one principle: We are all one family, one nation, and nobody is setting out to kill anyone.

You can have a different point of view than I do, but we still live in one home, and we only have one pie for all of us. So, let's divide it with the maximum benefit for everyone.

Rabbi Michael Laitman is the Founder and president of the Bnei Baruch Kabbalah Education & Research Institute, which is dedicated to teaching and sharing authentic Kabbalah. He is a Professor of Ontology, has a PhD in Philosophy and Kabbalah, and MSc in bio-Cybernetics.
www.laitman.com

Reprinted with permission.

"We claim all economic systems to be under the judgment of God no less than other facets of the created order. Therefore, we recognize the responsibility of governments to develop and implement sound fiscal and monetary policies that provide for the economic life of individuals and corporate entities and that ensure full employment and adequate incomes with a minimum of inflation. We believe private and public economic enterprises are responsible for the social costs of doing business, such as employment and environmental pollution, and that they should be held accountable for these costs. We support measures that would reduce the concentration of wealth in the hands of a few. We further support efforts to revise tax structures and to eliminate governmental support programs that now benefit the wealthy at the expense of other persons."

"We believe **private ownership of property is a trusteeship under God,** both in those societies where it is encouraged and where it is discouraged, but is limited by the overriding needs of society. We believe that Christian faith denies to any person or group of persons exclusive and arbitrary control of any other part of the created universe. Socially and culturally conditioned ownership of property is, therefore, to be considered a responsibility to God. We believe, therefore, governments have the responsibility, in the pursuit of justice and order under law, to provide procedures that protect the rights of the whole society as well as those of private ownership."

-- From *The Book of Discipline of The United Methodist Church*, Copyright 2004 by The United Methodist Publishing House. Reprinted with permission.

Is the Vatican Joining the 99%?

by Hunt Henion

Religious authorities seem to be in agreement on one thing. Whether Jewish or Catholic, Protestant or pagan, they all are calling for more ethical approaches to running the world, and a stronger sense of unity among all of God's children.

While many bristle at the idea of a "new world order," a recent statement by the Vatican makes it sound like that could be the answer to our prayers – and shouts and demands. In fact, their new report makes it sound like the wealthiest religious empire in the world is actually throwing in with the 99% who have been protesting for serious financial changes.

The National Catholic Reporter announced October 25th 2011, that the Pontifical Council for Justice and Peace was calling for a global authority to manage world economics in an entirely new and ethical way.

The 18-page document cited the reasons for the financial downturn to be behaviors like "selfishness, collective greed and hoarding of goods on a great scale." They said that world economics needed an "ethic of solidarity" among rich and poor nations, and it urged Wall Street power-brokers to examine the impact of their decisions on humanity.

Then, seeming to side with the oppressed masses over the established economic pros, the Vatican called on those who wanted to change economic structures to "not be afraid to propose new ideas, even if they might destabilize pre-existing balances of power that prevail over the weakest. They are a seed thrown to the ground that will sprout and hurry toward bearing fruit.

This report issued a strong critique of the global financial system, speaking of "the primacy of being over having," of "ethics over the economy," and of "embracing the logic of the global common good."

It also addresses the importance of "democratic legitimacy" and speaks of "shared government." So, it would seem that this new Vatican report demonstrates that those protesting against a broken and corrupt financial system are not expressing some unreasonable niche position. They are simply calling attention to obvious inequities that have now officially been recognized by the Roman Catholic Church!

Those who might be suspicious of this official Church position can take comfort in the fact many Catholic conservatives were not at all happy with the document. For instance, George Weigel, the conservative Catholic writer, took to National Review's blog to minimize the importance of this new document by saying that the Pontifical Council is "a rather small office in the Roman Curia". He also insists that their document "doesn't speak for the pope, it doesn't speak for 'the Vatican,' and it doesn't speak for the Catholic Church."

Actually, the Pontifical Council for Justice and Peace is not really a "small office." And this document is completely consistent with the papal teaching going back to Popes John XXIII, Paul VI and John Paul II. In fact, Pope Benedict's 2009 papal letter addressed to the bishops of the Church, Caritas in Veritate, spoke in no uncertain language about the need for a global political authority to oversee the increasingly complex world economy.

This new Pontifical Council document is extremely important, because while many view the Vatican as elitist, they are now clearly demonstrating that at least one of their important factions wants to be part of the solution. It would seem that the Vatican is on the verge of joining the 99%! And perhaps we are on the verge of the prophesied new beginning where "the lion shall lie down with the lamb..." Isaiah 11:6

Hunt Henion holds a PhD in Religious Studies and is the author of four books.
www.shiftawareness.com

Share Consciousness, Share the Earth

by Wendell Fitzgerald

When I was sixteen I realized that something was amiss with this world. Years later, I was introduced to a question that is known as the "**land question**". The question is, whose Earth is this, and for whose benefit is it? My introduction to this question was the start of a journey lasting nearly three decades. It has led me to believe that the "**land question**" is one, possibly the most fundamental, question that can be asked about the quality of life on the planet. I also now believe that the answer to it is the key to virtually every social, economic, political, environmental and even spiritual question we have today.

The current answer to the "land question" is that the earth is owned by no more than 15%* of us with the **most valuable** land and natural resources monopolized in the hands of far fewer. The monopoly of land and natural resources has historically been the root cause of the disparity of wealth in the hands of the wealthy. It also has been the root cause of poverty for the masses of humanity. The wealthy have used the income from land, all of it unearned in economic terms, in modern times to monopolize ownership of capital and other forms of wealth. Unfortunately leftists starting with Marx did not make and still do not make the distinction between land and capital and that is why most critical attention is directed toward capital and virtually none toward the monopoly of the earth. It is therefore crucially important to understand the land question in order to understand how control of capital and the modern financial sector came about. Regulation of capital, the financial sector and the monetary system may be called for but the root cause of the maldistribution of wealth and power on the planet will not thereby be dealt with. Failure to appreciate the land question and deal with it directly will merely guarantee the dominance by the few of the monopoly of wealth and economic and political power indefinitely.

The earth is available for the use of humanity upon payment of a price, and those who do not or cannot pay are not particularly welcome. We humans may have an official right to "be" but they do not really have a right to be "here". The right of access to the earth does not even appear in the Declaration of Human Rights. The earth, therefore, officially is not for the benefit of all humans.

Many people think that there are too many of us on the planet and that this is the root cause of poverty and the environmental holocaust that poor people inflict on the earth. Suffice it to say that from the perspective of the "land question" over-population is "blame the victim". I suggest that the "fact" of over-population has been uncritically accepted as a fundamental and unquestioned belief. On the flip side of over-population is the "**land question**" and because of that the solution to the land question holds the key to the solution of what seems to be over-population. These assertions are bound to trouble and even anger many. This is not to say that the earth is not over populated. It is to say that over population is the effect of a deeper cause and that limiting population directly is not an effective response. I call for an open mind.

Over the years I have found awareness of this most fundamental context of the relationship we humans have with the planet does not exist in the larger public discussion anywhere. As far as I can tell. even among those who today speak of the commons, this larger issue is not appreciated. This indicates to me that our relationship with our own planet, the literal physical ground of our beings, exists in our collective psychological shadow. If this is so, it is definitely not a good place for it to exist unexamined. If we are coming into an era of shared consciousness as many are predicting, I suggest that the "land question" will have to come to consciousness and we humans will have to learn to share the earth in some more appropriate way for the benefit of all. I expect an enhanced sense of unity to make this self-evident.

As a practical matter and perhaps if only as a bridge to the new economic paradigm, we humans will have to give up buying, selling and speculating with the body of our Mother for private profit. How humanity will manage its economic affairs in the future when the transformations of this age have been fully integrated remains to be envisioned let alone seen. One thing is sure. We will share the earth on the basis of equality and the age old fight for control of the earth, her land and natural resources will be at an end. Those who have profited undeservedly from this old paradigm will go on to be productive citizens wondering how it is that they could have ever thought of exploiting their fellows.

In the following paragraphs, we shall explore the connection between emerging unity consciousness and the land question. We shall see the crucial importance of access to land with regards to every aspect of life, and we shall inquire into what mechanism can be adopted to share it based on the principle of equality. I will suggest that tax policy as unlikely as it might seem at first blush is at the heart of the solution. I will suggest how a simple tax shift can be the key to solving many other issues. Lastly, I will suggest resources for further inquiry.

Since access to land is an absolute necessity of life, the right to life must of necessity include the right to adequate access to land. Ironically, as mentioned above nowhere in the grand declarations of the rights of humans to date is this right spelled out. Landlessness and insecurity of tenure seen in sprawling squatter cities such as the favellas of Brazil is the condition of many of our kind. In developed countries more recently, the loss of millions of homes to foreclosure brings the issue closer to home. These facts are just the tip of the iceberg of the story of inadequate access to land for a large segment of the world's population.

The landless, for the reason of owning no land, have little opportunity to provide for themselves, and as squatters dare not build anything of lasting value since it can be taken away at any time. These people own no land and little else. Landlessness, and inadequate access to enough of the right kind of land, has always been closely associated with poverty.

When thoroughly examined, it can be seen that landlessness is not only the most fundamental cause, but the root cause of poverty! This is true for developing countries as well as developed countries, even though the issue is fairly well obscured in the latter because in countries that are no longer predominately "agricultural", people have lost not only their physical but their psychological connection to the earth. In addition most criticisms of the economic status quo focus on the issue of capital while the larger and more fundamental question of the monopoly of the earth itself is unappreciated and ignored.

Closer examination of the "land question" reveals that failure to adequately address it is either the root cause of all else that is economically and socially dysfunctional, or is at least an essential causal factor. This is simply so because the land is an essential element in everything we do or produce without exception. The rules and practice regarding ownership and access to land and the economics involved enters into every thing! This is both good news and bad news. The good news is that there is something that hasn't been taken into account that holds great promise for the future of humanity and for the well being of the earth. The bad news is that it involves such a fundamental change that it triggers survival concerns for many and, thus, instinctual resistance even among those who would benefit the most. In addition powerful vested interests can be expected to oppose any change as they have for centuries. Ironically the pain caused by the current systemic breakdown of the economic and financial status quo is offering humanity the opportunity and motivation to rethink fundamental issues that otherwise could never happen.

Available statistics indicate that ownership of the earth is highly concentrated. It is estimated that 3-5% of people and their corporations own 85% of the most valuable land and natural resources. As stated before the relative monopoly of land and natural resources historically has been the basis for the disparity of wealth in all places and times. Land speculation with American farm land and land grabbing in Africa are just two examples of how the process of privatizing, enclosing and monopolizing the earth proceed unchecked to this very day.

The remaining non-monopolized, privately held land is owned mostly by tens of millions of homeowners, small farmers and other small holders. It is the large number of these micro landowners who support current land tenure policies not realizing that the system of land and natural resource monopoly by the privileged few is not in their best interests, in the interest of their communities, or that of the environment. Micro land owners are in touch in a very visceral way with the importance of adequate access to land. For this reason and because they/we have something in hand that is truly comforting to them, micro land owners are usually conservative in their/our outlook and the most sanguine protectors of property rights in general. Who can blame people for resisting poverty by tenaciously holding on to what insulates them from it, even though this results in protecting what does not work in our system of land and natural resource monopoly by a relative few?

Meanwhile a large percentage of people even in developed countries own no land. In the U.S. the figure is at least 40%. Generally, non-landowners must pay land rents all of their lives as part of the cost of renting housing with no possibility of garnering equity value in land or the houses they rent. Recently many non-landowners attempted to join the ranks of land owners by becoming home owners, but now many of them are back to renting after the bust of the so-called "housing" market. **The collapse of the "housing market" was in reality a collapse of a land speculation bubble**. So unconscious is this issue that even those who understand it the most do not call it by its real name. And because we do not call it by its name we are not looking to address it let alone solve it.

It is obvious upon reflection that the value of houses does not go up over time, but the value/cost of land and locations does. When individuals can no longer afford to pay they become what we in developed countries call "homeless". Homelessness is not merely to be without a house. It means they do not have a place to "be". I submit that the existential suffering this causes and the possibility of falling into it is what keeps the rest of us, even the good-hearted among us, on the straight and narrow accepting what we are told will keep us safe. It most fundamentally means that one is without access to land, landless, except at the price of being a criminal or a pariah. Even my liberal minded community of Ashland, Oregon refuses to allow the homeless the right to sleep overnight within city limits and it provides no homeless services beyond one portable toilet. Welcome to the land of good-hearted people. The homeless have dropped most, if not all, their illusions about the American dream and the illusory promises of capitalism/industrialism/free markets to benefit all.

Please understand that this is not to say that private ownership of land or natural resources for **exclusive use** is a bad thing, or that it will, or should, disappear as a necessary consequence of realization of Unity Consciousness. It is not to say that separative consciousness for the purpose of establishing appropriate boundaries is a bad thing or that boundaries will disappear. It is not to say that payment for access to land will cease, or should cease. It is to say that the **"land question"** suggests something more subtle and wonderful at work that humanity has yet to use to its great advantage.

The following discussion of economic principles involved in the **"land question"** can be the beginning of inquiry into what this might be.

I submit the following three basic things about the economics of land as the place to start. These things are well enough known to economists, mortgage bankers, Wall Street insiders, and those looking for big profits in "real estate", but not generally known by the public. There are also many other related principles that together illuminate the **"land question"** and suggest what to do about it. There are resources for further inquiry mentioned at the end of this essay.

First is the fact that **the entire economic value (measured in land rents and purchase price) of land and natural resources is created by the community of all people, and not by individual owners of particular pieces of the land or natural resources.** The absolute need for access to land of every individual without exception creates the market for land and together we create its value that did not exist before we came. As our numbers grow so does the economic value of land since the supply of land is fixed. Private individuals collect this value but they do not create it.

The fact that all of us create the value of land complements the idea that the earth belongs to all of us in common. Not only does the earth belong to all of us in common since we equally together create all of its value it might become obvious that that value also belongs to all of us in common. More about that later.

Second is the fact that **all government services have the economic effect of increasing the value of land.** This is so because public services make land more useful and thus more productive in a way that is measured in terms of what people are willing to pay for it. This is also true because community government is an extension of the population that is the heart of community that creates land value. Government services increase the value of land but do not increase the value of the improvements on land. This may not be obvious at first, but all economists (even though they never speak of it outside of the classroom) agree on this fact.

When private owners of land sell land, the purchase price contains that increased value, because the buyer can expect to receive the benefit of the community services even if the services are not used. For example. homeowners often complain of having to pay for schools after their children have grownup and no longer go to these schools. What they do not seem to realize is that the value of their land is enhanced by the existence of schools in their community. It is not hard to predict what would happen to land values in a community where the schools suddenly disappeared. The fact that our schools are under funded and their quality declining is having the same effect in slow motion.

Third is the fact that income from land and natural resources per se is wholly unearned. **Income from land is unearned** because the owner does not himself create the land or its value. The fact that one has to purchase land with hard earned money does not make the income from land earned. Income from land is no more earned merely because it is legal any more than the income from ownership of slaves was earned when it was legal. These forms of unearned income were and are equally a way to get something for nothing at the expense of others.

This is an aspect of the economics of land that may be shocking for many. Few want to admit that they get something at the expense of others. I am a land owner. I rent it and the house on it to others. I just no longer deny that I get an unearned income when I receive the rent for the land portion. Landed property owners who sneer at the poor on welfare are to be pitied. They are looking in the mirror and denying that they are just the same. This is the shadow at work projecting itself and ascribing one's failings onto others. This is tragic for those who blame and those who are blamed.

Homeowners often say that they are not receiving income from the land they own because they use it themselves to live on and do not rent to others. Well recognized in economics is that land owners who use their own land receive indirect or "imputed" income from land. Imputed income from land is the amount the owner of land would have to pay in rent if he had to rent his own or similar land from someone else. Not having to pay this rent is equal to a direct payment of the same amount to the landowner from the community that creates that value. This payment to the landowners comes directly from the community as a subsidy. Non-landowners do not have such a subsidy and in fact they are forced to pay it when they pay taxes. Either way it is an unearned value/income in the hands of the land owner. And, yes, it is true that landowners do pay some of this subsidy back to the community in that portion of the property tax that falls on assessed land value.

The existing property tax that falls on land values nowhere covers the cost of services that make land more valuable. In addition that part of the property tax that falls on the assessed value of improvements to land is substantial but it falls not on a value created by the community but on a value created by the individual property owner. Bare land speculators love this. Either way landownership is preferred over everything else in our economy and our tax system. We have been willing to sacrifice the wages of labor, the profits of real capital investment in the real economy and the value our homes to make sure landowners collect values they do not create. I suggest this is an amazing contradiction in our so-called free enterprise economy where property rights are protected so zealously. It is just that some property rights are more sacred than others and these others are to be sacrificed for the sake of the one.

Is there any doubt about who really is in charge of molding our tax codes? The land and natural resource owners historically were in charge of everything and they still are.

Remember, all economists agree with the principles stated. Ask them if you run across them. Few economists with some exceptions** ever talk about them, nor do most public intellectuals who profess to be critical of the "flaws" in the system.*** I suggest that what has been described above, along with many other related things, amount to a massive flaw in the free market/free enterprise system at the ground level – literally!

So, how might we use these simple principles of the economics of land and taxation to fashion a more just answer to the "**land question**"?

Over a century ago Henry George, an American political economist and social philosopher, suggested that we shift all taxation off of labor and real capital onto community created land values. Not only would this be just, and eliminate destructive taxation, but it could also provide enough revenue to fund all levels of government. Of course the politics of this are daunting but failure to understand the economics involved makes it impossible for citizens and politicians alike to know what they are up against. Failure to consider the fiscal and non-fiscal effects of such a tax shift make it impossible to see how many economic, social and environmental problems are related and how they might be solved or significantly ameliorated.

More than the obvious appeal of economic justice in taxation the most exciting things about this proposal are the economic consequences that solve myriads of problems without further effort or government involvement. Those familiar with whole systems analysis will recognize land value taxation as a high leverage change point. It is at the level of paradigm shift just below a shift in consciousness. Anything less is mere treatment of symptoms.**** Treating symptoms was the best we could do until now.

To adequately discuss the questions raised by the idea of land value taxation and the effects that would flow from it would take more room than is available here. To find out more about these ideas search the web for "Henry George" and "land value taxation." I also recommend going to Alanna Hartsok's Earth Rights Institute website at www.course.earthrightsrights.net and reading the information behind the "Quotes" and "SWOTS" tabs. You will find the many great minds that have endorsed George and the idea of taxing community created land values as well as some of the history of where it has been tried to good effect.

* Kevin Cahill, *Who Owns the World*, (Grand Central Publishing, 2010), page vii
** Herman Daly, Michael Hudson (the professor, not the journalist), Joseph Stiglitz

*** A notable new comer to this discussion is Charles Eisenstein whose book Sacred
Economics has recently been published and is available at: **www.northatlanticbooks.com/store/evolver-editions**
**** Donella Meadows, edited by Diana Wright, Thinking in Systems, (Sustainability Institute, 2008) chapter six and page 194.

Wendell Fitzgerald is a recovering attorney and the President of the Henry George School of San Francisco.

The Commons and Turangawaewae

by Alanna Hartzok

Police attacks on the Occupations are the current manifestation of the violent suppression of the peoples' rights to the planet's land and natural resources. This harshly exploitative power relationship stems directly from the amalgam of church/state that was the Holy Roman Empire, and the fundamentals have never shifted toward justice. The basic person/planet ethic of HRE is "dominium" - legalization of land acquired by conquest and plunder. As long as the few rather than the many "own" the planet, there will be brutality and unending war. I perceive that a not yet fully conscious reason why the Occupations are so fundamentally powerful is that this action takes and holds land as a commons. Pitching a tent and sleeping on land is a direct threat to the powers that be, because in our system the only way to acquire land is inheritance, purchase (with mortgage debt) or rent (to a landlord who has inherited land or purchased land via mortgage debt.) In our system there is NO INHERENT RIGHT to land as a birthright.

By the simple act of direct land occupation, the Occupation movement is first and foremost a land rights movement. The painful awareness of the abnegation of our fundamental rights to land is deep in the subconscious mind of the many. For millennia, reigning powers have unleashed violence and death upon myriads of assertions of land rights by the landless. These psychic scars in the collective mind-field are laden with fear and trepidation.

The Occupations have broken the fear barrier. Still, if people are "permitted" to stake claim to little city parks here and there, their next step might be to stake claim and hold more and more urban and rural land. The call of the Russian Revolution was Land and Liberty. The French Revolution was also triggered by the revolt of the landless serfs. Yet the land problem has not been solved but rather festers and erupts, showing itself to be an unhealed world wound, the source of our weltschmerz, the pain of the world we all are feeling right now.

If the powers that be were to permit the people to stake a direct land rights claim, freely and indefinitely, and land rights movements expanded, soon people would be building their own "free" villages and communities. They would discover that they do not need "jobs" to survive. This is the greatest threat to the powers that be. For without sufficient numbers in a "labor pool" competing with each other to drive down wages, the "job creators" would have to pay the highest wages possible or else people would self-employ on land, cutting deeply into their unearned profits.

The very first environmental party, precursor to the German Greens, was the New Zealand Values Party. Their platform contained a key policy based on the Maori land ethic of turangawaewae. Turangawaewae is one of the most well-known and powerful Maori concepts. Literally turanga (standing place), waewae (feet), it is often translated as 'a place to stand'. Turangawaewae are places where we feel especially empowered and connected. They are our foundation, our place in the world, our home. [1]

[1] See: Turangawaewae as foundation **http://www.teara.govt. nz/en/papatuanuku-the-land/5**

The Occupations are standing on Trangawaewae. And as you read this, the Occupiers are once again being thrown off the Commons. For information on what we can do about it, see my Earth Rights Institute online course: **www.course.earthrights. net**

Money--an Instrument of Elite Social Control

by John Spritzler & Dave Stratman

"Money is a new form of slavery, and distinguishable from the old simply by the fact that it is impersonal-that there is no humanrelation between master and slave."
-Leo Tolstoy, Russian writer

"It is well enough that people of the nation do not understand our banking and money system, for if they did, I believe there would be a revolution before tomorrow morning."
-Henry Ford, founder, Ford Motor Company

Perhaps the most surprising feature of the new society is that money is abolished. Why is this necessary and how does it make sense?

The economy of revolutionary democracy is based on the principle of "From each according to ability, to each according to need." It is a "Contribute what you can and take what you need" economy, not a 'If you give me this, I will give you that" economy. This means people share things rather than exchange them. Money, which is a means of exchanging things more conveniently than barter, is, therefore, not necessary in the new society.

Furthermore, buying and selling is not an equitable way for the wealth of society to be distributed. Goods ought to be shared on the basis of need. If someone who contributes to society is in need of food or shelter, he should receive them, whether he has money or not. (Most homeless in the U.S. are full-time workers whose jobs pay too little to afford them a home.) If somebody is sick and needs care, it is immoral that he should only receive as much health care as he can buy. The Golden Rule is to share, not buy and sell.

Money may not be necessary in a good society but it is; however, extremely important for a society based on inequality. In a society based on money, a single individual can accumulate a great deal of money and use it to buy many things and pay many people, and thus control the use of things and the behavior of people on a vastly greater scale than would otherwise be possible.

Money, thus, makes inequality easy to impose because it makes it easy to concentrate power in the hands of a few, even in a society like ours today that purports to be a democracy. Money enables wealthy people to buy the votes of politicians, make laws to benefit themselves at the cost of society and sway public opinion through their corporate media. A society based on money is incompatible with genuine democracy and equality.

On the surface it might seem that without money there would be no way to accumulate capital for investing in new enterprises. But if we look closely at what "capital" is, we see that capital accumulation for new enterprises does not require money in a society based on sharing.

Today, when a businessman wants to start a new enterprise, he needs money to buy or rent the necessary equipment and to pay wages for the necessary labor. In the new society, when people decide to start a new enterprise and the larger society democratically approves of it, then the people who carry out the enterprise may freely use the required land and natural resources and machinery, and the workers may freely take what they need to live on. The point is that in a money-based society, money is indeed important, but in a moneyless society it is not.

There remain two additional major reasons for not using money: money is an instrument of elite social control, and money poisons social relationships.

Money Is an Instrument of Elite Social Control

In an earlier time in America, the rich landowner or bank would extend credit to the tenant or farmer for seeds and fertilizer and food to sustain his family till harvest. At harvest the farmer would often find that his debt combined with the interest owed exceeded the value of his crop; with each passing year he would sink further into debt-peonage. In current times in the United States, a young person graduates from college saddled with gigantic loans, which by law he can never escape, not even through personal bankruptcy. He is in debt-peonage to the bank. He is forced by his debt to seek out the highest paying job he can find, no matter what career he would prefer. Economic pressures make him work at an unfulfilling job for a boss he may despise. The more successful he is at finding that high-paying job, the more pressure he is under to conform to capitalist values and keep his mouth shut.

At the same time his parents may carry a mortgage on a home worth perhaps half of what they paid for it. They are in debt-peonage to the bank. Someone with a car loan or needing health insurance is under similar pressure to find and keep a job and make the daily compromises necessary to stay employed in a corporate dictatorship. Young people under economic stress join the military and are trained to kill their class brothers and sisters on command. As the rulers crank up the economic pressure on families, more parents are forced to work two or three jobs and barely have time to share with their children. Money reduces life to a rat race.

The banks gain and exercise their power in society through the power of money. The power of the banks looms over all our life choices. They hold our lives in their hands. A society based on money enables the few who are wealthy to control the many who are not.

Money Poisons Social Relationships

In a society based on money, many human interactions are mediated by money, with one person using money to exert power over another. The more money plays a role in society, the less of a role is played by the Golden Rule: moral persuasion, mutual agreement, or reciprocity of good deeds among equals. Money suppresses the role of positive human values and replaces it with greed and domination.

In a money society, money confers on its possessor an almost magical power. If the owners of a corporation want a manager to fire long time employees in order to increase profits, they just pay the manager to do the nasty deed. No need to persuade the manager that it is a morally good thing to do. The owners of the corporation have a perverse power over the manager.

In the absence of money, social power comes from one's ability to persuade others that doing this or that is morally right or at least that it benefits them. It also comes from having relationships of mutual support: because one has helped others in the past, they want to return the favor. In the absence of money, social power is not power over people but power to act with people to accomplish goals that are shared.

It has long been said that the love of money is the root of all evil. Only in the absence of the power of money will people's moral feelings and their best values truly shape society.

John Spritzler is a Senior Research Scientist at Harvard School of Public Health and author of *The People as Enemy: The Leaders' Hidden Agenda in World War II*. He co-edits NewDemocracyWorld.org.

Dave Stratman is former Washington Director of the National PTA and author of *We CAN Change the World: The Real Meaning of Everyday Life (*New Democracy Books, 1991). He co-edits **NewDemocracyWorld.org**.

Ethical Ecological Economics: Sustainable Prosperity

by Cynthia Sue Larson, MBA

Can you imagine a world in which behaving ethically with environmental conscientiousness dramatically improves finances? Can you envision citizens of your neighborhood, city, and nation being consistently rewarded in the short-term for doing what's best for everyone and the Earth in the long-term? Answers to these questions will help guide us toward a 21st century renaissance of the highest order, as people around the world work with both top-down and bottom-up grass roots movements to restore balance to local and global ecosystems.

While most people don't automatically connect the words ecology and economy, nor see these fields of study as intrinsically intertwined with ethics, the truth is that our world has reached the point where success is required in all these areas in order for us to enjoy an excellent quality of life. We now have the opportunity to find ways to collaborate better as guardians of the Earth to avoid economic and ecosystem problems that may take us in unthinkably horrific directions.

Earth contains limited natural resources, many of which we depend upon without formally acknowledging their true value in our lives. The concept of ethics must be addressed when discussing ecological economics, because there must be genuine consideration for common-pool resources. Without true consideration, those individuals or groups striving to maximize individual profit are at risk for stressing ecosystems beyond their carrying capacity, or are at risk for leaving messes in the oceans or air for others to suffer with or clean up. While environmental exploitation is hypothetically preventable when everyone behaves ethically, all too many examples of environmental and resource exploitation suggest ethical behavior over the past several centuries has not been commonplace. An island of floating trash is now larger than any natural island in the Pacific Ocean where it resides, radioactive particles from Tepco's Fukushima Japanese reactor meltdowns continue to drift through the ocean and air, acres of BP oil still stain the beaches and waters of the Gulf of Mexico, and all manner of other pollutants flow through our oceans and sky. With so many environmental and economic crises lately, it's no wonder some people think the end of the world is nigh.

According to the Hopi, we're currently entering the fifth of seven predicted worlds. The good news from this perspective is that the world as we know it has ended many times already, according to our planet's indigenous peoples, and humans have successfully handled the transition to a new world more than once. When we listen closely to what indigenous peoples have to say, we learn that most indigenous cultures emphasize the importance of interconnectedness and honoring all life. Every act of gathering food from plants and animals is treated with sacred respect, by honoring the relationship between those plants and animals and the surrounding environment. Plants and animals are talked to, sung to, and honored by most indigenous people before they are hunted, gathered, and consumed. Indigenous people maintain ecological diversity by observing the complex relationships between plants and animals within their neighborhood ecosystems, and by addressing imbalances as they arise. This view of human being as caretaker is one that western society is finally getting around to adopting, and the idea of doing the right thing for everyone in the ecosystem fits into the idea of ethical environmentalism.

Ethics is the art of taking right action, even when it seems nobody is looking. Ethical behavior is necessary and essential because even with laws and rules, we can't always think of every possible check and balance to ensure short-term incentives best serve everyone's long-term interests. Contrary to Garrett Hardin's environmental economic model based on "tragedy of the commons," privatization has seldom been historically proven to save the environment. Privatization of the commons has instead often led to the ruin of ecosystems, due to demands for short-term returns without consideration for commitment to long natural cycles required for resource regeneration. Small family-owned interests often conscientiously manage their properties, such as my Swedish cousins who selectively remove trees from their forestland. In such small-scale operations, trees are carefully selected for removal in Earth-friendly ways that enhance the growth of surrounding groves, so even after hundreds of years of having been forested, the woods look as wonderfully wild as a nature preserve.

Larger corporate interests, on the other hand, have been known to publicly tout their corporate social responsibility while privately engaging in unethical activities overseas. The problem of greenwashing, or deceptively promoting the perception that a company's policies are environmentally friendly, is an ongoing concern, as some companies publicly posture as green, yet privately engage in questionable or downright harmful activities. Such lack of ethics has been more frequently coming to public attention, thanks to peoples' insistence on corporate transparency. An example of greenwashing can be found in Coca Cola's privatization of India's water resources while publicly touting environmentalism, leading the Polaris Institute to award Coca Cola with their first annual Corporate Greenwashing Award. Legislation and a top-down approach to setting and enforcing measurable environmental standards for such things as greenhouse gas emissions, levels of toxic contaminants, and proper use of carbon credits seem every bit as necessary as grass-roots bottom-up movements for adopting sustainable ways of living in harmony with nature.

Sustainable Development

The Brundtland Commission's 1987 report, "*Our Common Future*" defines sustainable development as "*development that meets the needs of the present without compromising the ability of future generations to meet their own needs*" according to currently accepted standards. This statement is a welcome change from near-sighted corporate mission statements of the past, which primarily focused on the bottom line and shareholder satisfaction, and it harkens to the sensibility of the Iroquois peoples who keep seven future generations in mind whenever making significant decisions or plans. The concept of ethics is explicitly included in the constitution of the Iroquois nations, which states, "*In all of your deliberations in the Confederate Council, in your efforts at law making, in all your official acts, self interest shall be cast into oblivion. Cast not over your shoulder behind you the warnings of the nephews and nieces should they chide you for any error or wrong you may do, but return to the way of the Great Law which is just and right. Look and listen for the welfare of the whole people and have always in view not only the present but also the coming generations, even those whose faces are yet beneath the surface of the ground – the unborn of the future Nation."*

In 2009, Harvard Business Review published a study whose results indicate that corporate sustainability is the key driver of innovation that also yields real financial rewards rather than extra cost. The report stated, "By treating sustainability as a goal today, early movers will develop competencies that rivals will be hard-pressed to match," providing a five-stage process companies utilize when adopting green business models. Large corporations such as Wal-Mart seem to have taken this advice to heart regarding taking a proactive approach to setting environmental goals, with sustainability goals that include: being supplied 100% by renewable energy, and creating zero waste.

The New Sustainability Champions

A recent study by the World Economic Forum and the Boston Consulting Group identified sixteen companies they call "the new sustainability champions" in emerging markets for utilizing eco-consciousness to their competitive advantage. One thing that stands out most about these highly profitable businesses is the innovative way they turn resource limitations and challenges into opportunities. Not enough water to make concrete? No problem for India's Shree Cement, who devised an air-cooling system for curing cement. High energy costs cutting into corporate profits? Not an issue for China's Broad Group, who harnesses "waste heat" from buildings. Each one of these sixteen companies has creatively discovered a way to more efficiently operate with reduced impact to the Earth, often getting ideas from employees who are actively encouraged to think creatively and share suggestions with management for financial and other awards and recognition. These companies are noted for embedding sustainability into their corporate culture and actively shaping their business environments, so their innovations are much more than a public relations campaign. This kind of ingenuity in emerging markets of companies around the world gives us renewed hope that all of our businesses can thrive even as they reduce the long-term adverse environmental impacts of their activities.

Gross National Happiness

The relatively small nation of Bhutan has found a marvelously creative way to keep a focus on sustainable nature-centered development, with its idea of Gross National Happiness (GNH) coined in 1972 by Bhutan's King Jigme Singye Wangchuck. Rather than emphasizing ever-expanding economic growth through the more prevalent Gross National Product (GNP) measurement of economic development, Bhutan's GNH provides a measurement of indicators of human happiness according to four broad indicators. Bhutanese Prime Minister Jigmi Thinley outlined these four foundational strategies in January 2011 as being: sustainable socioeconomic development, conservation of fragile ecologies tracking expansion of vegetation cover, promotion of culture, and good governance. Bhutan's focus on

The idea of gross national happiness is catching on in cities such as Seattle, Washington, which is the first city in the United States of America to measure gross national happiness, and the city of Victoria in British Columbia, Canada, is another city moving forward to survey its citizens on what makes them truly happy. The surveys go deeper than merely finding how satisfied citizens are on a 10-point scale, by exploring aspects of life that contribute to high ratings, and by asking people about specific factors known to influence well-being.

Just how well does GNH work toward bringing true environmental and economic prosperity to communities? It's still too soon to tell. But one thing is for certain. With communities adopting Gross National Happiness as a means to track progress and growth, an ethically environmental economy looks increasingly realistic... and a genuinely rewarding way of life looks to finally be in sight as being attainable for all.

Cynthia Sue Larson is the editor of the monthly Reality Shifters e-zine and author of several books, including the highly acclaimed, *Reality Shifts: When Consciousness Changes the Physical World*

We are their Hope!

Learn from yesterday, live for today, hope for tomorrow –
Albert Einstein

19945731R00173

Made in the USA
Lexington, KY
13 January 2013